4-H - A DEI
Love Story

HOW POSITIVE YOUTH DEVELOPMENT BECAME A BATTLEGROUND FOR DEMOCRACY

BY: JOHN-PAUL CHAISSON-CARDENAS, PhD, MSW, SHRM-SCP

Co-Author: LISA LAUXMAN, PhD, MBA

DEDICATION

To J & T, my personal learning laboratory for Positive Youth Development, who learned along with me to 'make the best better' using our family motto... *"Kind Words, Gentle Hands,* to my mother, who serves as my role model, to be open and caring to all, and to my brothers, well, they offered me the challenge to prove that I could do "it" as well, *if not better.* ☺.. *"To Make the Best Better",* 4-H Motto.

- Lisa-

This book is dedicated to my wife Angelica and my mother Chita, any bravery I may have - I got from them. Also, to Mama Alfa, and my querida Tia Ana. And finally, to Salome, B'alam (the Jaguar), because you, my girl, are going to change the world!

– John-Paul

It is also committed to all the Public Servants and DEIA Officers who have lost their jobs, and so much more, to the "War on Woke". Thank you for humbly protecting our democracy, our civil rights, our health, science, the truth, and so much more. We owe you as a nation!

THE 4-H PLEDGE

I pledge *my Head* to clearer thinking,

My Heart to greater loyalty,

My Hands to larger service,

and *my Health* to better living,

for my club, my community, my country, and my world.

FORWARD

By: Dr. Suzanne LeMenestrel

Unlike Lisa, I didn't grow up in 4-H. In fact, 4-H wasn't even heard of in the suburban university community where I am from. I was a Girl Scout and made it all the way through to Gold Award Girl Scout. As an adult, I became a Girl Scout leader and later a Gold Award mentor. My mom was a Girl Scout and troop leader, and I followed in her footsteps. However, like John-Paul, I became a 4-H convert. I went from thinking that 4-H was only a program for kids to show off their cows or sheep to being completely blown away by the compassionate and poised group of youth who I met at a National 4-H Conference in Washington, DC.

I was hired as a national program leader at the Department of Agriculture for my research expertise. My tasks? Build the evidence base to demonstrate the impacts of the 4-H program. Bridge the 4-H program with other programs across the federal government so that Cooperative Extension was no longer a "well-kept" secret. Create a way for 4-H programs to measure their outcomes. Evaluate the annual National 4-H Conference, a civic engagement experience for high school-aged youth from around the country. I also served as a mentor and support for college-aged 4-H alums who were recruited to serve as facilitators. One facilitator I worked with, a college student from Puerto Rico who is now a national journalist, prepared a group of teens to deliver a briefing to agency leaders at the Department of Justice. In just a couple of days, the youth researched factors that contributed to the school-to-prison pipeline. They prepared a PowerPoint deck and a compelling presentation. They practiced and memorized. And wow did they deliver!

What were the 4-H experiences that these youth had as children that led to this moment? How did they develop these leadership skills and the ability to examine such a complex issue that perhaps they had not observed or experienced before? I believed that 4-H was an equalizer, a key to leveling the playing field for all youth. 4-H didn't require pricey fees or dues or special equipment. Anyone could excel in 4-H and find their passion. Sitting in that conference room at the Department of Justice made me realize that 4-H really was more than "cows and cooking."

In this memoir written by two very different and outstanding scholars, the authors write about the promise of 4-H. The promise that 4-H fosters belonging and inclusion. Youth and adults are partners, and caring adults foster in youth a sense of independence, mastery, and engagement in communities and the world. 4-H could indeed play a key role in fostering a pluralistic democracy.

In a recent report from the National Academies of Science, Engineering, and Medicine (2025), the authoring committee found evidence that suggests participation in out-of-school time activities does support youths' confidence to influence political issues. I saw this confidence firsthand at the National 4-H Conference. These 4-Hers felt that their voices mattered. Perhaps they vigorously disagreed on their recommendations when they researched and prepared for their briefing. But through the carefully facilitated process, they emerged with a powerful set of recommendations.

This memoir is a love story to 4-H. It is a deeply personal and sometimes very painful story. But there is also hope. Hope in the power of youth voice, especially for those youth who have felt voiceless and who are marginalized by our society. I don't believe 4-H is just a promise. I believe that 4-H and other positive youth development programs have the power to change lives and to lift up all voices.

Reference: National Academies of Sciences, Engineering, and Medicine. 2025. The Future of Youth Development: Building Systems and Strengthening Programs. Washington, DC: The National Academies Press. https://doi.org/10.17226/27833.

Short bio: Dr. Suzanne Le Menestrel is a developmental scientist whose career has focused on positive youth development and out-of-school time settings. She holds a doctorate in human development and family studies from The Pennsylvania State University. She is an active volunteer in a youth-serving program for immigrant teens.

INTRODUCTION: TWO VOICES

This is a story braided from two voices—distinct in rhythm, rooted in different traditions, but committed to a shared promise: that pluralistic democracy is not only possible, but necessary.

One voice speaks in the cadence of civic infrastructure and constitutional ideals. The other sings in ceremonial tones, guided by Human and Civil Rights. Together, we strive toward a pluralistic democracy that refuses to succumb to fear, bigotry, and hate.

We come from different vantage points. Lisa's love language is public service—policy, legislation, and program design shaped by a generational commitment to 4-H and the Extension creed. John-Paul writes through the lens of Diversity, Equity, Inclusion, and Access, because he is shaped by war, migration, and a postcolonial sociology that questions the very institutions he has been asked to reform. Our styles diverge. Lisa is structured and deductive, a steward of systems. John-Paul is relational and ceremonial, a disruptor of Western logic. Yet both center on social justice and love (agape).

Lisa grounds her understanding in Midwestern Christian civic habits. John-Paul grounds his in Maya spirituality and the sacred story of maize. We do not proselytize; we name convergent values—welcoming the stranger, tending family, stewarding land, and honoring work done well—and we offer these values as a public grammar for belonging.

The Project

Our project is a comprehensive exploration of democratic pluralism, aiming to challenge and redefine the narrow, exclusionary model often associated with this concept. We advocate for a living democracy that thrives on the coexistence of Western and Indigenous, empirical and intuitive, civic and spiritual ways of knowing. This is not about assimilation; it is about creating a space where diverse perspectives can flourish without being diminished. Our project is a call to action, a manifesto for a more inclusive and vibrant democracy.

We are clear about the goal of the experiment: to honor policy and belonging in the same space, to test whether legal frameworks and ritual memory can be braided into practices that strengthen democracy rather than divide it. This experiment is not just theoretical; it's a practical exploration of how we can create spaces and practices that respect diverse cultural and knowledge systems while upholding democratic principles. It is a bold step toward a more inclusive and just society.

That experiment is urgent because pluralism is under assault. In recent years, legislative efforts, litigation, and cultural campaigns have reframed equity work as a form of political theater rather than a public service. Corporations that, after George Floyd's murder, were eager to publicize diversity initiatives have quietly scaled back or rebranded them amid shifting legal signals and public pressure. These shifts are not abstract; they alter who sits at policymaking tables, whose histories are taught in classrooms, and whether public institutions can serve as sites of historically honest learning and repair.

At the same time, large portions of the workforce and younger generations continue to demand accountability and a sense of belonging. Surveys and workplace studies from 2025 show that many organizations, including those in higher education and K-12, have maintained or quietly increased equity investments, even as public rhetoric shifts. Employees—especially younger groups—expect workplaces that promote equity and opportunity. These concurrent trends make our task unavoidable: how to defend the civic space where pluralism can thrive while also addressing the real pressures that threaten to narrow it.

Why Does Cultural and Perspective Braiding Matter

We trace histories that few modern readers expect to find side by side. Through these pages, we walk through the Morrill Act of 1862 and the Smith-Lever Act of 1914, the legislative frameworks that created land-grant universities and Extension systems, promising practical education to broad publics. We refer to the tribal lands taken to fund those institutions and the dual structures imposed by later legislation, such as the 1890 Act, which created separate provisions for Black land-grant schools. We honor the educators who, when excluded from the main stage, built civic classrooms in barns and basements, transforming scarcity into civic creativity.

We vehemently reject the current 'either/or' or 'zero-sum' policy approaches, which assume that one party's gain is inherently at another's expense. Instead, we lean on the idea that when we share, the bowl will be more plentiful.

Yes, Extension and 4-H have been tools of assimilation and instruments of civic uplift. They have fostered agricultural innovation and excluded Indigenous knowledge. They have trained leaders and reinforced hierarchies. Naming these truths is not an act of condemnation; it is an effort of truth and reconciliation. Because we believe that truth held with care can liberate the institutions we love and make them more honest, resilient, and generative.

This is why Lisa invokes Booker T. Washington's vision of farming as a means of belonging, asking how the four H's—head, heart, hands, and health—might guide reconciliation and civic formation.

In contrast, John-Paul hears Audre Lorde's warning that 'the master's tools will never dismantle the master's house,' and he watches for ways colonial logics are reproduced in government initiatives like 4-H. However, he also recognizes the transformative potential of strategic reclamation: when ancestral practices reshape imposed forms, they can turn instruments of domination into bridges of belonging. Like the Virgin of Guadalupe—an imposed icon that Indigenous peoples reanimated as a symbol of survival and resistance (La Lupita)—reclaimed civic symbols can serve as mirrors and prayers that reflect both survival and future visions. After all, the Bill of Rights was never meant for anyone other than male, white, Christian landowners, but today it has established the U.S. as a shining democratic beacon on the global stage— a position we hope to preserve.

Today's Political Landscape

The legal and political context matters because institutions are not neutral. Executive decisions and state legislatures have reshaped incentives for campuses, employers, and public agencies. The reverberations from major political decisions and subsequent administrative mandates have created a genuine sense of uncertainty for practitioners of diversity, equity, inclusion, and access working in public service or education. Employers and institutions now face conflicting and potentially unconstitutional enforcement guidance and shifting interpretations that affect how they design programs, hire, and sustain community work.

Public narratives have also become more rigid. Legislation in many states (such as Iowa), along with public campaigns and high-profile political messaging, have depicted Diversity, Equity, Inclusion, and Access (DEIA) work as partisan, anti-American, or as an illegal exercise of power. These campaigns succeed not only by influencing policy rather also by altering the story we tell about public service—turning accountability into a scandal and stewardship into an ideological test. These shifts are significant because the book asks: how do we maintain practices of belonging when the very language of belonging itself becomes contested?

Against this backdrop, our book presents an argument that democracy should be a practice of reciprocity and pluralistic governance, rather than a zero-sum contest for cultural dominance. We document the ways that law and policy can either foreclose or enable belonging, and we offer practical pathways—program designs, curricular choices, and civic rituals—that make cohabitation possible in contested spaces.

How to Read This Book

Please read our book as if Lisa and I are partners in tension. When Lisa names policy levers—funding streams, statutory design, and program metrics—she does so to show how civic architecture can be shaped to include, rather than gatekeep. When John-Paul tells ancestral stories and performs ritual frames, he does so to show how meaning is cultivated and how memory becomes a practice (what we may also call praxis) that sustains courage in the face of erasure.

Neither voice seeks to subsume or convince the other. Each interrogates the limits of their own logic and borrows what is generative from the other.

This means you'll encounter chapter structures that switch between analytical essays and narrative interventions, legal histories, ceremonies, program blueprints, and everyday practices for fostering belonging. We also include case studies ranging from a Midwestern county fair and community-building circles to informing legislative hearings or campus governance meetings. In simple terms, through storytelling, we share a practical manual for educators, leaders, and community organizers—with hands-on, applied tools to design inclusive public meetings, root civic learning in land stewardship, hold institutions accountable that fall short, and ritualize means to belonging—reciprocating, building resilience, and ensuring sustainability.

Our Invitation

This book is not a manifesto of certainty. It is a manual of practice for collective possibilities. We do not promise easy answers. We promise an approach that is inclusive, rigorous, humble, and generative. We invite leaders who care about civic life—educators, policymakers, organizers, and neighbors—to join a practice that merges policy craft with ceremonial intelligence. We invite readers to learn how to hold contradictions and to steward institutions so that they can become places where difference is neither a threat nor a nuisance, but an engine of democratic possibility.

We wrote this book because the stakes are high. Democracy will be shaped in the classrooms, on farms, in meeting rooms, and in prayer spaces of ordinary life. If pluralism is to survive, it must be made whole again and again, by people willing to bend toward Reverend Doctor Martin Luther King's arc of justice, to speak truth without annihilation, and to weave governance with memory.

This braid is our method and our prayer: a democracy braided of many voices, sustained by law and ritual, fierce in its tenderness, and uncompromising in its demand that our club, our community, our nation, and our world be rid of sexism, racism, homophobia, and so many other "isms" that seek to dominate rather than preserve the dignity of us all.

TABLE OF CONTENTS

PROLOGUE
(LISA)

It's August 2, 2018, and I'm sitting at my work desk. I answer the phone......

Some days are just etched in your memory. You remember odd items, sounds, smells, and what you were wearing. I had just gotten a phone call from my colleague, John-Paul Chaisson-Cárdenas, MSW (John-Paul), Iowa 4-H leader. He told me he had been fired for supporting LGBTQ+ youth. He was driving and sounded shell-shocked.

I said something, but I don't exactly recall what, other than I'm sorry this has happened or something like that. I put down the phone and wept. He and I were both people who had suffered because of our belief, our love for 4-H. It felt like the world was just imploding. I was no longer sitting at my Director, DY4-H desk. I had been removed from that position and was now sitting at a desk in another part of NIFA.

It's hard to believe that seven years have passed. In the Old Testament, seven years is symbolic, and though neither of us adheres to that faith, well, seven years seems long enough to wait to tell our story in our own voices.

How did this happen? Why did it happen? This book tells the tale of two leaders, John-Paul and Lisa, with dissimilar backgrounds and cultural upbringings, who shared a charge: a call to action to ensure that 4-H was open to all youth, regardless of their race, language, gender, disability, or who they love or what bathroom they may use.

Seven years later, the echoes of that phone call still reverberate—not just in our memories, but in the national conscience. The firing of John-Paul for advocating for LGBTQ+ inclusion in 4-H was not an isolated event; it was the beginning of a national pattern of institutional resistance to equity and belonging.

Today, as book bans rise, DEI programs are dismantled, and youth face renewed attacks on their identities; this story becomes more than a memoir—it becomes a mirror. It reflects the courage required to lead with love, and the cost of doing so in systems that often reward silence over solidarity. It reminds us that inclusion is not a trend; it is a moral imperative.

People need to care because the stakes are no longer theoretical. They are lived daily by young people navigating schools, clubs, and communities, which may or may not affirm their existence. When leaders like John-Paul and I are punished for protecting youth, it sends a dangerous signal about whose voices matter.

A Primer on the Land-grant Cooperative Extension System

When I was an undergraduate, I took two pre-service extension courses: one on "Teaching Adults in Extension" and the other called "Extension 101". For me, this is my reflection and interpretation of the history of the land-grant extension system and how 4-H is connected to the university land-grant extension system.

Many countries have attempted to emulate the United States' land-grant university model and its Cooperative Extension System. I am amazed by this formal educational framework which was established during the chaos of the most turbulent and divisive periods in U.S. history, the Civil War.

So, why is it called a "Land-grant"? Well, this is the not-so-pretty story where land was 'granted' by grabbing up tribal lands and distributing the actual land or the sale of those lands to establish the university. A Land-grant university is an educational institution for higher education that receives federal funds for teaching, research, and outreach (extension). There is at least one Land-grant institution in each state and territory of the United States. Typically, it is considered a public institution and is governed by the state through an appointed entity known as the Board of Regents.

The Land-grant university system is attributed to the Morrill Acts of 1862 and 1890. The intent was to establish higher education for the 'sons & daughters of the toil'. The first date, 1862, established at least one institution per state, while the 1890 date reflects the expansion to be more inclusive for historically black colleges. The Equity in Educational Land-Grant Status Act of 1994 expanded the land-grant status to tribal colleges. Initial curricular areas for education included agricultural arts, the mechanical arts or engineering, military science, and what was also known as the domestic arts. The idea was to create an opportunity for all, regardless of gender, race, or economic class.

The Cooperative Extension System was established through the Smith-Lever Act of 1914. The Smith-Lever Act further expanded the Land-grant university's mission to 'extend,' which means to translate science into practice for the citizens of their states. Seaman Ashahel Knapp is considered to be the 'Father' of Extension, whose work helped lay the foundation for the 4-H clubs. There is a pedestrian bridge connecting the USDA's main administration building, the Jamie L. Whitten Building, to the South Building, named *Seaman A. Knapp Memorial Pedestrian Bridge.* To me, it was really cool to see this piece of history, as the Whitten Building is the only federal agency with a presence on the National Mall.

The U.S. Cooperative Extension System (CES) is the country's largest non-formal educational network, drawing on the expertise of federal, state, and local partners to provide practical, unbiased information produced by researchers through centers and universities to the public. At land-grant universities, faculty and staff serve the state, along with extension professionals and staff at the local level, such as in counties or parishes, who serve communities. These individuals may hold 'extension' titles. However, for me, it is reciting the Extension Professional's Creed that honors the legacy and affirms my role in extension—focused on people, education, facts, lifelong learning, and making a difference in others' lives.

This public institution that provides public service to everyone within a community, state, country, and our world is, for me and all, framed as public servants—our higher calling.

Extension Professional's Creed

I believe in people and their hopes, their aspirations, and their faith; in their right to make their own plans and arrive at their own decisions; in their ability and power to enlarge their lives and plan for the happiness of those they love.

I believe that education, of which Extension is an essential part, is basic in stimulating individual initiative, self-determination, and leadership; that these are the keys to democracy and that people, when given facts they understand, will act not only in their self-interest, but also in the interest of society.

I believe that education is a lifelong process and the greatest university is the home; that my success as a teacher is proportional to those qualities of mind and spirit that give me welcome entrance to the homes of the families I serve.

I believe in intellectual freedom to search for and present the truth without bias and with courteous tolerance toward the views of others.

I believe that Extension is a link between the people and the ever-changing discoveries in the laboratories.

I believe in the public institutions of which I am a part.

I believe in my own work and in the opportunity I have to make my life useful to humanity.

Because I believe these things, I am an Extension professional.

Once I achieved five years of service, I was eligible to join Epsilon Sigma Phi, the Extension Professionals Honorary Society, and receive the Extension Worker's Creed, which hung proudly in my various offices as an extension professional.

4-H Ties to the Land-grant Extension System, 4-H as an IDEAL

Everything is connected. 4-H is usually the first program a youth gets involved in at a land-grant university. Therefore, 4-H is tied to the research and evidence-based extension system of these universities. Additionally, 4-H's relationship with the land-grant extension service is based on legislation from the years that established these programs: 1862, 1890, and 1994.

There is an irony for me, that while our country was so divided, where one state had to enter as a 'free' state and another as a 'slave' state, that then led to the Civil War, a war about who was 'free' and who was not free, a slave. Yet, the land grants were established to provide access, equity, and opportunity. For my paternal family side, they left Tennessee to move to Kansas to be in a 'free state,' though Kansas at one time was known as "bleeding" Kansas due to the bloodshed that occurred.

The creation of the land-grant university system is quite an accomplishment, yet, inherently flawed from the beginning, with something sacred being taken away from those who held the land.

The initial 1862 institutions were primarily focused on white, rural youth. The 1890s, which followed, were established as separate, yet 'equal' institutions. However, the inequity was and still is on how they are funded and supported. The separate yet equal based on racial characteristics continued with the formation and support of the 1994 or tribal colleges and institutions. These separate yet targeted institutions also perpetuated biases in programming.

The democratizing and yet pluralistic efforts allowed for youth, those under the age of 19 years of age, to belong and participate in extension youth programming. 4-H considers its birth to be 1902, when rural educators set out to create a four-fold human development program to educate through hands-on, experiential learning in a non-formal setting. These tomato, corn, and canning clubs provided youth with practical experiences in the latest translation of science into practical methods. 4-H was incorporated into Cooperative Extension through its establishment with the Smith-Level Act of 1914. 4-H has transitioned and adapted through the decades.

The inequities in the funding and support still exist between the 1862s, 1890s, and 1994s. For me, it isn't easy to understand how we continue to perpetuate, through the Farm Bill, a siloed funding approach to the U.S. Cooperative Extension System. I mean, the word 'cooperative' is in the name of Cooperative Extension. The system is flawed; yet, if we were to start over today, would we honor and respect the diverse needs of our communities, of our people, and their need and desire for an effective and efficient system to translate science into practice? Bureaucracies tend to hold onto their structures till they are no longer effective, and the seeds of their destruction are inherently within them.

4-H has been referred to in the past as a 'movement', yet a movement has a life cycle; it is created, it grows, it achieves success or failure, and then it dissolves, ceases to exist, and dissipates. Sometimes movements have a charismatic leader. 4-H is more than a 'movement'. For me, 4-H represents an ideal, an adherence to something 'bigger', much like the founding documents for the United States.

It is why the **Constitution**, which, as it starts out, "*We the People of the United States...*"

We the People of the United States, in Order to form a more perfect Union, establish Justice, insure domestic Tranquility, provide for the common defence, promote the general Welfare, and secure the Blessings of Liberty to ourselves and our Posterity, do ordain and establish this Constitution for the United States of America.

And the Declaration of Independence which states,

"We hold these truths to be self-evident, that all men are created equal, that they are endowed by their Creator with certain unalienable Rights, that among these are Life, Liberty and the pursuit of Happiness."

and 4-H Pledge which states,

*I pledge my **Head** to clearer thinking,*

*my **Heart** to greater loyalty,*

*my **Hands** to larger service,*

*and my **Health** to better living,*

for my club, my community, my country, and my world.

These foundational documents speak to me, my heart, and my soul, for they all aim to create an "ideal," defined as either a guiding principle or a standard of high ethical behavior; a model of something without equal in principle or value. This ideal envisions a world and environment where all can flourish. It is about the collective, collaborative world to which my public service—first instilled in me through my club and community as a 4-H'er, and later for my country and my world —was committed. I pledged myself as a U.S. public servant. 4-H, as an IDEAL, is what I and others strive for and continue to pursue—"To Make the Best Better," as the 4-H Motto states. This 4-H Ideal is rooted in public institutions that are meant to serve the people and ensure that everyone has access to that service.

1

I"BLEED GREEN"AND THE HARMONY HUSTLERS (LISA)

I 'bleed' green, as in my family, my three brothers, and I say we owe our existence to the 4-H program. 4-H was foundational to me as it shaped through lived experiences who I believe I am today and the values I stand for. Our parents were from neighboring counties in Kansas and met at an older youth 4-H camp, where, with only a two-year age difference, Dad was a counselor and Mom was a camper. Dad had transformed his 4-H dairy cattle project into a registered Holstein-Friesian herd, and when they married, they named the business Ja-Sal Holstein-Friesian as their first names are Jack and Sally. My parents bought out my paternal Sexton grandparents' farm and settled in to raise the four of us.

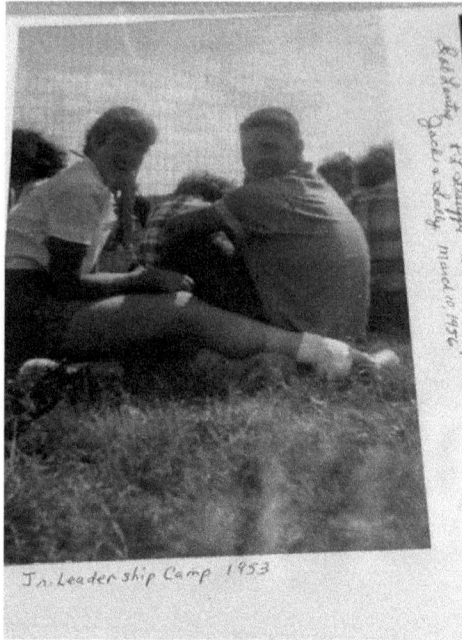

Photo of Mom & Dad
Jack and Sally, Lisa's parents, met at Jr. Leadership Camp, Rocks Spring Ranch

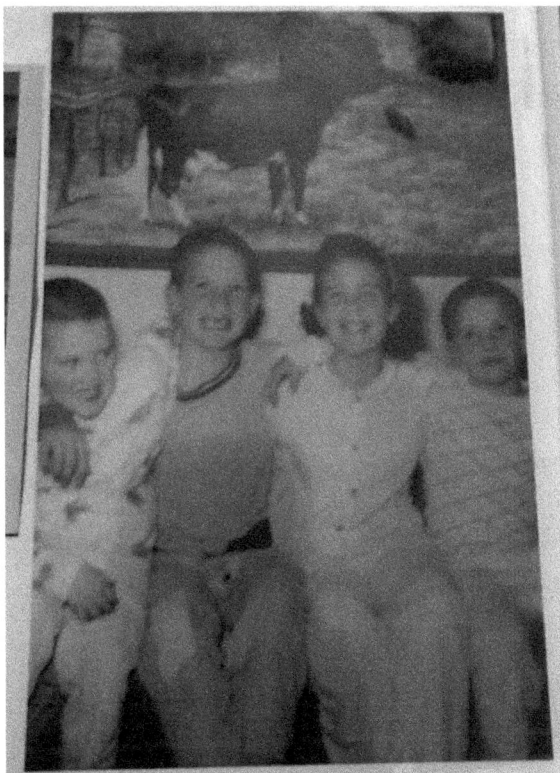

Photo of 4 Kids + Cow Painting

Lisa and her 3 brothers sit underneath their Uncle Dick's painting of a cow their dad owned

We were kids who lived 15 miles from town, so going to get groceries was a big deal, and though we had neighbors close by, we were also fortunate to have our first cousins just around the corner in a section of land, or one square mile. We could walk through the pasture faster to meet up. Life was spent doing chores, carrying buckets of grain, pitching out the manure from the barn and stalls, and assisting with the milking. Before studying genetics in school, I learned how to read bull stud books and pick the best bull to breed my dairy heifer and cows to increase their potential offspring's milk production

11

and butter fat. As the only daughter and oldest child, I became the chief cook and bottle washer, so it was my job to initiate the prep for the lunch and dinner meals during haying and various crop harvest seasons.

It seemed like it took forever, yet finally reaching the age of 8 by January 1st, I was old enough to join the Harmony Hustlers 4-H club. I was so excited to join 4-H, and with my first dairy calf, Trixie, my dad made for me a baling hay twine halter so I could teach her to lead. Baling twine is a strong cord used to bind bales of hay or straw. Visualize a small calf resisting being pulled in one direction. I soon learned that tugging led to a struggle, while providing a slight amount of slack allowed Trixie and I to move together. This life skill is one that has been repeated many times with not only animals, as I learned with groups, to give a little to move in a forward motion. As I had no older siblings, I truly looked up to the older 4-H'ers who were my neighbors and some even my relatives. They made me feel like I 'belonged', was a part of something by joining this club. I was still learning cursive writing as I affixed my name to the club roster. These older 4-H'ers inducted me into the 4-H club and taught me how meetings were structured and conducted. In fact, a replication of the new member induction ceremony with me as a new member was used in the model meeting competition. We won the model meeting competition at the county and regional levels. Then we presented it at the state 4-H camp, Rock Springs Ranch, where Governor Pearson attended just ahead of the historic Topeka tornado.

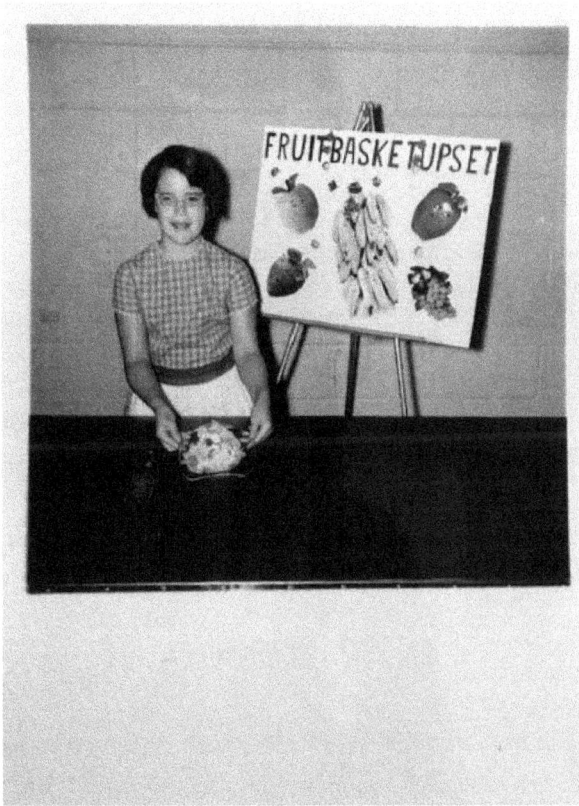

Fruit Basket Upset Demonstration
Lisa holds in her hands the product with the demonstration poster's title "Fruit Basket Upset"

My first demonstration was titled "Peppermint Fluff". A demonstration is an opportunity to 'show and tell' how to do something. Here I was teaching folks in my 4-H club how to make a peppermint ice cream milkshake. As a dairy farmer's daughter, we could get gallons of ice cream, butter and other dairy products from the milk cooperative. A specialty treat was to have peppermint ice cream with actual chunks of peppermint. My demonstration was quite simple – just a glass of milk and a scoop or two of peppermint ice cream with a couple of quick stirs with a long spoon to make it 'fluffy'.

Giving a demonstration does require one to do two things at once, to organize your thoughts and speak while doing something, and to be able to address questions when asked. This was my first foray into public speaking, and as a life skill, it has been something that I have used throughout my life.

Demonstrations and project talks provided me with opportunities to develop skills, including speaking confidently despite being nervous, and to collect my thoughts cohesively. These skills ultimately helped me excel in both debate and forensic events in high school and led me to quiz out of speech as a freshman in college. It was a skill set that I drew upon for presentations at the federal level when sharing about 4-H to other federal agencies, presenting on the first-ever Positive Youth Development (PYD) Research Agenda, and speaking to National 4-H Congress and 4-H Conference delegates. I also believe that it helped me read the audience, engage with them, and convey my beliefs and support for PYD practices. I will admit that I still get butterflies and experience sweaty palms when asked to speak. I draw upon all the techniques from those early 4-H club experiences and take a deep breath, which helps, and smile, as my first 4-H agent, Larry Riat, would remind us that it takes more muscles to frown.

I was a member of the Harmony Hustlers 4-H Club, and my dad, who was once a member, served as one of the club leaders. I learned from Peggy Chronister, the female leader, about parliamentary procedure, Roberts' Rules of Order, how to write a check as the club treasurer, and how to write a news report on our club meetings, which were submitted to the Abilene Reflector-Chronicle. Later, I also learned how to represent the club at the county 4-H Council, a county-wide group with two youth and two adults—one male and one female—representing each club in the county. The Council was responsible for all county-wide activities, and I served on the first-ever interstate exchange committee. While I was in my first 4-H agent position, the Harmony Hustlers 4-H club celebrated its 50th anniversary. Club alumni reflected on the skills they learned that were put to good use in life, such as keeping records, leading meetings, using parliamentary procedures, having fun, and making a difference in their community.

Between my three brothers and me, the four of us explored 4-H projects and activities in a variety of topics that interested us, including entomology, geology, electricity, woodworking, foods, dairy foods, clothing, gardening, photography, dairy judging, leadership, citizenship, reading, and public speaking, along with several community service projects. I mention this because 4-H was a family affair for us, with parent-child involvement that I cherish for the memories and even extended to aunts, uncles, and grandparents. I remember going to a tree farm where I learned about different leaves and types of trees as my grandpa worked there during the off-season. It was a field trip. There was also a field trip organized by my mom so I and others could learn how cheese was made. I was surprised to see the food dye dumped into the vat to make the cheese 'yellow'. My youngest brother was puzzled when he finally joined the club and became 'official' since he had participated all along.

4-H was an essential part of our rural lives, with church and school being the other key pillars. It was a multi-generational experience for me, as my Grandma Stauffer was a clothing leader, and my mom would ship me off to stay for a week to finish my clothing projects. We would watch her favorite soap opera while doing hand stitching on hems, securing buttons, and completing well-pressed darts. One year, my brother and I not only won county fashion revue awards, but we also competed at the state fair, earning purple ribbons. I modeled the clothes I made, which included a jacket, shirt, and long skirt, while holding a pair of pants. My brother modeled a purchased suit and tie outfit. My aunt and various local women made sure I learned how to cook nutritious meals, knit, and crochet, while also tending the garden. You know, the garden was my responsibility until the tomatoes began to set and ripen, and suddenly they became my dad's tomatoes to tend. I cherish the memory of him in his overalls, checking the vines and plucking the ripe ones, just before his life was cut short.

Those moments with all the adult women and men created lasting memories and bonds. I learned how to calculate, by hand with a pencil that had an eraser, the price per hundredweight of what my cows produced in milk to determine the cost-benefit and loss. We, my brothers and I, had an opportunity to each own up to 4 animals, and that allowed me to purchase a sewing machine, which I still have, contact lenses, a bicycle, buy my first car, a manual 3-speed with no air conditioning, a Honda Civic, travel to Europe, and pay for 3 of the 3.5 years I attended at Kansas State University.

Caring for my community was integral to my 4-H experience. As a club, we canvassed for the American Red Cross, the Cancer Society, brought meals to people in our neighborhood who were ill or had a death in the family or needed assistance to finish harvest. The Harmony Hustlers were recognized for our club's service to our community. And key to the service was that it didn't matter if we 'liked you', we were there for you. Neighbors were there for each other, and so was our club.

As a high school graduation gift, I had the chance to travel to Washington, D.C., on a two-week bus trip to the 4-H Citizenship Short Course. During that trip, I learned about our country's civic engagement, how a bill becomes a law, met some members of Kansas' House of Representatives, including K. Sebelius, J. Skubitz, D. Glickman, and Senators R. Dole and J. Pearson. I also toured national monuments and made lifelong friends from across Kansas as we sang around the Washington Monument at night.

I remember, in particular, Joe Skubitz—though he was not my elected representative—he had been a former teacher. He pulled all of us Kansas 4-H'ers aside and showed us all the cool places to stand in the Rotunda. He even closed the door so we could take a quick snapshot, and a guard opened the door to ask if everything was OK. He quickly replied 'yes' with a wink to us. He made an impression on me as someone who was authentic, real, and down-to-earth among our elected officials. I see now how that experience nudged me closer to becoming a public servant in D.C.

4-H allowed me to travel beyond the 45 minutes to my maternal grandparents' house. My first 4-H travel experience was an interstate exchange trip to Fergus Falls, Minnesota, where my host family took me to Bemidji to put my feet in the headwaters of the Mississippi. My family hosted for several interstate exchange trips, which allowed my brothers and I to experience different parts of the country yet share with others our 4-H experience. From those early travels, as I met and experienced how others live, my views have been broadened, I take note of how resilience shapes others' lives, and I seek to find the similarities, note the differences and respect them. It led me to realize that until I know someone, really know them, it is easy to lump them into categories 'them' and 'us', which is dehumanizing and fails to acknowledge that within each of us is a desire to 'belong', to feel 'connected' and to be recognized as we are.

The trip's timing to D.C. was unique as the nation was preparing for the Bicentennial. We did a stopover in St. Louis to go up in the Arch, and then spent the 4th of July in Columbus, Ohio, with fireworks, and then on to an overnight stay and tour in Gettysburg before going to the National 4-H Center. Preparations for the next year's Bicentennial celebrations were in progress across the country as a buildup for this historic excitement which for me provided an opportunity to reflect on where we were as a country and where we were headed.

In Gettysburg, I felt the presence of those lives sacrificed for their causes yet honored by Lincoln in his address where Lincoln's speech resonates yet to me still, tying his Gettysburg Address to the Declaration of Independence to even this present day, "...*our fathers brought forth on this continent, a new nation, conceived in Liberty, and dedicated to the proposition that all men are created equal*" ... *that the nation, shall have a new birth of freedom, and that government of the people, by the people, for the people, shall not perish.*"

The words " ... the *government of the people, by the people, for the people, shall not perish.*" reminded me of my high school government teacher who challenged us to remember the privilege it was to have a voice, to register to vote and to be engaged in government using these words. Later, I was able to see, as I walked the streets of D.C., the historical placards that reminded one of the Civil War, the assassination of President Lincoln and the paths through the District taken by John Wilkes Booth. To serve, to be humble, and to do without seeking glory or fame were messages I received on that trip and were ones that I later took to heart in my role as a public servant.

Coming to D.C., to our nation's capital, was awe-inspiring; to tread where Jefferson, Lincoln, the Adams and so many others gave of themselves for me, for us, for our country, well, it truly made all the 4-H community service efforts even more poignant as I realized I wanted to continue to serve "... my community, my country and my world", in the 4-H pledge in some capacity. Though I had not settled yet on my career as a public servant, this was a turning point. You see, I had thought to study computer science and enrolled at Kansas State University in their program that fall. I remember struggling in the weeks before school started with my decision, and my mom suggested I try computer science for one semester and then decide what path to take. That's what I did. I changed my major three times yet still managed to graduate in 3.5 years. It meant I took between 18 to 22 credits most semesters while living at Clovia, the 4-H Women's Scholarship House.

Because of 4-H, I became familiar with Kansas State University (KSU) through my participation in various state-level 4-H events, such as 4-H Round Up and dairy judging. This familiarity eventually led me to live at Clovia, the Alpha Chapter, where I served as President, was the chief shower cleaner, and cooked early morning breakfast for 64 women. Here, one put into practice service to others as we all relied on each other to perform our tasks; otherwise, food was not on the table, and the house was not kept clean. I can guarantee to you that no one ever got 'foot fungus' while I cleaned the showers! Cooperative living is an experience for someone such as me who did not have any sisters. I suddenly acquired 63 Clovia's sisters who provided experiences and opportunities to practice my empathy, tolerance, as after all, not everyone gets along easily or is as neat a freak as you are, and support when someone had those moments of success and failures. We had two levels of an open-air sleeping porch, which meant electric blankets were necessary when the temperatures dropped. We were randomly placed with 3 others to share a room where we hung our clothes and had a desk for a year. We went through a pledge process where we learned the history and traditions of Clovia. You soon learned who to go to for studying assistance and who to go to when you wanted to have fun. Singing was just a part of living at Clovia, and one of my favorites is still "I'm a Flaming Clover". Sharing our evening meal together was a nightly event. We practiced on Wednesday evenings in formal dining settings, so we were prepared if or when we were invited to such events. Several of my Clovia sisters are and have served as extension professionals. 4-H provided me with so many wonderful relationships!

In the summer before I graduated from Kansas State University, I traveled for 4-H internationally for six weeks on the People to People Citizen Ambassador Program (CAP) to the European countries of the Netherlands, France, Germany, Switzerland, Denmark, back to the Netherlands, and England with five days in Moscow, the now former U.S.S.R. capital. We were a group of about 60-some youth and adults, with the group composed mostly of Kansas 4-H'ers ranging in age from 16 to 22. Most of us had never been overseas. Our chaperones were from Kansas, Eldon and Millie Weaver, and another was a volunteer leader from the state of Georgia. My friend Cindy and I traveled to the state of Georgia when invited to attend David and Debo's 20-minute wedding. Mylie and Weve would stop in to visit, whether in Kansas or in Arizona, where they eventually ended up wintering. Close connections were made with each of these 4-H travel experiences

While on the Citizen Ambassador Program, we had homestays in each of the countries. In my trip diary, the emphasis that was placed by State Department and CAP Officials reflected on homestays, our roles as citizen ambassadors, and this trip wasn't a tourist trip; it was one of diplomacy. Two or more youth were placed together in the homestays, so we were able to debrief after each stay. In my Denmark homestay, my host father showed me pictures of my home county in Kansas and Rock Springs Ranch, as his daughter had been a Rotary scholar at the University of Kansas. And, in Switzerland, I met youth who knew some of my K-State friends because of their mutual FFA experiences. I also met people who knew the IFYE, International 4-H Youth Exchange delegate, Bertie Baumgardner, whom my grandparents had hosted and whom I had met as a child when she visited our family's farm. It emphasized to me how connected we are to each other.

There were also opportunities to visit cultural sites such as Versailles, Notre Dame, Anne Frank's house, see Delftware being made, and watch Swiss cowbells being crafted. Camaraderie developed on the bus trips with our driver, Henk, who spoke seven languages and tolerated our singing. The trip offered a glimpse into others' daily lives, fostering a two-way dialog with U.S. 4-H'ers.

My time in Moscow brings up the memory of going through passport control stations where the guards would chuckle over my last name, Sexton. I also recall how our guide would also say "… and after the Great Revolution…" to point out structures that were quite utilitarian-looking. These rather ugly structures contrasted with the stores where Faberge eggs were on display and to a monastery next door. The utilitarian and dual purpose of the structures was evident when we took the subway, as it was deep, well-lit and felt like a possible bomb shelter. I saw Lenin's Tomb as we were hustled in and out by guards with guns. We knew our rooms and luggage had been searched, and once back in the Netherlands, it felt like a relief to be 'free' again. I do recall that some of us reached down to touch the ground.

An award trip to the National 4-H Congress in Chicago as the state 4-H dairy winner at the end of my 4-H membership career led me to meet my future co-worker, Janet Rediker. A few years later, she called to ask if I would be interested in being a 4-H Agent in Lyon County. I applied, was accepted, and graduated from KSU a semester early, allowing me to start on January 2nd in a month-long training program with Martha Murphy. My first three months were ones where 12 inches of snow fell regularly, and I didn't get to tour the fairgrounds or see Anderson Hall in Lyon County, since plowing the fairgrounds wasn't a priority. I was hired as the first female 4-H agent in Lyon County. Up to that point, only men had served as 4-H agents, and the position was seen as a 'trainer' position to become either a home economist or an agricultural agent.

When one is the 'first', it creates an informal opportunity to be a role model, to serve as an opportunity for young girls to see themselves also in this position. I recall that on my visit to the county in preparation for the interview, I was invited to tour the county with the ag agent and county extension director. One question he asked me while we drove around was if I cried easily, to which I replied, "No, I wear contacts". He found that response funny and appeared to accept me, as I was subsequently hired. When I look back on that 'tour', I now know it was a test of acceptance with the ag agent. So once my training month was over, I was at my desk when I received a phone call. I answered politely, "Hello, this is Lisa, how may I help you? This male voice said something like I'm "Herman Haney, and I want to know how long to leave my roosters in with my hens". And, I said, "Let me place you on hold, and I'll check". What I didn't know at the time, it was a prank from the neighboring county ag agent planned with my ag agent. They were hoping for me to say, "Just a minute" and hang up. Only I thwarted them. It led to a lot of laughter by my ag agent, who came in to tell me about the prank and introduce me to one of my extension colleagues. Yes, hazing was a part of my first position while I tried to assert myself as an adult, since I was working with adults who were as old or older than my own parents. These experiences led me to serve, I hope as a better mentor to new hires, as I never wanted anyone to have those experiences thrust on them.

I completed ten years in the position. It was my first role as a public servant, an extension professional. I was told during my first week that two things worked 'perfectly'—the county Fair Queen contest and the fair livestock sale. Although it wasn't my intention, listening to the leaders and families involved made it clear that both needed some adjustments. This showed the importance of listening to the clientele. Change is inevitable, yet can be fostered, and my role was to be that change agent.

Of course, I heard the youth who said the adults were taking over too much of the program, which created an interesting challenge since I was barely four years older than some of them. This sparked serious conversations with some adults who viewed my support for the youth as 'threatening,' but it also strengthened my resolve to ensure the youth had a voice while respecting the adults' roles. After all, the 4-H model of youth development, Positive Youth Development (PYD), is built on a partnership between youth and adults, regardless of age or gender. In some respects, it reflected what I was experiencing in my position as I was regarded as a 'youth' to the 'adults' I was working with. I sought out advice from other extension agents, who informed me that there were cyclical and systemic challenges. One challenge, besides partnering with youth and adults, was to address the gap between the number of potential youth and those who were at present served/engaged in the program.

As required by law, I established an expansion and review committee, and I worked to create a cadre of opportunities that promoted inclusivity through school enrichment and short-term project clubs. This led to the creation of two more 4-H clubs and outreach within a school where seven global languages were spoken. It also ensured that the expansion and review committee was representative of the county's demographics and was more than just a 'one and done' committee. This led to some interesting discussions about whether youth who only wanted to be part of the county-wide horse project club also had to belong to a community club. This discussion was sidestepped by considering short-term, 4 to 6-week after-school project club offerings in 3 local schools led by youth and adults. *Navigating what was comfortable and yet still led to opportunities was truly a learn-by-doing experience for me as to what was the 'edge' for others' comfort zones.*

I managed to gain support as a female 4-H agent from the 4-H parents and received a backhanded compliment when a 4-H dad said to me, 'You're not too bad for a female 4-H agent,' while assisting at the sheep show. I suppose one could say that having three brothers gave me the impetus to prove that girls can do anything boys can do, only better. What sustained me during those first three years was my faith. I read "The Power of Positive Thinking" by Norman Vincent Peale. I wrote quotes onto 3x5 cards and carried them around with me. I still have the book and a 3x5 card which says… "God is with me, God is helping me, God is guiding me. Affirm it, visualize it, believe it, and it will actualize it." I have a highlighted section. (pg. 105) " Have faith in God (that's positive, isn't it) for verily I say unto you, that whoever shall say unto *this* mountain (that's specific) be thou removed (that is, stand aside) and be thou cast into the seas (that means out of sight. And "If God be for us, who can be against us, "where one is to say it 10 times each day (p. 25). In the book, there is a quote from Emerson, "They conquer who they believe they can…. Do the thing you fear, and the death of fear is certain." (pg. 24)

I struggled, though, to find balance in my work-life with the birth of my first child. My spouse at that time would say to others, "I have to babysit my kid cuz the wife is working", when I had night and weekend 4-H activities. He was challenged, though, by another woman who questioned him, asking, "Isn't he your kid, too, so why is it babysitting?".

My oldest son was initially a trooper and attended many functions until he was a year old. I requested to take a sabbatical to pursue a master's degree in business administration, which led me to leave my first 4-H position to become a Convention and Visitors' Bureau (CVB) Director. I left the 4-H position as I thought overall it would be a positive for my family, since a county 4-H Agent works lots of nights and weekends. During my tenure as a CVB Director, I yearned to find my way back to being an extension 4-H professional. Over the next two years, I applied for about 30 some positions and interviewed for 3. In one position, I was 8.5 months pregnant and had a telephone interview. When I was told the date for the in-person interview, it was my due date, and I knew I couldn't travel by air due to my pregnancy. I was told by that extension director then that they would not proceed with interviewing me since I couldn't attend in person. Yet, I missed the 4-H program, and when my second child was a year old, I took a position as a Pima County 4-H Agent in Tucson, Arizona.

In Arizona, we embraced an inclusive outreach and engagement approach within the Arizona Cooperative Extension System under Dr. Shirley O'Brien's leadership. Here, diversity was expanded beyond civil rights compliance, and we were challenged to engage with all potential audiences through outreach and programming.

This led to opportunities to work with various other youth programs such as park and recreation, military child and youth programs, after-school programs, Boys and Girls Club, and Boy and Girl Scouts, to find and complement each other's program niche. I also had the opportunity to learn from my Hispanic colleague, Lita, how to engage and adopt the best approach to work in a more diverse environment than I had experienced in Kansas.

4-H in Arizona for me was more than a rural versus urban engagement. It was about outreach and engagement within a county the size of the state of Massachusetts, including a tribal reservation, and a population of nearly 1 million. How to engage and be authentic with the target audience was critical. Through my work as a Pima County Extension 4-H Agent, I had opportunities in many areas. One was with the Tucson Police Department, where I taught clowning as a tool for identity development in the Gang Resistance and Education Training Program (GREAT) to middle school youth. These youths were identified as 'wanna be' gang members. Identity development through clowning was a way to help youth understand who they want to present to the world each day. Sometimes, trying on a new persona allows you to shift and change how others perceive you. First, everyone looked in the mirrors to see themselves as they are. Then I discussed the types of clowns, petite and grotesque, and how both color and features created that type of face. By using cold cream and food coloring, we created a color palette and a base color for their face. Each youth initially crafted their face on a piece of paper. Some youth then worked in pairs to paint each other's faces. I remember one young man having several girls work on his face. Later, the sergeant in charge said he was surprised to see that the young man allowed them to do that. I guess he was one they were observing based on potential affiliation.

Working with the Arizona School for the Deaf and Blind provided an opportunity to engage with youth who have disabilities. Here, more tactile experiential learning was used. My extension colleague, Joe Hiller, expanded my awareness and connection with tribal programming through Indian Country Extension (ICE) and emphasized the importance of respecting their sovereign nation status. For me, it reminded me of my roots in Kansas and the sacredness and stewardship of the land.

One experience gave me insight and increased my awareness of what it was like to be in the 'minority' at a multi-cultural event where youth and adults representing the local tribal communities and South Tucson gathered. I was one of two straight, white women. I remember playing "Two Truths and One Lie" with this group and how all present thought my one truth was that I played Dorothy in the Wizard of Oz because I was from Kansas. That was my lie, and it just emphasized how perception creates bias.

While working for the University of Arizona, I acquired my M.A. and Ph.D. in Educational Psychology. Faculty and staff could take courses and receive reduced tuition, so I was able to work full-time and take classes part-time as a single parent. One class where we conducted peer review as primary, secondary, and tertiary reviewers allowed me to apply the skills I gained in that class when I was the Children, Youth, and Families at Risk National Program Coordinator. After about five years as a county extension agent, I applied and accepted the position to move 'on campus' as the Curriculum Coordinator for 4-H. Being on campus led to other experiences where I took on various roles, such as interim volunteer extension specialist, acting Assistant Director of 4-H Youth Development, and Special Advisor to the Extension Director for Outreach and Engagement.

With my youngest son in his final year of high school, my career path then led me to Washington, D.C, to work on the Children, Youth and Families at Risk (CYFAR) program on an Inter-Personnel Act (IPA) from the University of Arizona where my role was to lead a transition to an expanded competitive grants program to include the 1890 institutions. The term 'youth at risk' was and still is a term that causes me pause. I had grantees ask if it could be changed to "Children, Youth and Families at Risk Are Resilient and be CYFAR-squared. When I raised this internally, at CSREES/NIFA, I was told that one person opposed changing the name as it would not emphasize the need and the population, would not resonate and would take political goodwill to make the case to change it.

This IPA assignment lasted until February 12, 2010, when I assumed the position of Director of the Division of Youth and 4-H, as CSREES (Cooperative System for Research, Education, and Extension) was reorganized into the National Institute of Food and Agriculture (NIFA) within the USDA.

Taking the oath of office and pledging to the Constitution was a tremendous honor. In my 4-H experiences, a key component of my 4-H club was community service. We volunteered for many key causes such as the American Heart Association, American Red Cross, water well testing, and other key civic engagement opportunities that were presented. When I came to D.C. to work for the federal government, it was coming full circle from my initial 4-H Citizenship Short Course trip (later called Citizenship Washington Focus). My friends from other countries who have had required military service came to my mind as I reflected that a tour of duty in our nation's capital would provide all an opportunity for public service, to gain a better understanding of how to govern, and how a government of the people works.

I would tell youth and adults that they too, could come and work for the federal government. After all, I, a Kansas dairy farmer's daughter, had not seen myself in this public servant position. To help others see themselves, I would encourage 4-H'ers to come visit our office, and I made a point of having student interns, especially programs such as the 1890 Scholars, HACU, Hispanic Association of Colleges and Universities, the Thurgood Marshall Scholars, another Historically Black College and University scholarship program and the federal government internship program, Pathways.

It is important to see oneself in a role; to experience and try it on. I was trying to grow others for public service, to pay it forward.

In my role, I was responsible for 'right-sizing' staffing, building connections, competency, and capacity within NIFA, USDA, and then across the federal system for 4-H. The team I led was exceptional, and those amazing colleagues remain some of my dearest friends.

We revisited the National 4-H strategic plan, created an organizational system for public-private partnerships, built a system of accountability and program quality, raised awareness of demographics, and sought ways to engage and expand opportunities with our Land-grant partners for 4-H.

This led to making sure 4-H was at the table with the Department of Justice's Office of Juvenile Justice and Delinquency Programs (OJJDP), the White House OSTEP, Office of Science, Technology, Education Programs, members of the career staff's federal Interagency Working Group on Youth Programs (IWGYP), which enabled DY4-H to re-configure National 4-H Conference to have youth voice at the table on issues pertinent to about 15 other federal agencies as well as the House and Senate Agriculture Committees. In addition, with the Center for International Programs, (CIP), DY4-H and CIP, both within USDA NIFA, established an informal International Youth Development Working Group with other career federal employees interested in international positive youth development.

When serving on the Office of Juvenile Justice and Delinquency Programs (OJJDP) committee, I was the career employee behind the USDA political appointee or principal, and I sometimes sat at the table where Judge Gordon Martin from Massachusetts served. He was a staunch supporter from Massachusetts for 4-H and had, in his early career, been a "freedom fighter". During this time, 4-H programs were funded via 4-H Council (our national private partner) to support expansion opportunities using Children, Youth, and Families at Risk (CYFAR) programs that worked with audiences supported by OJJDP.

My work included domestic and international, as there was a strong interest in all the entities that had "4-H" in their title or used a translation of the word "4-H". My work assignments took me to Iraq, Pakistan, Tanzania, and Georgia, and I had the opportunity to meet with visitors from Turkey, Nigeria, the Netherlands, Japan, and Korea. Additionally, I participated in a 21-day youth engagement scoping mission for Feed the Future programs funded by USAID in Tanzania.

Everywhere I went, I found 4-H alums serving in public service, whether on the House or Senate Agriculture Committees and in other federal agencies, while there were others who said they wished they could have been in 4-H as youth, to which I would reply that you still can be… as an adult volunteer leader.

4-H is and has been a vehicle for me to network, build connections, competency, and capacity, and tout that 4-H is where my tagline, "youth and adults who work together to create sustainable community change."

2

NOT YOUR "TRADITIONAL" 4-HER (JOHN-PAUL)

I am most definitely not your typical 4-H kid. But I have come to bleed green like Lisa. Reflecting on my life, I realize that I had no prior contact with 4-H before applying to be the State Director and Leader of the Iowa program—except for one possible instance. As a high school student in Cheyenne, Wyoming, I cleaned the stables after the 4-H and FFA youth had completed their events before the state fair. I am not sure if it was a significant fair event or something more local, since I took the job purely to earn some money and did not learn about 4-H or FFA. However, since I worked in 4-H, I have often wondered why I was never invited to participate in the youth program in Cheyenne.

Let me give you some context. It was the late 1980s, during Frontier Days in Cheyenne, Wyoming. "The Daddy of 'Em All," they called it. Back then, it felt like there were more horses than people. I was a Spanish-speaking Guatemalan kid, new to Cheyenne, and definitely not part of the horse crowd. I didn't own animals. I didn't wear boots. I didn't know the difference between a bridle and a halter.

Most days, I felt like I was watching someone else's movie, just standing off to the side. The horse kids were something else. They were up before sunrise, brushing, feeding, and training. They moved with purpose, like they'd been born into it. 4-H and other youth equestrian events weren't just fun; they were serious. Discipline, money, and time. These kids didn't mess around. They didn't have time for small talk or outsiders, especially not me, the stable boy. Or, like some of them referred to me, "spick".

But then there was June. She was the fair queen. Not just because of the sash and crown, but because she carried herself like she belonged to the fair. Her roping boots were scuffed from real use, her jeans faded from long days in the saddle, and her cowboy hat sat low over her eyes like it had seen a hundred sunrises. I remember watching her ride—her horse, "Refugio" (a Spanish word for refuge). Her horse responded to the slightest shift of her weight as she turned the corners in her event. She didn't yank or kick when she led the horse. She floated.

In hindsight, I wonder if it was her horse's name that first caught my attention. In those days, you did not hear Spanish very often in Cheyenne, at least not in public. Whatever it was, "Refugio", connoted the memory of my Mama Alfa's (my Abuelita) whispered prayers over to the Virgen of Guadalupe, to the milpa that knew our names, and the wind that spoke to me in…. Well, maybe a bullhorn, it was Cheyenne after all, the windiest city in North America.

But getting back to "Refugio", it may have resonated with my inner soul, since we didn't plan to leave Guatemala—we fled. My mother, a teacher and community leader, had become a target during the war. One day, she disappeared. When she returned, she was changed. She never spoke of what happened, but we knew: it was time to leave Guatemala. We packed what we could into suitcases and boarded a plane to Houston the next day. No farewell, no ceremony.

Just escape. I left behind my home, the women who raised me, the language of my childhood, and the streets where I first saw what happens when human and civil rights are suspended in a society.

I didn't talk to June much at first. I didn't know how, and my English was "muy malo". But I watched. She wasn't loud. She wasn't showy. She was kind in the way that made kids like me, who didn't fit, who were different, who came from far away, feel at home. She taught me to love things without me ever knowing it. About country music. About how to stand tall even when you feel small. About how belonging doesn't always come with an invitation—it sometimes comes with a glance that says, "You're okay." June didn't change who I was; we never became great friends. But her gentle and welcoming confidence made me realize, maybe I didn't have to apologize for being me (just a Spanish-speaking stable hand, a "spick"), simply by being her. She was a true 4-Her.

White Maize: El Norte

What can I say, I loved Frontier Days; after all, what was there not to love for a Latino teenage boy?

There was food, girls, and music! While the first two is self-explanatory for a teenage boy, I am not sure most people realize that Country music, for me, feels like the soundtrack of mi tierra. The feeling it brings to me reminds me of the marimba back home or the cumbia that gets everyone moving at a family party. It's got that same earthy pulse, that same way of telling stories about love, loss, and holding on to what matters. When I hear Western Swing or old American folk tunes, I think of my Mama Alfa, who used to sing corridos or play rancheras from Mexico on scratchy radios. It's all connected – music born from land, labor, and longing. If you ever doubt that, listen to George Strait and compare his lyrics with Shakira. George Strait's music feels like a quiet hug—steady, familiar, like the way my Mama-Alfa, my grandmother, and the matriarch of my familia used to speak when she didn't want me to worry.

"You'll need a home to come home to/ Son, we all need a refuge [...]

No matter the dreams you're chasin', never get above your raisin' | May the simple things be amazin'."

– From George Strait's Cowboy and Dreams album (2024)

With that said, George's music talks about home like it's a place you can drive to, but for me, home is oceans away, so my heart still longs for the smell of street vendors cooking, the sound of my language echoing in the streets, and the laughter of my cousins Macky, Chicky, and Chato, who I love seeing when I go home. When George sings about returning home, I close my eyes and imagine stepping off a plane in Guatemala and feeling whole again. Country music might wear cowboy boots, but it dances with the same heart as cumbia: proud, rooted, and full of soul.

Similarly, Shakira, who at the time was gaining notoriety in Latin America as a rebellious teenager with black hair, has a voice in Spanish that carries something raw and visceral—like she's dancing through heartbreak. She sings with vibrato, fire, and vulnerability, and when she talks about identity, my identity, I feel seen.

"Tú eres mi amor, mi alegría, la verdad de mi vida, mi bebé que me salta a los brazos de prisa, tú eres mi refugio y mi verdad (Oh, yeah), Tú eres mi amor, mi alegría, la verdad de mi vida, mi bebé que me calma el alma con risas, Tú eres mi refugio y mi verdad."

– From the song, Mi Verdad, performed by Mana and Shakira in 2015, after the birth of her second child. Also, the tune that my daughter and I danced to at her Quinceañera.

I remember being a teenager, trying to adapt to a new country, a new school, a new version of myself, and especially a new language – English. Her music taught me that I don't have to erase where I came from to belong here in the U.S. That my journey as a human being, my accent, my memories, my longing to be more—they are not weaknesses. They're proof that I am worthy of my voice "being", something that inspired me to write this book. In those lonely high school and early college days, where street fights, drugs, alcohol, and homelessness were my daily experience, I played their songs to feel less alone. They didn't fix the ache, but they gave it shape.

Most important from a practical sense was that the Daddy of 'Em All always coincided with my birthday and meant that I could earn some extra money. As a growing teenager who was constantly in need, hungry, and living in a trailer or, at times, couch surfing with friends, that was a good thing. Please know that I am not complaining about my life in Cheyenne; it gave me grit and some wonderful friends who are still on the journey with me today. Plus, it let me see Chicago live, a band that I idolized as a kid in Guatemala—got to love you some brass.

Hun Hunahpu – Reborn from Yellow Maize Seeds

As I write this book today, I realize that what I consider "normal" might not be the same for many traditional 4-Hers in the U.S. For instance, growing up in Guatemala, I had a pretty normal life as a kid and teenager – or at least, I thought I did. When my dad, a U.S. citizen, left us to return to the States, my mom, Gladys, or Chita as everyone called her, who was a teacher, raised me, along with my grandmother, Mama Alfa, the family matriarch who helped me stay connected to my indigenous roots, and my aunt, Ana, who sparked my social justice interests. All these experiences have shaped who I am today.

After all, I have many amazing and ordinary childhood memories from my life in Guatemala, including going to school at San Sebastian, playing ball – using balls on the streets – with balls made from old socks – and having my first big crush. So, it is only with an adult lens that I began to understand that my "normal" was a little different from most 4-Hers in the United States. For example, while many traditional 4-Hers were playing cops and robbers, cowboys and Indians, soldiers, or battling with their friends, my entire childhood was marked by a constant Dirty War.

Red Maize: Blood

At the heart of this dissonance is the Guatemalan Civil War, which lasted from 1960 to 1996 and is recognized as one of the longest and bloodiest conflicts in Latin American history, enduring 36 years and resulting in over 200,000 deaths, according to "official" counts. However, these official figures notoriously underestimate the true death toll, especially among indigenous communities, where international human rights groups report that about 83% of war victims were Maya Indians living in remote areas, as well as those who opposed the government, such as academics, clergy, and particularly journalists.

Journalists and other truth tellers are always targeted by dictators and fascists, and that was no different while I was growing up. This is because they threaten the architecture of control. In regimes built on fear, propaganda, and manufactured silence, truth-tellers become dangerous. Independent media exposes corruption, amplifies dissent, and gives voice to those the regime would rather erase. That's why authoritarian leaders—from Pinochet to Putin—don't just censor; they intimidate, imprison, and even assassinate. The pen, in these contexts, isn't just mightier than the sword—it's a matchstick near a powder keg. Journalists disrupt the illusion of unanimity, and in doing so, they remind the public that freedom is still possible. As the ACLU, Freedom House, and the UN have documented, attacks on journalists—from smear campaigns to transnational repression—are not anomalies; they are strategies. Because in the eyes of a dictator, a free press (even comedians) isn't just inconvenient—it's insurrection.

This brings me to the war. The "Dirty War," initiated by U.S. political and military intervention, began with a CIA-backed coup in 1954 that led to the Guatemalan military overthrowing the country's democratically elected president. This conflict, which I will elaborate on in the next section, is particularly relevant to my work with 4-H, as it has deep roots in a rural and agricultural context that contrasts sharply with Midwestern upbringing.

In Guatemala, one of the original banana republics, agriculture is often characterized by small, terraced, and labor-intensive plots that cultivate crops like coffee, bananas, and various vegetables across diverse microclimates. In contrast, Iowa's current agricultural landscape is dominated by flat land, large-scale, and highly mechanized operations that primarily produce vast monocultures such as corn and soybeans. Therefore, I will provide a brief overview of these contrasts to illuminate the personal connection of land and agriculture to my immigration story and academic and professional orientation.

Please note that the term "Dirty War" in this book refers to the Guatemalan Civil War, which is the textbook example of a conflict that blurred the lines between war and repression. Historians and other scholars do not see "Dirty Wars" as battles between armies but clandestine campaigns where the state or government uses terror to silence dissent, often under the guise of national security or anticommunism. It is also important to note that many human rights advocates, especially those among First Nations and indigenous communities and scholars, classify this war as ethnic cleansing and, in some contexts, genocide because of the racialized nature of the war.

In the early mid-1950s, President Jacobo Árbenz, with a mandate from the country's electorate, was passionately advocating for the redistribution of unused land from large, elite foreign estates, including the famed United Fruit Company, a predecessor of Chiquita Banana. This is a critical chapter in global agricultural history, as it challenges the profound cultural differences in how many, if not most, people living in the U.S. relate to the land, particularly in a farming or agricultural sense. It also echoes how, mechanically, Native American land dispossession occurred in North America. This includes the checkered mark on how Land-grant Universities, and by extension, 4-H, were founded.

Returning to the story, it's important to note that President Jacobo Árbenz tried—but ultimately failed—to restore traditional Maya communal land ownership, a system dismantled in the 19th century by Guatemalan dictator Justo Rufino Barrios. Barrios, aiming for a "modern" capitalist economy, oversaw the widespread dispossession of Indigenous lands and the rise of industrial agriculture using the same techniques that were coined in the western U.S. many years earlier.

Decades later, Árbenz's efforts to revive communal land practices were labeled as "communist" by the CIA, justifying his removal by the Eisenhower administration with the support of the United Fruit Company. This dismissal ignored the historical reality that Maya communities like the Q'eqchi', K'iche', and Mam had practiced communal stewardship for centuries—rooted in ancestral cosmologies, collective identity, and reciprocal relationships with the land. These traditions continue to influence Mayan and my spiritual heritage today.

Black Maize: PYD and the Journey to Xbalanque

Today, like the sacred black corn at the heart of Maya creation stories—dark, vital, and full of promise—Positive Youth Development (PYD) serves as a living seed that has spread across 4-H and its sister organizations worldwide: Boys and Girls Clubs, Girl Scouts, Boy Scouts, YMCA, and Big Brothers Big Sisters. Just as our ancestors saw black corn as the source of life and memory, PYD honors each young person's innate wisdom and capacity to grow. In 4-H's "progressive" youth work, we see more than a method; we see a milpa where youth plant questions, cultivate skills, and reap the transformative power of community.

Black corn reminds us of our roots and our responsibilities. In the same spirit, PYD has always been a grassroots movement—a living laboratory for pluralistic democracy where youth learn not just to inherit the world but to challenge and remake it. I cherish 4-H because it mirrors the Maya tradition of participatory rites: young people step into circles of belonging, voice their visions, and together weave new possibilities far beyond inherited boundaries.

This sacred ethos echoes in the closing words of the 4-H Pledge: "for my club, my community, my country, and my world." Like the four colors of Maya maize—white, yellow, red, and black—these concentric commitments remind us that caring for the individual, the village, the nation, and the earth are inseparable. At its core, 4-H stands as one of the most expansive Diversity, Equity, Inclusion, and Access (DEIA) initiatives on the planet, nourishing rural youth who often sustain the very lands that feed our cities and fuel global economies.

Yet, as we honor this living kernel of PYD, we must reckon with forces that would wither its promise. White grievance movements— MAGA, Anti-woke, English-only, Reconstruction Backlash, the

Southern Strategy, Jim Crow—rise like droughts threatening our communal fields. Their nostalgia for a narrowly defined past rejects the plurality and abundance inherent in both black corn and the inclusive vision of youth development. For example, central to Make America Great Again's (MAGA) appeal is a politics of white grievance—the belief among some white Americans that they are victims of systemic discrimination, despite enjoying continued structural advantages. This narrative, amplified through right-oriented media and political rhetoric, frames demographic change and racial equity as threats to national identity, fueling skepticism, resentment, and resistance to pluralism. While MAGA draws on exclusion and nostalgia for a narrowly defined and exclusive past, our work must center belonging, critical consciousness, and the empowerment of all youth—especially those historically marginalized. In this contested landscape, Positive Youth Development must be more than a framework; it must be a counterforce to division, rooted in justice and the full humanity of every young person.

Thus, the "War on Woke" appeal is a politics of scarcity – a zero-sum game: the belief that some must lose their seat at the table for others to gain voice. But black corn teaches a different wisdom: that diversity of color and flavor enriches every ear, every hand that plants, and every mouth that eats. In this contested landscape, Positive Youth Development must be more than a framework; it must be our living antidote to division—rooted in justice, nourished by belonging, and celebrating the full humanity of every young person.

3

JOLOCH:
TAKING UP THE GREEN
(JOHN-PAUL)

At this point in my story, readers may ask themselves, how did a Guatemalan immigrant with no experience in 4-H become one of the organization's most historic, or, more accurately, infamous and controversial leaders in its 120+ year history?

It all started in the early 2000s, when I was the Multicultural, Equity, and Civil Rights coordinator at West Liberty schools in West Liberty, Iowa. At that time, my mother worked at a local PYD organization based in Iowa City, Iowa, called United Action for Youth or UAY. I was at the time working in inner-city Chicago, supporting gang-affiliated youth and families. There, I worked in Latine and African American neighborhoods and housing developments such as Cabrini Green, Taylor Homes, and especially in Humble Park, where I also lived. However, because I am very close to my mom, I had an itch to live near her, and my family had moved to Marion, Iowa.

In the late 1990s and early 2000s, West Liberty was undergoing a profound demographic and cultural transformation—mainly driven by its growing Latino immigrant population, especially families of

Mexican origin. By the 2000 Census, Latinos already made up over 40% of the town's population. By 2010, West Liberty became Iowa's first majority-Latino town. During that time of massive Latine and immigrant growth, which some white West Liberty residents referred to as "the plague", I was recruited by the district to be their first Multicultural and Equity Coordinator (later renamed Equity and Civil Rights District Coordinator). As the Multicultural and Equity coordinator, I worked with key school officials and a dear friend of my mother, Carmen Sosa.

Carmen, a PhD educator from the University of Iowa College of Education, was the driving force behind our small group of West Liberty school educators (part of the district's newly established Diversity Committee) in writing Iowa's first system-wide dual-language program, which supported kids teaching kids. Specifically, English-speaking and Spanish-speaking students teach each other's language in class, while taking their core subjects (e.g., Math, Science, and History) in both languages.

The $3.2 million federal grant we secured to establish the West Liberty system-wide dual language program was different from most Federal Title VI programs at the time. Carmen and I, among others, argued in the grant proposal that the dual language program was not remedial; in fact, we argued that dual-language teaching was – or had the potential to help Limited-English and Native-English learners "perform at significantly higher levels than their peers of the same age, experience, and environment in one or more domains," which is the classic definition of a Gifted and Talented program.

This framing was reminiscent of what I would later learn was the heart of Positive Youth Development (PYD), which boldly focuses on developing and fostering the strengths, competencies, and positive qualities in young people to enable them to thrive and contribute meaningfully to their communities.

Once funded, West Liberty's dual language program evolved from our initial effort, which focused on elementary school, to middle school and beyond. Later, a set of scholars at Yale would evaluate the program, which would eventually become a national model for dual-language education in rural communities experiencing rapid demographic change.

It was during the dual language program's ramp-up that I met Cathann, a local extension professional with a dream of bringing 4-H to the same Latine and immigrant students I was serving. At first, I saw Cathann as a possible resource for my students, but I had no way of knowing how influential she would become later in my life and career. This included teaching me how to work with young people in a very different way (PYD) than I was trained to do as a regular school educator. Instead of traditional teaching, she introduced me to the philosophy underlying Positive Youth Development and how to work with youth from their strengths and aspirations, rather than their deficits. My mother, Cathann, Carmen, and I, together, did some great work to empower all youth in West Liberty and surrounding communities, especially among Latine, migrant, and immigrant communities.

After I left West Liberty schools to serve as the National Training and Technical Assistance Director at the National Resource Center for Family Centered Practice at the University of Iowa, I did not see Cathann for many years until I received a surprising call from one of her staff members, who out of the blue encouraged me to apply for the position of State Director and Leader of Iowa 4-H.

At the time, I was the Interim Executive Director at the Cedar Rapids Commission on Civil Rights; thus, I had little to no contact with youth programs. I applied to 4-H because of a "why not" mentality, and it seemed like an exciting challenge that aligned well with my passions; it also paid significantly more than I was making at the commission. I never thought that an off-the-cuff decision to apply would change my life in such a profound way. I also wish I could tell you that I was the best "traditional" candidate for the position, but that would be a lie. I was not, but I may have been what 4-H really needed at that time – a bold disruptor. Additionally, I had worked with youth of color and immigrant youth for most of my career, a skill that is sometimes lacking in extension.

On the day of my interview, my first meeting was with Cathann, who was serving as Iowa State University's (ISU) Vice President for Extension and Outreach at the time. It is notable that in my interview, she asked me no questions. Zero, nada, zilch --not even "how are you doing today?" Instead, she began to tell me about the beautiful history of 4-H and how PYD was supposed to work. She spoke fast and continuously for the full 90-minute interview, like a history teacher teaching a pupil.

She also handed me a paper and ordered me, she did not ask, to memorize the 4-H pledge immediately before my next interview meeting with the extension county officials and community leaders. I immediately connected with the head, hands, heart, and health language in the pledge, for it reminded me of the Maya "Joloch". In the traditional Maya farming system of milpa, Joloch, the leaves and stock of the maize represent support, community, and life. This is because Mesoamerican milpa is a biodiverse garden typically featuring the "Three Sisters" of corn, beans, and squash, and their interdependent symbolic meanings arise from how these plants interact to sustain both the farm and the community.

Ironically, although it was not part of the formal interview questions, I was asked by one of the committee's volunteers (an outstanding long-term 4-H leader from Dallas County) to lead the recitation of the 4-H pledge before sitting down for the interview.

Looking back, I'm not sure why Cathann chose not to ask me any questions during the interview. Maybe she understood how resistant some "Traditional 4-H" leaders could be toward outsiders. Perhaps she was looking for someone "diverse"—what we now call a DEIA hire—or maybe just a token to perform. But I choose to believe she saw something else: a disruptor. Someone who could, in the spirit of civil rights icon John Lewis, stir up "good trouble" within a venerated institution, and do so with love.

Whatever the case, I paid close attention to Cathann 's oral firehose. I then mimicked her 4-H vocabulary and history, repeated the frames she provided, and added my not insignificant professional expertise, gained from working with youth from diverse backgrounds. Lo and behold, a few weeks later, I became Iowa's 4-H Director and Leader … right before the Iowa State Fair.

4

DEIA & "TRADITION": FAIRS, CLUBS, AND THE CHANGING FACE OF 4-H (JOHN-PAUL)

"The paranoid, real or pretended, always secretes its pearl around a grain of fact."

—Arthur Miller, reflecting on The Crucible, the Red Scare, and McCarthyism

I love 4-H! I love its generational rhythm; the way that generations of grandmothers and grandfathers, parents and children pass down the sacred knowledge of daily life, raising animals, and building community with care and intention. Head, heart, hands, and health – the four "Hs". That rhythm is real. It's rooted, adaptive, and sacred, like a milpa that remembers every hand that's touched it. But I've also seen how "tradition"—and yes, I wrap that word in quotation marks deliberately—can calcify around grievance, especially when wielded by those clinging to a myth that falsely perpetuates immutable privilege.

In 4-H, as in the broader American landscape, tradition can be a grain of truth or a pearl of paranoia. For example, in today's politics, MAGA's invocation of "tradition" is not a return but a reinvention—a nostalgic sleight of hand that conjures a past that never truly existed. The "again" in Make America Great Again gestures toward a golden age that excluded too many of us (Women, Native, Latine, Black, individuals with disabilities), collapsing complex histories into feel-good symbols while erasing the labor, pain, and resistance of those who were never invited to the table.

This isn't conservatism, which I can honestly relate to because my father is a Conservative but still kind and respectful to others; it is not restoration, which would involve including others in the idea of the golden age. Instead, like in the play, it is a curated political mythology designed to justify power, not share it. In the play, Arthur Miller dramatizes the Salem witch trials of 1692, where fear and suspicion spiral into mass hysteria, leading to the wrongful persecution and execution of innocent townspeople, especially forthright women such as Rebecca Nurse and Martha Corey. At its core, the play is a searing allegory for political repression – originally McCarthyism, but its resonance endures.

Today, similar dynamics unfold in the backlash against "wokeness," scientific consensus, and free speech. Just as Abigail Williams manipulates public fear to silence dissent and consolidate power, modern political figures have weaponized cultural anxieties to suppress opposing views. For example, MAGA elites such as former Governor Noem (now United States Secretary of Homeland Security) and current Iowa Governor Reynolds have passed laws demonizing diversity initiatives and the professionals who have dedicated their lives and careers to fostering a sense of belonging in our institutions.

DEIA professionals who, contrary to popular caricatures spread by the War on Woke, are not language police or "woke HR hitmen".

They are the organizational cultural gardeners, trauma-informed strategists, and bridge-builders across generations, identities, and systems. Their work, which is not limited to race or gender, is expansive, intersectional, and deeply rooted in the sacred task of restoring belonging where it has been denied.

These anti-woke efforts, which restrict academic freedom, echo the play's themes of institutional overreach and ideological purity. In both Salem and contemporary America, the danger lies not in witches or woke ideology, but in the zeal to punish difference and silence truth. The Crucible reminds us that when fear overrides reason, justice becomes the first casualty of mass hysteria.

Diversity, Equity, Inclusion, and Access (DEIA) professionals, and I emphasize professionals, because many of us, like myself with over 30 years of experience, have dedicated our careers and scholarship to building a profession grounded in research, ethics, and professional standards—such as the Standards of Professional Practice for Chief Diversity Officers from the National Association of Diversity Officers in Higher Education, which state the following:

The National Association of Diversity Officers in Higher Education (NADOHE) has established standards of professional practice for chief diversity officers (CDOs) in higher education. Given the complexities of differing institutional types, missions, historical legacies, and current contexts and the varied professional backgrounds and trajectories of CDOs, institutions will inevitably differ in the details of the application of these standards in terms of critical features including, but not limited to, (a) the organizational structure in the portfolio of the CDO, (b) the allocation of human, fiscal, and physical resources, (c) the optimal degree of centralization versus decentralization of equity, diversity, and inclusion (EDI) efforts, (d) the processes of building institutional and organizational capacity, (e) the unique organizational manifestations of institutional change, and (f) the specific focus and metrics related to mechanisms of accountability. CDOs play the central administrative role in guiding, facilitating, and evaluating these processes on behalf of the institution (Williams & Wade-Golden, 2007, 2013). The highest levels of commitment, responsibility, and accountability reside throughout institutional leadership, in which cabinet-level CDOs serve as the principal administrators to advance mission-driven efforts through highly specialized knowledge and expertise. Through the standards of professional practice that follow, NADOHE provides guidance and support to individuals serving as CDOs, as well as to the institutions where they work.

- *Standard One: Chief diversity officers have ethical, legal, and practical obligations to frame their work from comprehensive definitions of equity, diversity, and inclusion—definitions that are inclusive with respect to a wide range of identities, differentiated in terms of how they address unique identity issues and complex in terms of intersectionality and context.*

- *Standard Two: Chief diversity officers work to ensure that elements of equity, diversity, and inclusion are embedded as imperatives in the institutional mission, vision, and strategic plan.*

- *Standard Three: Chief diversity officers are committed to planning, catalyzing, facilitating, and evaluating processes of institutional and organizational change.*

- *Standard Four: Chief diversity officers work with senior campus administrators and, when appropriate, governing bodies (e.g., trustees or regents) to revise or remove the embedded institutional policies, procedures, and norms that create differential structural barriers to the access and success of students, faculty, and staff who belong to marginalized and oppressed groups.*

- *Standard Five: Chief diversity officers work with faculty, staff, students, and appropriate institutional governance structures to promote inclusive excellence in teaching and learning across the curriculum and within cocurricular programming.*

- *Standard Six: Chief diversity officers work within a community of scholars to advocate for inclusive excellence in research, creativity, and scholarship in all fields as fundamental to the mission-driven work of the institution.*

- *Standard Seven: Chief diversity officers are committed to drawing from existing scholarship and using evidence-based practices to provide intellectual leadership in advancing equity, diversity, and inclusion.*

- *Standard Eight: Chief diversity officers work collaboratively with senior campus administrators to plan and develop the infrastructure for equity, diversity, and inclusion to meet the needs of the campus community.*

- *Standard Nine: Chief diversity officers strive to optimize the balance between centralization and decentralization of efforts to achieve equity, diversity, and inclusion throughout the institution.*

- *Standard Ten: Chief diversity officers work with senior administrators and members of the campus community to assess, plan, and build institutional capacity for equity, diversity, and inclusion.*

- *Standard Eleven: Chief diversity officers work to ensure that institutions conduct periodic campus climate assessments to illuminate strengths, challenges, and gaps in the development and advancement of an equitable, inclusive climate for diversity.*

- *Standard Twelve: Chief diversity officers work with senior administrators and campus professionals to develop, facilitate, respond to, and assess campus protocols that address hate bias incidents, including efforts related to prevention, education, and intervention.*

- *Standard Thirteen: Chief diversity officers work with senior administrators and campus professionals to facilitate and assess efforts to mentor, educate, and respond to campus activism, protests, and demonstrations about issues of equity, diversity, and inclusion.*

- *Standard Fourteen: Chief diversity officers are committed to accountability for advancing equity, diversity, and inclusion throughout the institution.*

- *Standard Fifteen: Chief diversity officers work closely with senior administrators to ensure full implementation of and compliance with the legal and regulatory requirements for the institution.*

- *Standard Sixteen: Chief diversity officers engage in their work in ways that reflect the highest levels of ethical practice, pursuing self-regulation as higher education professionals.*

Consequently, as a national expert in DEIA, I frequently remind institutions that equity is not a silo—it's a comprehensive system. Yes, race and gender matter deeply. But our work reaches further. We build structures that honor veterans' transitions, support disabled employees, and create trauma-informed spaces for youth shaped by poverty, exile, and systemic harm. We also fight for language access so that non-native speakers and neurodivergent individuals (like me, as a dysgraphic) aren't excluded from vital information. We redesign emergency protocols to include mobility, sensory, and cultural needs. We advocate for flexible work, due process, restorative justice, and mental health inclusion—not as trends, but as necessities. We push for digital equity in rural and low-income communities, and we confront environmental injustice where pollution hits hardest. We affirm ancestral knowledge in classrooms and protect the dignity of those reentering society after incarceration. We also make space for spiritual pluralism—recognizing many sacred calendars, Indigenous cosmologies, and the right not to believe at all. DEIA is not just about who's in the room. It's about how the room is built, who it serves, and whose humanity it honors. This is systems work. This is justice work. And it belongs at the center of every institution.

While this quiet yet vast effort of replanting respect and worth may lack glamour, it holds profound importance in today's political

51

world. Often misunderstood, politicized, or overlooked, it remains a sacred act. DEIA professionals nurture people's sense of belonging within an organization—removing weeds of exclusion, enriching the soil of justice, and sowing seeds that might grow only generations later. We do this not for praise, but because we remember what it's like to be excluded. Stubbornly and with conviction, we believe everyone has the right to feel like they belong in any and all public spaces and institutions.

Arthur Miller understood this widespread duality deeply. Born in 1915 and shaped by the Great Depression, Miller became one of America's most acclaimed playwrights, known for Death of a Salesman and, as mentioned earlier, The Crucible. He wrote The Crucible in 1953 as a direct response to the "Red Scare," when Senator Joseph McCarthy's anti-Communist crusade turned patriotism into a weapon. Similar to today's "War on Woke," Miller saw colleagues and friends abandon and betray each other under pressure to "name names," and when he was called to testify before Congress, he refused to cooperate. His warning was not abstract—it was a shout in the dark, a warning to us all at a pivotal moment in U.S. history.

As a refresher, the Red Scare was a period of intense anti-communist paranoia in the United States, spanning the late 1940s through the 1950s. It was fueled by Cold War tensions and political opportunism (e.g., United Fruit Company in Guatemala wanting land reform so they could create a monopoly) and, like today's "War on Woke", it saw widespread accusations, blacklisting, and loyalty tests and investigations by the U.S. government—often targeting educators, artists, and public servants who were falsely labeled as "communists" for advocating for civil rights or progressive change or questioning dominant narratives.

The First 250 Days

In a chilling echo of the Red Scare, the Trump administration is now aggressively pursuing a campaign of retribution against perceived political enemies, weaponizing federal agencies, including the Civil Rights Divisions within each government unit, to silence dissent and punish opposition. Within the first 250 days of his second term, Trump directed criminal investigations into over 100 individuals and organizations, including former officials like **New York AG Letitia James,** Dr. Anthony Fauci, U.S. Ambassador to the United Nations John Bolton, former FBI Director and longtime federal prosecutor James B. Comey, progressive law firms, DEIA Professionals, and even student protest groups. Executive orders have targeted colleges and universities, including mine, demanding the dismantling of diversity programs and audits to ensure the elimination of Critical Race Theory and instilling "viewpoint diversity," (which is vague language for affirmative action for conservatives) while ICE arrests and revoked security clearances have become tools of intimidation. Much like the loyalty tests of the 1950s, these actions serve not to protect national security but to enforce ideological conformity and punish those who challenge MAGA orthodoxy.

Today's climate of fear has metastasized into a campaign to suppress free speech and criminalize progressive activism. One stark example is Trump's executive order designating "Antifa"—a loosely defined term that simply means anti-fascist, a stance we once unified around in our fight against Mussolini and Hitler—as a domestic terrorist organization. Like "communism" during the Red Scare, the term lacks legal clarity, making it a convenient tool for ideological persecution. First Amendment scholars have described this move as a "permission slip" for state and federal officials to target speech they don't like, or oppose their perspectives or policies. . Under new leadership, the FBI has reportedly purged agents who investigated Trump and the January 6 insurrection, replacing them with loyalists tasked with probing an ever-growing list of political opponents. These tactics echo the paranoia-driven surveillance of the Hoover-era FBI, where dissent was treated as treason and civil liberties were sacrificed in pursuit of national purity.

This is because the "War on Woke" is not merely a cultural backlash—it is a calculated effort to dismantle pluralism, punish resistance, and consolidate power through fear. It mirrors the rhetoric and repression strategies used by military strongmen in Guatemala, who invoked national security to justify silencing critics and maintaining control. In both contexts, the real threat is not ideological diversity, but the authoritarian impulse to erase it.

Back then, and echoing today, the Red Scare also targeted the "progressive 4-H movement" within extension, especially those promoting inclusive, community-based youth development. As the Red Scare swept through public education, over 500 anti-communist groups paralleling Moms for Liberty today—a group that now works on censoring ethnic studies, history, and LGBTQ+ books, teachers, librarians, and topics—began to emerge to scrutinize teachers, extension agents, and youth programs.

At that time, the National Education Association established a Defense Commission to protect democratic values in education, but the environment was tense. Leaders focusing on equity, cultural responsiveness, or collective action in 4-H programs risked being labeled communists or subversives. Similar to today's "War on Woke," 4-H initiatives that aimed at empowering rural youth through cooperative learning or civic engagement were sometimes met with suspicion, especially if they challenged racial hierarchies, the "Americanization" narrative (e.g., Manifest Destiny, the City on a Hill, or the Lost Cause rhetoric), or traditional power structures.

It is in that light, I restate the difference between "traditional" 4-H as being rooted in nostalgia and conformity, often promoted as "Christian" nationalist and "patriotic"; and "generational 4-H," which focuses on transmitting love, knowledge, and genuine citizenship—not just as in US Citizen, but as the value of actively contributing to our community and society.

As a result, great and welcoming 4-H leaders were once again being quietly punished, sidelined, silenced, or pressured to dilute their vision by the "traditionalists" who have labeled all DEIA as "indoctrination." This contrasts with today's "generational" 4-Hers, who focus on love, family, and community. Meanwhile, "Traditional" 4-H emphasizes power, control, and defining who belongs and who does not.

Like in The Crucible, where Miller used the Salem witch trials to expose how fear masquerading as fidelity can destroy organizations and communities. The same dynamic echoes in "traditional" 4-H: a mythologized version of rural youth development that resists pluralism, even as the authentic tradition celebrates it. This book walks into that same political fire by narrating how the Twin Heroes in Maya mythology descend into Xbalanque (the underworld), not to destroy tradition but to retrieve its sacred fire and replant it in new soil.

For those readers who may not have experienced 4-H in the heartland, I will refer to many traditional (no quote marks) as generational 4-Hers from this point forward.

Contrasting "Traditional" and "Generational" 4-H

Generational 4-Hers see county fairs like the playoffs, and the State fair is like the Super Bowl. This is especially true of the Iowa State Fair, which brings in over a million visitors each year. So, a few days after I was hired, and as the Iowa State Fair gates swung open, I decided to walk through the Bruce L. Rastetter 4-H Exhibits Building for the first time in my life, which I must admit inspired a sense of midwestern reverence. It's not just the building's scale—41,000 square feet of love for youth, creativity, and learning. It was the palpable tradition emanating from its bones.

For example, when I entered the building, its stories seemed woven into every corner. I saw quilts created by a first-generation 4-H'er honoring her German grandmother's migration to Iowa, a LEGO robotics project built by a farm kid dreaming of engineering something like the Hubble Telescope, a fashion show where contestants had only $20 to spend on their outfits, and, one of my favorites, a mural that combined maize symbolism with messages of equity and belonging. These aren't just exhibits; they're declarations of identity, resilience, and vision. As a new state 4-H leader, I immediately realized that this building was more than just brick and glass; it was a living archive of Iowa's past, present, and future. It was hallowed ground.

As I left the main exhibit building and headed out into the youth barns and show arenas, the rhythm shifted into hustle and bustle with thousands of youths tending to their animals with quiet confidence— market lambs, dairy heifers, heritage swine—all raised with care and purpose as part of a century-old generational tradition. The pens were lined with hand-painted signs, sleeping bags, and always in the background – music, sometimes from the grandstand or rides, or impromptu musical instruments, or just an iPhone playing its speakers to death.

Even when I went past the last arena, the trailer park at the Iowa State Fairgrounds is more than a place to sleep—it's a vibrant, intergenerational village of 4-H families who turn the fair into a full-on lifestyle for 11 days. Some families have camped there for decades, passing down traditions like early morning livestock prep, late-night exhibit reviews, and communal meals, most on the grill, under awnings strung with green clovers. It's not uncommon to see grandparents helping grandkids polish their best show boots or rehearsing for their upcoming communication events. For many, the Iowa State Fair is many things—music, midway, and spectacle. Still, for many generational 4-H families, it is a yearly pilgrimage of love to support and recognize kids for their hard work. Finally, it is about community pride and bragging rights.

Nevertheless, it was easy to see that something was going on below the surface. This is because in 2012 and 2013, efforts to expand Iowa's 4-H programming into urban communities sparked concern among "traditional" stakeholders who feared the initiative would dilute the organization's agricultural roots and alienate mostly white rural participants. Thus, when I showed up at my first fair, there were entire groups of extension, 4-H, and fair leaders that would test my 4-H chops, state their dissatisfaction, or walk away when I said hello.

My initial interpretations of these interactions drew from "official" narratives promoted by National 4-H and Iowa State Extension leadership. Specifically, that 4-H was experiencing an "existential crisis" due to a decline in enrollment in the program between 2004 and 2014, during which the number of Iowa 4-H participants dropped by over 32,000, from 127,309 to 95,225. However, as soon as I began to converse with local Iowa community 4-H stakeholders, I found that most of them were not really concerned about the drop in participant numbers. Instead, I heard a lot of concern about identity, "tradition", and the notion that rural kids should not share "their" resources with those from "urban" areas.

As a vocal county extension director, who also served on the local fair board and judged 4-H livestock, pointed out, in Iowa, the backbone of 4-H funding depends on local Extension Councils, which are crucial for maintaining county-level programs. These councils are made up of locally elected community members, who were almost all white and rural. Their responsibilities include distributing public funds to support county staff, facilities, and outreach efforts aimed at local youth.

Their financial choices directly impact the availability and range of 4-H activities, from traditional livestock projects to registration and travel for state, national, and even international events and programs. This means that even in predominantly urban counties, and often despite their demographics, extension funds primarily benefited white rural youth.

This county director, who I will call Chad, also expressed the opinion that if we aim to serve "those kids," a phrase he used for diverse and urban youth, the county extension offices would have to: a) redirect funds from the existing rural white youth, which he compared to a form of Affirmative Action, and b) shift the focus from being a leadership program to "an at risk youth program," thus conveying a racialized view of leadership and who is considered or should be a leader. Notably, this county leader was not isolated in his thinking, as I heard many explanations along those philosophical lines, ranging from simple logistics questions to far-fetched racial replacement theories, such as those that have now become staples of the "War on Woke" campaign. Other county extension and fair officials blamed the influx of migrant workers working in Iowa fields and immigrants working in meat, pork, and poultry plants for the crime, drugs, poverty, and disinvestment in their agricultural communities.

This framing exposed a definitional dissonance within the 4-H program. Specifically, if the "traditionalists" believe that the 4-H program is about "rural kids" and "agriculture," why aren't migrant youth working in the fields, and immigrant communities working in industrial agriculture (e.g., meat and

poultry plants) considered "real" 4-Hers? Why are they lumped in with the "urban" kids as secondary recipients of PYD?

However, most 4-H stakeholders that I spoke to at the fair that year, including many multi-generational farm families, county educators, and Iowa State University Extension faculty and staff—many of whom were 4-H members and have long been the backbone of the 4-H program—mourned what they considered the "Golden Age" of 4-H and their rural communities. This narrative refers to the mid-20th century, especially from the 1940s through the 1960s, an era marked by a dramatic expansion in 4-H reach and influence. During this time, 4-H evolved from a rural agricultural program into a national youth development powerhouse, utilizing its traditional Club model, which shares deep connections with other now-struggling youth development organizations, such as the FFA and the Boy and Girl Scout organizations.

In addition, because agriculture 4-H efforts were and continue to be supplementally financed and supported by industry associations like the Iowa Farm Bureau, Iowa Corn Growers, Pork Producers, Soybean Association, Cattlemen's Association, and Midwest Dairy, which have played a critical role in developing that rural identity by funding scholarships, shaping curriculum, and ensuring that 4-H remained relevant to Iowa's evolving agricultural landscape. Thus, it created a mythical but racialized 4-H Golden Age, during which 4-H became a rite of passage for many rural white youths and established itself as a respected institution in American rural life by promoting what were communicated as "American" values—though these are actually universal human values—such as leadership, land stewardship, and civic engagement, while simultaneously denying access to native, migrant, immigrant and youth of color.

Thus, it is essential to understand both the organization's funding systems and the Golden Age narrative since it undergirds and maintains the "traditional" culture within 4-H. This means that 4-H growth isn't just about participant numbers; it also involves heartland, national, and racial identity, community memory, and rural change. That's why many "traditional" 4-H leaders and alumni cling to it so tightly, even though modern 4-H is no longer solely about rural club or animal culture. In other words, these conversations at my first state fair exposed a significant rhetorical and cultural gap between 4-H at the state and national levels and local 4-H stakeholders.

However, it is also essential to challenge some of the secrets around Miller's "pearls". For example, based on my analysis of the participant data from that period, the decline in 4-H participation in Iowa was primarily caused by a combination of agricultural, demographic, and cultural changes. Many of these shifts can be traced back to the lasting impact of the farm crisis in the 1980s. In other words, it was the farm crisis, rather than immigration, that devastated rural communities. This crisis led to the closure of thousands of family farms, a wave of bank closures, and a significant decline in population in small towns. The 1980s farm crisis was a perfect storm of economic and political factors that severely affected rural America, particularly in the Midwest.

For those of you who are not from the heartland or an agricultural setting, in the 1970s, farmers were encouraged to expand aggressively, borrowing heavily as grain prices soared and land values skyrocketed. But by the end of the decade, inflation surged, and the Federal Reserve responded with steep interest rate hikes—making farm loans unaffordable and pushing many into financial ruin. Under the Regan administration, Iowa farmland lost up to 60% of its value between 1981 and 1986, and agricultural banks began to fail under the pressure. With foreclosures sweeping across the Midwest, the social fabric of rural communities unraveled. The crisis accelerated the decline of family farms, triggered rural exodus, and paved the way for the rise of mass industrial agriculture.

In addition, the economic and emotional toll of the Farm Crisis fractured local institutions, such as local public schools, many of whom were forced to consolidate and close due to the lack of students, local church congregations dwindled, and generational continuity in farming gave way to industrial farms owned by multinational conglomerates similar to the United Fruit Company in Guatemala, thus weakening the community and generational club-model pipeline into 4-H. Between 2017 and 2022, the U.S. lost over 140,000 family farms, and Iowa continues to feel the ripple effects. In simple words, it was not immigration that hurt 4-H and rural Midwestern communities; it was just capitalism, being capitalism.

Thus it is essential to note and validate that during that time, land dispossession from generational farm families, suburbanization (which was driven by US policy), changes in traditional gender roles, and especially television, video games, and movies further diverted youth interests away from generational 4-H agriculture programs such as showing livestock, creating static exhibits (e.g., photography and art), and what at the time was called Domestic Arts and Home Economics, which were expressly framed as girl's programs. It is also important to note at this point that while MAGA-oriented talking heads often misrepresent this last economic and demographic reality to stoke racist, sexist, homophobic, and anti-immigrant dog whistles, which frame non-white and non-rural people as invaders, as in my West Liberty example in Chapter 2 ("the plague"). As a result, the reality within the loss narratives is much more complex than the "they came to take what is mine" because new populations were also responding to massive social and economic change forces.

For example, in the 1980s and 1990s, a quiet yet profound transformation occurred in rural communities across Iowa and the

Midwest. Specifically, Urban families—many of them Black, Latino, Southeast Asian, and immigrant—began moving into small towns that had long been considered homogeneously white. Many of these groups were first displaced from cities by push factors, including deindustrialization, predatory urban renewal, rising housing costs, and deteriorating public infrastructure. Many others were drawn by pull factors, such as the promise of affordable living, safer neighborhoods, and the opportunity to raise children in quieter settings and with good schools. However, most were drawn to rural communities by both the push and pull factors of the day.

Adding to that demographic shift, refugee resettlement programs, some started by republicans like then-Governor Ray (1969 to 1983) after the Vietnam war, brought Southeast Asian families to places like Iowa, while immigration reform in 1986 allowed many Latine urban and migrant workers to settle more permanently in rural communities, changing what once had been a seasonal, migratory labor force which began to root itself in rural communities like Muscatine, Sioux City, and Marshalltown, shifting from temporary fieldwork to year-round employment, school, and family life.

At the same time, rural Iowa economies were being reshaped by the rise of large industrial plants—especially in meatpacking, food processing, and agribusiness. These facilities required a stable, low-wage workforce, and immigrant families filled that gap. As seasonal migrant labor wound down, permanent immigrant populations grew, bringing cultural richness, resilience, and new forms of community to towns that the farm crisis and population loss had hollowed out.

In other words, this wasn't just economic adaptation—it was a complete redefinition of rural American identity. I emphasize this because, me and my family are some of those "New-Iowans". Personally, I put myself through college by working at meat packing plants in Kansas. In addition, while I was in Iowa, I worked with many of these new arrivals, which revitalized schools, churches, and civic life, even as they faced exclusion and structural race and class barriers. A legacy that continues to inform my work today, particularly as I consider how youth development, DEIA, and institutional change must reflect the full complexity of rural America.

5 FROM THE HEAD

CLOVER- – A FEDERAL PERSPECTIVE (LISA)

The term "Head Clover" was one that was used to describe my role or position at the federal level. That label was one that I would cringe when it was used. It felt presumptive and also like a term one would use for 'royalty,' while I was more comfortable with less "I" and more "we" to describe the efforts being done. I resonate more with the acronym 'TEAM" or Together Everyone Achieves More". My staff would also tell you that I like to use alliteration to convey key concepts such as "3Cs - Connections - Competency - Capacity", or the 3 P's - Programs, Policies and Partnerships" and have a catch phrase to use much like an 'elevator speech' to describe 4-H to others who lacked familiarity... *"4-H is youth and adults working together to create sustainable change in their local communities."* I would also tell both internal and external audiences that *"4-H is the federal government's _model_ Positive Youth Development program."*

I used a 'formulaic equation' to describe **Positive Youth Development** as *"**Positive Experiences + Positive Environments + Positive Relationships + Positive Risks = PYD"**.* And another equally important sentence was provided to me by one of USDA's attorneys assigned to NIFA which gave me a short, sweet and to the point concise sentence to use:

"4-H is open to all youth." Note, there is nothing that follows the period, which is important to me for access, equity and opportunity, outreach and engagement, is an 'evergreen' part of 4-H.

Initial Connections as Director, Division Youth and 4-H

During my tenure from February 2010 to June 2018, as Director, Division Youth and 4-H, or 4-H National Headquarters (4-HHQ) it was easier to do outreach and engagement if I considered it like being in a 'county extension office'. I could see from my office building the various federal agencies that represented similar entities that I worked with when I was in the county. I would point out, there's education, there's housing, there's health, there's juvenile justice, etc.

Critical to the success of outreach and engagement was being able to define what you had to offer to someone else. We, the DY4-H national program leaders and program specialists were able to connect with key agencies for example on education where a bullying focus had been initiated, with housing on opportunities for youth in housing projects, with juvenile justice where youth were now seen as potential agents for change versus problems to be 'fixed', and with all the science agencies such as NASA (National Aeronautics and Space Administration), CDC (Center for Disease Control), and even the Library of Congress.

We began to target who to leverage for the land-grant university extension system and its outreach into all communities with other federal agencies. When you do not have funds, you leverage your connections.

NIFA- Internal Connections- Challenges & Opportunities - Why 4-H?

It was easier to deploy an external marketing strategy for myself and the DY-4H team. Internally, it was more challenging. There were many transitions as NIFA was being set up, including how to say the actual name for the National Institute for Food and Agriculture or "NIFA". It might have a short or long "i" pronunciation, such as "Neefa" or "KNIFe-A" or "Nifa". During my first three years as Director, DY4-H, there were several folks who were acting or who served as Director of the NIFA. The position as NIFA Director was to be up to 6 years and to be more or less non-partisan, to bridge the terms of an administration. Yet, once we had an appointed NIFA Director who stayed more than two years, they challenged me and the DY4-H staff as to *why 4-H was even a part of NIFA.*

To meet and counteract this internal challenge, the DY-4-H team and I embarked on creating a marketing strategy and implementation plan. To gain a better understanding, the DY4-H team conducted focus groups to understand what others knew or thought about 4-H within NIFA. It led to understanding the perceptions and biases we faced internally as to what 4-H is/was. Engagement with national program leaders and program staff was created through the revamping of the National 4-H Conference. Strategically, we created advocates for 4-H and our team when NIFA staff were involved with 4-H youth and adults.

In addition, DY4-H was challenged as to the demographics for 4-H. This led to both internal and external to DY4-H conversations on data collection and examining the myths surrounding ES-237.

Granted, no internal NIFA funding resources were dedicated to developing our marketing strategy and implementation plan, yet we were asked to put forward proposals for possible future USDA federal budget requests. 4-H National Headquarters was also used as the name for DY4-H, as that resonated more with our land grant extension stakeholders as to the role the division played. So, we created and shared an internal 4-H National Headquarters Strategy Plan and put forward a business proposal to the NIFA Director. We also conducted an internal program review of DY4-H during my tenure.

Initial Challenges – GEN-2704, FOIAs, HSUS

I faced some interesting challenges that were either carry-overs from CSREES, the Cooperative System for Research, Education, and Extension, and my predecessors, as well as ones that popped up in my first three months on the job. I was challenged on how to handle the complex transition and ultimate demise of:

- 4-H GEN-2704, which stood for "group exemption number "and "2704," referred to the federal tax-exempt status exemption for 4-H. This issue pissed off all my former state 4-H program leader colleagues and extension directors due to changes to IRS regulations, and

- 'Permission' granted to our private non-profit partner, National 4-H Council, to carry out a licensing strategy for product marketing, to which there was a FOIA, a Freedom of Information Act, submitted. FOIAs require extensive research and detailed legal responses.

The third challenge emerged shortly after the National 4-H Conference held March 20–24, 2010, in Washington, D.C., when the Humane Society of the United States (HSUS) delivered a breakout session titled "Animal Instincts: Service Learning and Animal

Welfare". As a result of this session, the National 4-H Council lost scholarships for the 1890s from a key donor who opposed HSUS. Additionally, USDA had to respond to key legislators, stakeholders and submit a public notice on USDA's website as to how information must not be biased and accept all viewpoints, and we, DY4-H, would change our practices for workshops at the 4-H Conference.

I quickly realized that being a middle manager in the federal government was not so much fun, especially with some of these challenges that were started before I took my position.

Organizational Shifts - Internal- -Mapping Positions to Priorities

Internally, there was the organizational transition from the former CSREES, Cooperative Research, Education and Extension System, to the National Institute of Food and Agriculture, NIFA. In that process, there was both physical rearrangement as well as reassignment of staff; I needed to rightsize staffing as I had three national program leaders, one for youth development research, one for afterschool programming, and myself as I continued to direct the Children, Youth and Families at Risk program, CYFAR, and seven program specialists and program assistants. Over the next eight years, I navigated hiring processes for additional program leaders in the areas of civic engagement and volunteerism, learning and healthy living, vulnerable populations, which also expanded to include CYFAR, military child and youth programs, and 4-H Science. These positional priorities were ones to align with NIFA, USDA, and the administration's priorities.

Workforce Employability and Preparation - 4-H Emergence

A critical priority, workforce employability, emerged initially with me and Beth Birnstihl putting together a 'big idea'. This was pitched and called "Charting the Future," which was the first-ever joint meeting between representatives from the Public Private Partnership Working Group (P3WG), the 4-H Mission Mandate Teams (Healthy Living, Science, and Citizenship), 4-H National Headquarters and National 4-H Council at the National 4-H Youth Conference Center on April 3rd, 2013. The charge to the group was to look at big ideas and to frame a strategic programmatic direction with identified key priorities for system-wide discussion. The main idea that emerged was that *4-H Youth will be prepared to be productive and contributing members of the world workforce.*

Organizational Shifts - External- Who is in charge of 4-H?

However, for the "Charting the Future" initiative to proceed, significant changes needed to occur within the 4-H organizational structure. Prepare for a lot of the 'alphabet soup' that the federal system is known for. To clarify this, I'll suggest a way to make it simpler. If the next one or two paragraphs become too confusing, refer to this:

- DWG & the PWG become the P3WG, which becomes the PLWG

- Why is this important? Organization matters in systems to be effective.

Here's a more detailed timeline... In 2010, Dr. Glenn Applebee led the Directors Working Group (DWG) along with Dr. Dan Kugler. The PWG, or Partners Working Group, included representative state 4-H program leaders, 4-H Headquarters, and the 4-H Council. As USDA

NIFA was being established, I had to navigate both these groups as well as the Extension Committee of Policy (ECOP) under APLU, the Association of Public and Land-Grant Universities, after internal discussions and due to the absence of F4-HN Deputy Director Kugler, my responsibilities, shared with Dr. Caroline Crocoll, covered F4-HN - Family, 4-H, and Nutrition, which later became the Institute of Youth, Family and Community (IYFC) under NIFA.

It sounds like alphabet soup at times, and there was a gradual transition, which I oversaw from the PWG and DWG to the Public-Private Partners Working Group (P3WG), which included regional representatives of directors and state 4-H program leaders from the five extension regions, 4-H HQ, and 4-H Council representatives. The P3WG tackled youth protection, setting up standards within the 4-H system, along with crafting "4-H Guiding Principles":

- Positive Youth Development

- Partnership

- Learning

- Youth Potential.

ECOP, or the Extension Committee on Organization and Policy, also started to question and examine the 4-H organizational structure. Two extension directors, Elbert Dickey from Nebraska and Gaines Smith from Auburn University, convened a 4-H Summit with representatives from the 4-H system. Afterwards, an ECOP 4-H Working Group, made up of five state program leaders and five extension directors, reviewed the report and shared their findings.

"Givens:"

- USDA/NIFA controls the 4-H name and emblem and their use

- USDA/NIFA and the National 4-H Council had a formal working agreement (MOU now expired.

- Cooperative Extension at the land grant universities develops and delivers 4-H/youth programs.

- Neither the land grants nor ECOP has a formal agreement with either USDA/NIFA or the National 4-H Council outlining their respective responsibilities and contributions to 4-H

- ECOP has no structure in place to represent, set policy or conduct negotiations between land grants (and their Cooperative Extension 4-H programs) and USDA/NIFA and the National 4-H Council.

The working group proposed to "develop a proposed MOU/Partnership Agreement with USDA/NIFA in collaboration with National 4-H Council as a guide for ECOP to negotiate a formal working relationship with both," with overarching themes to:

1. Articulate that leadership for 4-H programs is the responsibility of Cooperative Extension at the land grant universities and USDA/NIFA, with the National 4-H Council enhance and support the mission and goals of 4-H and

2. Call for Extension Directors and 4-H Program Leaders to become much more active in the leadership of the 4-H program at the national level.

A more general theme was to call for USDA/NIFA to work through/with ECOP and all CES directors and administrators to facilitate and institutionalize matters of *structure, personnel, policy, and to set the program direction for 4-H and a proposed structure for USDA/NIFA that would provide 4-H support needed from the federal partner"*. The devil is always in the details as to how that is to be accomplished.

ECOP established a standing 4-H Committee comprising representative regional extension directors and state 4-H programs, with ad hoc representation and non-voting members from USDA NIFA's 4-H HQ and the National 4-H Council.

That left the P3WG to consider its next steps and where it fit within this emerging organizational structure. First of all, the P3WG, Public-Private Partners Working Group, resembled the emerging ECOP 4-H Committee, which led the P3WG to rename itself and establish itself as the Program Leaders Working Group (PLWG).

I was tasked by NIFA leadership to work with others from extension, crafting the tripartite MOU with USDA NIFA, ECOP, and National 4-H Council. This MOU was signed on the 100th anniversary of the Smith-Lever Act on May 14th in Washington, D.C., which established the Cooperative Extension System. And, again, the devil is in the details as to how to operationalize the MOU.

These organizational transitions and gyrations and alphabet soup acronyms may sound confusing, yet for me, it was how I navigated crafting a system where transparency, authenticity, accountability, respect for each other, and a more cohesive approach emerged. I worked with the PLWG leadership to create a relationship between the ECOP 4-H Committee, which enabled the 4-H ECOP Committee to define roles and responsibilities, which allowed the Program Leaders Working Group (PLWG) to exist and for them to operationalize and carry out national programming efforts as needed and/or directed by the ECOP 4-H Committee.

These efforts included creating a chartering system that addressed both long-term and short-term needs, such as working groups, task forces, and study groups. Initial chartered working groups included: 4-H Shooting Sports, Vulnerable Populations (renamed Access, Equity, and Opportunity), Professional Development, and Learning. For me, the result was a structure in place to discuss trends, challenges, opportunities, and emerging issues related to program accountability and quality.

It reminded me of my early efforts to create a structure for the Lyon County 4-H Council, where youth and adults worked together to set program priorities and run the events they supported and valued. I once was asked why they voted on which events and activities to hold each year, and my reply was "It's your program, not mine" ... as my role was to facilitate and guide.

The bottom line is if you got lost in all the acronyms for navigating the system change, there's one thing to know—organization matters. To be effective change makers, one must understand roles and responsibilities within a foundation of respect, the 3 R's. Recall, I mentioned earlier that I enjoy alliteration.

National Strategic Plan - Evergreen Themes

The P3WG was the initial entity involved in revitalizing the National 4-H Strategic Plan, with 4-H National Headquarters (4-H HQ) facilitating the process. Key P3WG members, along with Doug Swanson and myself, presented a plan to advance the effort in summer 2014, outlining the premise, process, and timeline. During summer meetings, state program leaders revisited the themes from the 2002 strategic plan and concluded that the themes were 'evergreen'. There was discussion to ensure the plan was workable, used actively rather than shelved, and that everyone could see how their program level— club, county, or state—aligned with the national plan.

As the ECOP 4-H Committee was stood up, they put forward a goal in 2016, which would never be met due to what happened to DEIA and LGBTQ+ programs.

4-H Grows: A Promise to America's Kids (2025)

In ten years, 4-H will reflect the population demographics, diverse needs and social conditions of the country. This vision has the elements of inclusion, caring adults, involves at least 1 in 5 youth, and the volunteers and staff reflect the population.

Let me back up, and say that in 2014, John-Paul and I met as he took on a role with the P3WG then to the PLWG.

ES-237 - Data Collection Queries + Program Quality and Accountability

4-H demographics were limited and presented challenges because they were gathered using a form called "ES-237," which stands for "Extension Service form number 237." This form needed to be published in the Federal Register for approval before any changes could be made, and it was collected separately from the annual program information collected by the extension systems. DY4-H staff discussed data collection in 2014, while others within the 4-H system expressed concerns and a desire for changes in 4-H enrollment. Issues related to how to define and gather data were also discussed at P3WG meetings.

At the same time, efforts were underway to report to "Common Measures" from the National 4-H Council. Internally, Dr. Suzanne Le Menestrel was developing program quality and accountability, which included data collection and measures, with others also exploring the program theory of action for 4-H PYD ("Positive Youth Development Integrating Research and Practice", 2025, Arnold and Ferrari, editors).

Meanwhile, the NIFA Director and Civil Rights Division Director were conducting state 4-H program audits to assess the engagement, outreach, and participation of potential youth audiences. It was only after several of these audits had begun that my team and I became aware of them. One could say a 'perfect storm' was forming. As someone who is 'geeky' enough, this reminded me of the efforts to build an evidence-based system to explain why and how 4-H positively impacts the lives of youth and adults.

In 2016, I shared a presentation with state 4-H program leaders during NAE4-HA a presentation called "ES-237- Myth and Mystery."

4-H Shooting Sports

4-H has a strong, vibrant 4-H Shooting Sports program. In my roles at the state and federal levels, I supported extension professionals and volunteers who work with youth in archery, air rifle, shotgun, muzzleloading, and more. I even took 4-H shooting sports training to better understand my cross-eyed dominance issue.

To demonstrate national support for 4-H Shooting Sports, they were among the first entities to be chartered under the PLWG; otherwise, the national committee that supported the training and national event essentially bore the sole liability. The 4-H Shooting Sports program acknowledges the sensitivity around gun use, the violence, and school shootings that have happened, and adheres to safety standards and respect for firearms and their use.

2015 - APivotal Year - Theme of Inclusivity

Vulnerable Populations - Identified and Champions Sought. Dr. Bonita Williams was hired by me in 2012 as a Vulnerable Populations National Program Leader. She managed CYFAR grants and led a Vulnerable Populations Working Group, which developed a presentation and a call for champions within the 4-H system.

In 2015, Dr. Bonita Williams, along with other extension professionals, launched the Vulnerable Populations Working Group's efforts. They contributed to the development of a program for underserved and underrepresented youth populations, as well as a framework created by the Working Group that incorporated PYD principles. Using a PYD perspective, they emphasized that all young people need support and opportunities to successfully transition to adulthood.

The focus of the PYD approach is to help youth acquire the knowledge and skills they need to become healthy and productive adults. PYD builds on young people's strengths and recognizes their unique contributions. They used a four-fold approach as outlined:

- Implementing the PYD approach requires *preparation of the organization, adults, and youth.*

- Adults must examine their views of *young people* and work to *see them as "resources"* rather than "problems to be fixed."

- *Policy and practice must be reviewed* to ensure that they support the PYD philosophy. If they contain barriers, they need to be revised.

- *Training* can assist in this process. *Young people also need preparation* to be able to fully participate in the opportunities provided to them.

For NIFA, vulnerable populations were defined as demonstrating that these are groups exposed to high risks within five dimensions: developmental, emotional, mental, physical, and social.

These same populations—which comprise a large and growing percentage of our country's young people-- disproportionately contend with conditions that often compromise healthy development and access to support for it, even as they carry rich cultural resources and cultivate strength and insight through adversity.

The working group sought 'Champions' to work within these groups:

- Immigrant Youth

- Youth in Foster Care

- Special Needs/Youth with Disabilities/(Physical/Mental) Intellectual Disabilities

- Underserved/Underrepresented/Diverse Racial Ethnic Youth

- LGBT Youth

- Incarcerated Youth

- Disconnected Youth

- Homeless Youth

SPL Professional Development Track NAE4-HA - Portland, OR

In 2015, a state 4-H program leader's professional development session was conducted in Portland, OR, at the NAE4-HA (National Association of Extension 4-H Agents, now known as the National Association of Extension 4-H Youth Development Professionals). John-Paul was instrumental in the session's agenda and flow; I was invited to do a brief presentation.

The theme of inclusivity was emerging in many places and continued from the 2015 work to the 2016 National Program Leaders Meeting in Tucson, AZ.

Here's' how inclusivity was defined as a priority:

Inclusivity – To overcome institutional structures and systems to diversify programs that reflect the demographics in each state.

> *Launched – 2015; Identified in Portland, 2015. To be prioritized in Tucson, 2016.*

Connecting the Threads of Access, Equity, and Inclusivity

4-H, in my experience, has evolved from its beginning roots, where it was an opportunity to educate, to translate science into practice with rural youth. First with rural youth, more than likely white youth and then to youth of color with the 1890 institutions. This was considered until the Civil Rights Act to be 'separate yet equal,' though that too merged with the adaptation to youth in urban settings. In 1973, with the change in the 4-H Pledge to include the words '... *and my world'*, 4-H continued to expand beyond all lines and boundaries on a map.

4-H's umbrella of access, equity and inclusion continued to evolve, to craft and create for youth wherever they lived, whenever they could be involved, before, during and after school times, episodic or shorter-term to longer-term, more defined experiences. 4-H's content has also expanded so that youth will find relevant and relatable content for AI.

4-H, during my participation as a youth and my career as an extension professional, has continued to evolve and adapt to the youth's needs. These expansions for outreach and engagement might appear to some to be an endorsement or support for specific types of lifestyles. 4-H represents the ideal that all may belong. To ensure that all may belong, education, training and research of evidence-based programming is necessary.

Wrapping up DY4-H or 4-H HQ's Story

4-H HQ/DY4-H did our own marketing and communication plan, our own DY4-H Strategy and business pitch, and then led on a national level the revitalization of the strategic plan, data collection plan to transition ES-237, crafted a program quality and accountability plan, changed national 4-H conference to be a youth-voice amongst federal agencies, defined a PYD research agenda at the federal level, worked with CDC, NASA, OSTEP, Library of Congress, and others to leverage extension professional expertise - led by or facilitated by the 4-H HQ NPLs, national program leaders.

We never saw any additional funds and had Ag in the Classroom 'revolt' at being part of 4-H HQ. It was weird to have others also conduct the tractor/farm safety stuff, in NIFA, and for others to lead on the ag education programming, as it wasn't seen as '4-H'.

It was easier to work with other federal career employees on domestic and international youth programming than to work within NIFA and USDA. 4-H was seen by some within the USDA as just a conduit for them to push their stuff out as political appointees. On the other hand, working with others who had a 4-H background, like fellow 2024 National Hall of Fame inductee Krysta Harden and her staff at USDA, allowed us to do some fun and exciting things.

It is hard to 'sell' something to those who already have an idea of what you are and what you represent, though they never really spoke to you about what you were doing or did. We had no control over the funding yet were expected to make states comply with Civil Rights. We had no funds attached to support ES-237 and data collection, yet were responsible for ensuring that the federal register was completed. Contractors who supported us were pulled off the task as the software and system architecture were so very old, and the priority was to update and complete the grants funding system, as well as the extension reporting system.

As I reflect back, we, 4-H National Headquarters, thrived and truly created connections, developed competencies and enhanced capacity. I am proud to have worked with such an awesome and amazing dedicated 4-H HQ staff. For me, it was so much fun to come to work with others who shared the 4-H love.

We all carry biases based on our life experiences. I had to develop awareness and acknowledgment of my own implicit biases. That is an ongoing, lifelong endeavor, and I am grateful for 4-H as it provided and still provides me with experiential learning or learn-by-doing opportunities.

Remember, I adhere to 4-H is open to all. There are no caveats, no restrictions, nor exceptions to that statement. That is why I love 4-H and truly 'bleed green'.

6

NEW IOWAN
BRINGING DEIA WORK INTO
4-H
(JOHN-PAUL)

Before the New Iowan Initiative, Iowa was already changing—but quietly, and not always willingly. The state's reputation for farmer stoicism masked a deeper unease: a shrinking workforce, an aging population, and a growing disconnect between who Iowa had been and who it was becoming. In the early 2000s, the numbers told a story. Unemployment hovered around 4.2%, which sounds good, but that wasn't the whole picture. Rural counties were hemorrhaging young people to urban centers or out-of-state opportunities. Employers in agriculture, manufacturing, and healthcare struggled to fill jobs, not because there weren't openings, but because there weren't enough workers with the right skills—or support systems—to take them. Around the University of Iowa, where I worked and taught, the running joke was that Iowa's biggest export was young workers.

This is because young people appear to be leaving Iowa in steady waves, drawn by opportunities they couldn't find at home. The state's economy, while stable, offered limited upward mobility—especially in rural areas, where industries such as agriculture and manufacturing now dominated. Many towns lacked access to higher education, cultural diversity, and entertainment. As college graduates looked toward cities like Des Moines, Chicago, Minneapolis, or Denver, Iowa's small towns felt the loss not just economically, but emotionally. It wasn't just a brain drain—it was a hope drain. The departure of youth signaled a deeper disconnection between Iowa's traditional identity and the aspirations of its next generation. But it was also a consequence of the root damage created by the farm crisis.

Politically, Iowa was caught in a quiet tug-of-war, which is why the media later named it a purple state. Governor Tom Vilsack, a Democrat elected in 1998, was navigating a legislature that was increasingly skeptical of immigration and wary of government-led social programs. Nationally, post-9/11 anxieties hardened attitudes toward newcomers, even as Iowa's economic survival increasingly depended on them. The tension was palpable: a state that needed immigrants to thrive, but had not yet reconciled that need with its cultural narrative. The Iowa of the early 2000s was still shaped by its agrarian mythos—self-reliant, insular, and slow to change. However, beneath that surface, the demographic shifts were undeniable. Between 1990 and 2018, Iowa's Latino population grew by 480%, and towns like Marshalltown, Storm Lake, and Denison saw dramatic transformations.

The New Iowan Initiative emerged in this fraught moment—not as a panacea, but as a principled intervention. It was a bet on belonging. Governor Vilsack responded—not perfectly, but with courage. The program started as a pilot under the Department of Workforce Development, with regional centers helping immigrants with job placement, legal services, ESL classes, and acting as cultural brokers or interpreters. It also supported new Iowans in navigating their communities, which I always called welcoming centers. Most of the time, these were simple tasks like providing guidance on how to apply for a job, getting directions to register children for school or translating weather alerts into different languages so that people in Iowa knew what to do during a tornado. That last one was lifesaving in Iowa!

The Initiative was built on a deceptively simple framework: a few regional centers, some leveraged funds from employers and local stakeholders, and monthly reporting. But its impact was quietly transformative. This is because of a built-in reframing, hidden in the program name—The New Iowan Initiative—which recast immigrants not as burdens to be managed, but as neighbors to be welcomed. It recognized that belonging requires more than sentiment; it demands infrastructure.

Translation, transportation, and support were not just services— they were scaffolds of trust.

As I revisited local papers from that time, I found vivid examples of this philosophy in action. In Ottumwa, the center became a lifeline for Amina, a Sudanese mother of two who arrived with no English and quickly found work, childcare, and a mentor. In Marshalltown, where the meatpacking industry draws workers from around the world, the Initiative helped launch multilingual safety trainings that restored dignity to the workplace. In Storm Lake, a town where over 80 languages are spoken, it fostered parent-teacher dialogues that had long felt out of reach. As their superintendent put it at the time: "We stopped asking why parents weren't engaged. We started asking how we were making it hard for them to show up." For a while, these weren't isolated stories—they were quietly building an architecture of belonging.

Over time, some of the New Iowan Centers became community hubs, not just for services, but for living and learning. I recall that Cedar Rapids had a program in the church basement that hosted weekly storytelling circles, supported childcare needs, and was run by a wonderful woman named Paula from Ecuador. These spaces were not just transactional—they were relational. They allowed people to show up whole, to be seen, and to contribute. They were, in essence, microcosms of the Iowa we were trying to build.

To me, the New Iowan Initiative was never just a social program—it was a DEI community-building experiment. It operated under Iowa Code § 7E.5 and § 15.108, which authorized the Department of Workforce Development and the Department of Human Rights, my department, to collaborate on immigrant services. However, one of its simplest but most effective interventions was the submission of monthly reports detailing service usage, community engagement, and outcomes.

Each of these reports became a kind of testimony—proof that the Initiative wasn't just symbolic. It was working. We saw increased school enrollment, improved workplace safety, and stronger community ties. Employers began to understand that investing in belonging wasn't charity—it was strategy. And for many immigrants, these centers were the first place they felt truly seen.

Still, the political winds shifted. In 2010, after a wave of Republican victories in the state legislature, funding was slashed. Plus, there was Steve King.

Iowa U.S. Representative Steve King, someone I ran into a lot in my work, was once a powerful conservative voice in Congress, was ousted in the 2020 Republican primary after years of mounting controversy over his inflammatory and racist rhetoric. Known for making provocative statements about immigrants and defending white nationalism, King faced bipartisan backlash after a 2019 New York Times interview in which he questioned why terms like "white supremacist" had become offensive. The fallout was swift: Republican leadership stripped him of his committee assignments, effectively sidelining him in Congress and weakening his influence on agricultural and local policy—critical issues for Iowa's 4th District. His diminished clout, combined with growing discomfort among constituents and party leaders, paved the way for State Senator Randy Feenstra to challenge and defeat him in a five-way primaryHowever, before Steve King left, he was an animating force behind the passing of "English Only" laws in Iowa

But the ultimate effect was that the welcoming centers staff were laid off. Services reduced. The rhetoric around immigration hardened. Suddenly, the language of welcome was replaced by the language of enforcement. Still, the work continued. Volunteers stepped in. Churches opened their doors. Youth organized their own circles. The Initiative became less of a program and more of a memory.

But from this lost opportunity, as a silver lining, my practice evolved, although it took years for me to understand how. Much later, while serving as the policy lead for the Northwest Area Foundation, I learned about ABCD—Asset-Based Community Development. ABCD gave me a new language. ABCD begins with a simple but radical idea: communities are defined not by their deficits, but by their strengths. Instead of asking what's missing, ABCD inquires what's already growing—what skills, relationships, traditions, and institutions can be nurtured from within.

A vivid example of this method was El Mercado in Minneapolis, a project I would later be involved in on a small scale. El Mercado was a lively Latinx marketplace that grew not through top-down planning but from the entrepreneurial spirit of local residents, most of whom were immigrants. Instead of viewing immigrant communities as just recipients of aid, El Mercado saw them as key cultural and economic contributors. It became a place where vendors sold tamales, textiles, and herbal remedies—where elders shared recipes and youth learned business skills. The market didn't just generate income; it fostered a sense of belonging. It showed that when development starts with trust in a community's own assets, the result is not only sustainability but also dignity.

Thus, giving people their dignity is not a gesture; it's an affirmative restoration. In DEIA work, dignity is the foundation upon which equity is built. It means recognizing that every person carries worth that is not contingent on credentials, fluency, or proximity to power. When institutions honor dignity, they stop asking "How do we fix them?" and start asking "How do we make space for their brilliance?" Dignity shifts the lens from deficit to abundance. It allows a refugee mother to be seen not as a burden, but as a bearer of wisdom. It allows a queer youth to speak about their truth without apology. It enables a janitor to be acknowledged as a culture keeper. DEI without dignity is just compliance. But when dignity is centered, policy becomes healing, and inclusion becomes transformation.

To me, this was the beginning of a journey of restoration that I am still on today. The New Iowan Initiative taught me that policy can be a form of love. That infrastructure can be a form of welcome. That belonging is not a feeling—it's a practice. And that even in a state like Iowa, where change often comes slowly, seeds of transformation can take root. You just have to be willing to plant them.

Journey to Xibalba

In the Popol Vuh, one of the Mayan codices, the Hero Twins—Xbalanque and Hunahpu—descend into the Maya underworld, Xibalba, to face a series of deadly trials. They're not the first to try: their father and uncle were defeated their years before. But the Twins outwit the Lords of Death through cleverness, sacrifice, and transformation. In the end, they don't just survive—they restore balance and bring forth maize, the sacred food of the people.

When pondering this story, it is important to culturally understand that the Hero Twins journey isn't about themselves (e.g. Orpheus); in Maya tradition it's about community renewal. They go into the darkness to retrieve what was lost and replant it for future generations. As someone who has spent a lifetime advancing equity, I believe deeply that democratic pluralism is not just a political ideal—it's a lived practice. It's the recognition that our societies are strongest when they embrace complexity, when they honor difference, and when they build systems that allow every voice to be heard and valued. In the United States and abroad, I've seen how the promotion of Diversity, Equity, Inclusion, and Access (DEIA) is not ancillary to democracy—it is its lifeblood.

Additionally, my professional practice, scholarship, and analysis emerge from a space of liminality (present in this book by the image of the hummingbird), which is informed by my life experiences, academic research, and professional expertise. Thus, I have perceived the world from the "rim", never really belonging to the gravity well of any given social sphere. Let me illustrate that idea further. As I wrote about in earlier chapters, my moral and professional compass is informed by the reality that I am the light-skinned child of a U.S. military intelligence man, a photographer, from Alabama (and a MAGA supporter), but also was born into a powerful matriarchy of Mayan teachers and activists from Guatemala.

This is why my approach to DEIA is rooted in Maya cosmology, where leadership is communal, cyclical, and spiritually grounded. I carry that wisdom into every boardroom, classroom, and policy space I enter. For me, promoting democratic pluralism means honoring ancestral knowledge while forging new pathways. It means listening deeply, acting boldly, and never losing sight of the people whose lives are shaped by the systems we seek to transform. All of these are grounding qualities of a 4-H leader to me, but more importantly (to me), it is my spirituality.

Linked to that, as my elders named me in ceremony, I am Ts'unu'um (Tzen, Tzun, Tzan in Mexica and Purépecha), the hummingbird. In Maya spirituality, the hummingbird is a creature of profound liminality, existing in the sacred threshold between the human and spiritual realms. Born from a divine breath and a carved jade arrow, the hummingbird was not molded from mud or maize like other worldly beings, but from intention and wind— hummingbirds are the messengers that carry thoughts, prayers, and desires across realms.

Their ability to hover in stillness, to move in any direction without disturbing a single petal, marks it as a being untethered by the rules of gravity or time. In this way, Ts'unu'um or the hummingbird becomes a spiritual courier, darting between the visible and invisible, the living and the ancestral, the present and the forbidden. When a hummingbird appears, it is said to be delivering love from someone far away or gathering the energy of a soul in transition. Its flight is not random— it is always a ritual. And in that motion, it opens a portal, however brief, where the barriers between worlds thin, and the sacred becomes perceptible. For Maya communities, this liminality is not abstract—it is embodied in every encounter with the hummingbird, a reminder that the spiritual world is never far, and that our thoughts, when carried with grace, can reach beyond the boundaries of flesh and time.

It is in that context that I am drawn to organizations, spaces, and people where individuals live in a state of liminality, not one or the other. This orientation led me to start The Transition Facilitator Group, a consulting firm specializing in leadership, organizational change, and transition, which I ran for many years. I may open it again when I retire, as I love that type of organization-building work.

Similarly, even before joining 4-H, I have always worked for and on behalf of youth, families, and communities, and have had the privilege of sharing in many of their self-earned successes. This is especially true for youth, families, and communities that have been overlooked or erased. I attribute this orientation to the three powerful women who raised me, my life experience in Guatemala, and my status as an immigrant to and from the United States.

Unfortunately, I must also admit that, unlike the hummingbird, I have a second, more passionate side, and it is centered on one truth: "I hate bullies." It is this latter statement that has driven me to work and advocate for, and on behalf of, marginalized youth, families, and communities by promoting and protecting the human and civil rights of the populations I have served. Looking back, I can say that for many, I was the ideal 4-H leader to be "bold and disruptive," but I also realize that, for others, I may have been a harbinger of undesired change—especially if they happen to be one of those "traditional" 4-H stakeholders who believe that 4-H is only for white, rural, straight, Christian, and particularly if you are committed to a MAGA (Make America Great Again) perspective that sees DEIA or "woke" as discriminatory.

In hindsight, I've come to understand my five years in 4-H not as a long tenure, but as a catalytic one—brief, volatile, and transformative. Like a chemical catalyst, I accelerated change without being permanently altered in form, though the emotional and spiritual toll was undeniable. That metaphor feels especially apt given the backdrop of my own upbringing in a war-torn country, where civil and human rights were not just denied—they were systematically erased. That early trauma shaped my instincts, sharpened my resolve, and made the fight for youth inclusion feel not just professional, but ancestral.

This is why my work in positive youth development and civil rights advocacy has never been separate. They are braided together—

like maize in the milpa—each strand nourishing the other. I first began to articulate this connection as a Latino Affairs Commissioner under then-Governor, later U.S. Secretary of Agriculture, Tom Vilsack, where I saw how government policy could either uplift or erase entire communities.

7

NEW IOWANS, OR ARE IOWANS ACTUALLY LATINOS? (JOHN-PAUL)

In the corner of my office sits a weathered copy of the Popol Vuh, its pages inscribed with my name, my school—San Sebastián—and my fifth-grade class, Grupo B. It is the only book I carried in my suitcase when my mother, baby sister, and I fled Guatemala. That book is more than memory; it is a remnant of my roots, a fragile tether to a homeland I was forced to leave behind. For those of us who have migrated north under duress—immigrants, refugees, exiles—the ache of absence is not abstract. It is visceral. It lives in our tongues, stripped of ancestral language; in our bodies, displaced from sacred soil; in our spirits, longing for the milpa and the mountains that once held us.

I identify as Latine or indigenous depending on the context, a contradiction born of colonial erasure: my Mayan language taken so I could learn Spanish, Spanish which was replaced by English when I arrived in the cultural mecha of the United States, Cheyenne, Wyoming, as a broken teenager. I am an immigrant twice over—first fleeing racial animus against my mother in Georgia, then escaping political persecution in Guatemala, where my mother's advocacy for her poor and indigenous students made us targets. My spirituality is a syncretic braid of Mayan cosmology and Catholic liberation theology, shaped by Monsignor Girardi, who, for simplicity's sake, I will call my school principal, who taught that education must serve justice or it serves nothing at all. After we left, Monsignor Girardi was murdered—stoned in the eyes, ears, and mouth—for writing the Guatemalan Truth and Reconciliation documents. His death, like my family's displacement, is a wound that never fully closes. And yet, in the sacred story of maize, in the teachings of the Popol Vuh, I find a map back to myself. We are not merely connected to maize; we are made of it. To say this is not poetic—it is genealogical. And in the absence of home, I hold onto that truth like a seed waiting to be replanted.

Monsignor Juan José Gerardi was a Catholic bishop, human rights advocate, and the director of the Oficina de Derechos Humanos del Arzobispado de Guatemala (ODHAG). He was assassinated on April 26, 1998, just two days after presenting Guatemala: Nunca Jamás (Guatemala Never Again), a landmark report documenting over 55,000 human rights violations during the country's 36-year civil war. The report, compiled by the Catholic Church's Recovery of Historical Memory Project (REMHI), attributed the vast majority of atrocities—including massacres, disappearances, and torture—to the Guatemalan military, state police, and paramilitary forces. According to Prensa Libre and El Periódico, Guatemala's major newspapers, Gerardi was brutally murdered in the garage of his parish house, which was annexed to my school building, struck in the head with a concrete block. His death sent shockwaves through Guatemala and the international community, symbolizing the high cost of truth-telling in a country still haunted by impunity. Though the government initially attempted to deflect blame, a court later convicted members of the military of orchestrating the killing. Gerardi's assassination remains one of the most emblematic cases of post-war political violence, a chilling reminder that even in peace, speaking truth to power can be fatal.

La Gente del Maize

But let me digress, Maya people traditionally call ourselves "La Gente del Maize," the people of the corn. A theme that is present in our Guatemalan and Mexican national literary canon. For example, Miguel Ángel Asturias, the Nobel Prize-winning Guatemalan author and diplomat, gave literary and spiritual voice to the Indigenous soul of the Americas through works like Hombres de Maíz (Men of Maize). In this novel, Asturias weaves myth, resistance, and poetic surrealism to honor the sacred relationship between Indigenous peoples and maize—a bond that transcends agriculture and enters the realm of cosmology.

In Asturias' book, La Gente de Maíz are not merely characters; they are embodiments of ancestral wisdom, guardians of the milpa, and defenders of a worldview rooted in reciprocity and reverence. Asturias challenges colonial logic and capitalist exploitation by portraying maize not as a commodity, but as sacred flesh, echoing the Mayan Popol Vuh's creation story, something that I am also attempting to do in this book. His narrative becomes a political and spiritual act, reclaiming Indigenous identity and reminding readers that to violate the maize is to violate the people themselves. Through Hombres de Maíz, Asturias offers a lyrical, defiant homage to those who live in rhythm with the land, whose very being is made of maize.

That understanding has been the true north of my life. My raíces—our word for roots—have guided decisions that could not be navigated by policy alone. They informed how I enter a room, how I set a table, whom I invite to speak first, how I measure the success of

94

a meeting by who returns, not by who agreed. Those roots shaped me when I worked alongside mostly white rural farmers during my time in the administration of then-Governor Tom Vilsack—who would later become the U.S. Secretary of Agriculture in the Obama-Biden years—and Lisa's former boss. They shaped me again when the question of naming arose, and I chose "Maize" for one of Iowa 4-H's most successful and nationally recognized programs serving Native American, migrant, immigrant, and Latine communities. I will share that example at the end of this chapter, but the name itself matters now, because naming is a ceremony. It tells you where something belongs.

This name is also of import because many of us formed by Mesoamerican cultures and spiritualities, Corn—Maize—is more than a plant or a cuisine. It is the sacred flesh of humanity, the golden gift from the gods, the axis around which life spirals. It nourishes the body, yes, but also the story—our ceremonies, our cosmologies, our social agreements. In the Popol Vuh, the sacred text of the K'iche' Maya, the first humans are formed from masa, maize dough. The claim is as radical as it is intimate: our very essence is rooted in this plant. Corn is the heartbeat of the milpa, the field made sacred by cycles of planting, tending, and harvest that mirror birth, death, and renewal.

Deepening that parallelism, in Guatemala and Mexico, Indigenous artisans have long practiced a powerful form of spiritual resistance and cultural continuity by crafting Catholic religious statues from maize—transforming colonial symbols sitting in Catholic churches into vessels of ancestral meaning. These statues, often depicting saints or the Virgin Mary, were molded from corn dough or layered with maize husks, grounding them in the sacred material of creation as told in the Popol Vuh.

But the true act of syncretism lay within: hidden inside these figures, where indigenous artisans placed spiritual icons, offerings, or symbols from their own cosmologies—jade beads, copal resin, feathers, or miniature carvings of Maya gods. This quiet defiance allowed Indigenous communities to honor imposed Catholic and Christian religious mandates while preserving their own sacred narratives. The statues became double-coded: outwardly Catholic, inwardly Maya, embodying a theology of survival where maize remained the flesh of divinity and the conduit of ancestral presence.

It is in that light that Maize is not a flourish or a metaphor for us. It is the oldest truth we know about ourselves, repeated like a prayer from field to kitchen to story circle, our own kind of Genesis, written not in ink but in kernels and husks. In our tradition, maize is not merely food; it is essence and spirit, akin to the "mana" spoken of in Native Hawaiian belief. We are not merely connected to maize; we are made of it. To say this is not to speak poetically—it is to speak genealogically. But more importantly, for me, it was the roots, the raíces that kept me whole.

The Hummingbird Between Guatemala and Iowa

For me as the hummingbird, the one in between, this sacred relationship spans geographies, connecting the volcanic soils of Guatemala with the rolling green fields of Iowa. In Guatemala, maize is prayer and memory, carried in the hands of abuelas and woven into daily life with a steadiness that defies the interruptions of history. Tortillas slap from palm to palm; steam lifts from a comal; kernels keep the pace of a day. In Iowa, corn is industry and abundance, a backbone of rural economies, a symbol stitched into caps and roadside murals and field signs that punctuate the horizon. One land speaks in terraces and small plots etched into hillsides; the other in section lines and grids and precision planters that hum across prairie winds. Life is even in its state slogan at the time – Iowa, a place to grow.

Under the difference in scale and machinery lies a kinship of reverence. Corn sustains communities in both places. It anchors ritual and marks time. It gives language to belonging. For those of us who have migrated or been replanted, maize is a bridge—a golden thread that ties ancestral wisdom to new soil. It reminds us that even when the postal address changes, the root system can remain intact.

I guess I carry milpa within myself like a lit ember, blowing on it gently in foreign seasons until it glows again.

Every time I go home to see my parents in Iowa, I recognize the familiarity of rows that seem to run forever, that dull green rippling under a sky as wide as any ocean. I see the grain elevators rising like sentinels and barns that reflected the stubborn endurance of winter. I also recognized the people—those who study the sky like a ledger, the farmers who place a hand on the soil and truly understand the day's work. That is the kinship maize promises: a shared accountability to land and to one another.

Furthermore, this belief that maize is body and breath is encoded in our stories, ceremony, and art. Some Mayan traditions, including the Popol Vuh, teach that white maize formed the bones—purity, structure, the architecture of being. Yellow maize became vitality—the muscle, strength, and movement that carry us through a day. Red maize is blood—the sacred current of life and the thread of ancestry. Black maize formed the eyes and hair—mystery, night, and the doorway into what is not seen but must be acknowledged.

The Story of the Popol Vuh

The Popol Vuh is one of our last remaining foundational texts, a record of the oral traditions that survived conquest, conversion, and centuries of interruption. It was transcribed into Spanish by Father Francisco Ximénez in the early 18th century, its roots reaching back to a 16th-century Quiché manuscript and further still into the storytelling gatherings that preceded any pen. In it, the gods attempt to make humans from mud. The mud dissolves in the rain because, as we say in the heartland, they were too wishy-washy. The gods then attempt to create humans again, this time from wood. The wooden figures were so inflexible that they could not change, remember, or speak gratitude to their creators. They also did not care for their world or their makers because they had a wooden heart. Each of those forms fail because they lack K'i'ik'—breath, energy, the animating force that ties flesh to spirit. K'i'ik' is the bridge between worlds, the bond between inflexibility and lack of form, the gust that turns matter into kin.

The story continues until the gods form humans from masa, from the dough of maize. It is then that we speak and sing, that we hold memory and obligation. It is then we can name our gratitude and our responsibilities. In this telling, life does not begin at the boundary of skin; it begins at the boundary of relationship—between seed and soil, body and breath, ancestor and descendant. K'i'ik' makes the ordinary sacred, not by removing it from the world but by deepening its ties. However, K'i'ik' cannot occur when the heart is too rigid or too soft, which is why Mazza paste becomes so symbolic. In this context, it also represents how programs must be designed - not so inflexible that participant voices cannot be incorporated, and not so wishy-washy that participants become lost.

Counterintuitively, when I first learned about K'i'ik', the explanation offered to me was simple: it is the breath that moves through a body and the breath that moves through a people, the same wind that lifts a field of corn and the same wind that becomes a prayer. To this day, when I walk a field and the stalks shift as one, I think of that breath, how it moves through a community and makes it more than a collection of individuals. It makes us a people.

Thus, for me, the maize story is not a myth; it is a declaration. It says, "We are born of the land, of the diversity of milpa, of the cycles of planting and harvest." It says we are not separate from the earth; we are its children. It says abundance is a shared practice, not a solo performance. This understanding shapes everything I do—my teaching, my work, my advocacy. It connects me to 4-H youth and families who still work the land, and to those whose land now is a raised bed on an apartment stoop or a community plot beside a city library. It teaches me to lead with humility and to cultivate with care. It insists on interdependence as method and outcome.

In a society that often prizes individualism and extraction, the milpa calls me back to reciprocity and ceremony, to a sacred obligation to grow together. When I enter a room to build or rebuild an organization, I bring that ethic with me. I ask first: What is the soil like here? Who are the elders? What stories have been harvested too early? Where is the shade, and who needs it? Where is the water, and who has been denied it? The questions are agrarian because the work is about growth, and because people and communities can bloom. Institutions are fields; cultures are soils. If we want a different harvest, we must work the ground differently.

The Raíces of Generational 4-H as Compass

In this approach to DEIA and PYD, raíces is more than a metaphor; it is a governance tool. Roots reveal what a plant can survive, what it can store, and how it can bend without breaking, which is why I believe Generational 4-H has a central role in shaping the future of 4-H. Thus, in my leadership style, raíces means honoring memory while making room for the new. It means checking which practices hold meaning and which traditions merely persist out of habit. It means tracing the path of nourishment—are resources reaching the tips of the system, or do they pool near the trunk? It means asking who is sheltered and who stands alone in the wind.

This is where my Maya orientation met the practical world of policy and programs. When I later chose "Maize" as a program name, I did so because I wanted the work to inherit the responsibilities embedded in that story—interdependence, reciprocity, memory, and breath. I wanted any young Latine or indigenous 4-Hers entering a room with a 4-H Maize banner to feel the quiet assurance that their gifts and histories were presumed to be assets, not anomalies. The story preceded the design.

But as I stated in the last chapter, in truth, my 4-H journey began before any official title, while I worked on the "New Iowan" initiative as Iowa's Director and Commissioner of Latino Affairs under Governor Vilsack. The work placed me at the heart of a rapidly changing cultural landscape where migration, identity, and belonging were being renegotiated in real time. My days were spent in Iowa hometown school cafeterias, union halls, church basements, and city council chambers, where overlapping languages were braided into a single conversation about how to live together well. I was not merely advocating for policy. I was helping communities imagine themselves anew, often through youth-led efforts, bilingual education, and grassroots organizing.

In those rooms, my maize stories came to life. I learned to map a town by its social roots: who everyone calls when there is a problem, which uncle runs the Saturday soccer league, which grandmother has

100

a key to the church kitchen, which teenager is the first to try something risky and then translate the experience for friends. I learned the cadence of shift changes and how to schedule so parents did not have to choose between feeding their families and participating in their communities. I learned that youth will lead if adults unlearn the habit of speaking first.

The values I carried into 4-H—pluralism, inclusion, and belief in the power of young people to shape their own narratives—were forged there. From immigrant families, particularly in rural Iowa, I learned the discipline of hope: to keep showing up even when the rules seem to rearrange themselves overnight. I learned the grammar of resilience: how to conjugate "we" in a new language while holding the old one close, how to translate dignity across counters and forms, how to insist on the fullness of a life not yet recognized by systems.

Those lessons shaped the leadership I later brought to other large organizations: listening as a strategy, honoring lived experience as data, and building structures that reflect the full spectrum of our communities rather than asking communities to contort themselves to fit a narrow structure. If maize teaches anything, it is that monoculture impoverishes. Diversity—of seed, of soil, of method, and especially of people—creates resilience.

Through the New Iowan initiative, we set out to ensure that communities like Marshalltown, Mason City, West Liberty, and Fort Dodge could serve as model sites for integration. We wanted newcomers—many of them Latine—to find meaningful employment, housing, education, and a sense of belonging, not just a place to sleep between shifts. The timing was not incidental. Iowa was facing a massive, looming workforce shortage. The data were uncompromising; the math did not bend to ideology. Our launch was the state's official acknowledgment that our future strength lay in embracing diversity rather than resisting it.

The practicalities mattered. We supported credential evaluations for professionals trained outside the United States so that college professors (such as my mother) did not become night-shift janitors by default, and engineers did not end up stuck behind a register because a licensing board could not imagine their training. We collaborated with school districts on dual-language programs and family engagement practices that treated bilingualism as an asset and parents as partners. We worked with employers to move beyond transactional hiring and into long-term investment—mentorship, training, transportation supports, predictable scheduling—recognizing that a person is not a slot to be filled but a neighbor to be welcomed.

Thus, my role in the Vilsack administration was to advocate fiercely for culturally responsive policies, dismantle barriers to workforce and professional licensing, and amplify the voices of immigrant families eager to call Iowa home. But I did not experience the work primarily as "economic development" or "workforce strategy," though it was certainly both. I experienced it as an insistence on dignity, resilience, and potential—a refusal to waste talent or deny contribution. The families I met were not asking for special treatment; they were asking to be seen accurately, to be measured by their gifts and their work rather than by the color of their skin, place of their birth, or who they love.

Corn as common ground between Iowa, 4-H, and Guatemala

In those rooms, I learned to start where common ground was easiest to find—corn. I began to joke, especially when speaking to rural Iowans for the first time, that Iowans are actually "Latinos," specifically Maya Indians, but just do not know it yet. It always drew a nervous laugh, and in that laughter a door opened. Humor did not erase differences, but it softened the defensive postures we carry when we are told a change is coming. It allowed me to point to shared values—family, hard work, and corn—without accusing or pleading.

From there, we could talk plainly. Iowa produces 2.63 billion bushels of corn for grain each year – a crop that Mesoamerican Indigenous peoples domesticated. In simple words my people gave Iowa the corn that Iowa now exports to the world. The same maize that is woven into my spirituality is the state's economic engine. Thus, I asked my audience if we could honor that convergence without fear, which they always affirmed. This simple act allowed us to tell true stories about a shared inheritance—how a seed shaped continents and how it can shape a conversation in a church hall on a quiet Iowa Tuesday night.

However, my joke carried a hook, and the hook had a promise: if corn matters to you, then a piece of my story is already familiar to you. If family and work matter to you, then we have someplace to stand together. If you have ever prayed for rain or watched a forecast like a gambler checking odds, then you know something about dependence and hope that I know, too. If you have seen dispossession because of the farm crisis, my people have also – which is why we immigrated here.

Corn became a translation device. It allowed me to show the immigrant, the youth of color, and the urban dweller—the new Iowan—not as an abstraction, but as a neighbor with a different map to the same field. That's why Iowa coined the term "Dreamers" to refer to those children brought by their parents but who had no papers.

There is also an etiquette to entering communities, what social workers and anthropologists call rapport, that predates any civic training—an etiquette shaped by kitchens and porches. You do not arrive empty-handed. You start by listening. You compliment the bread before you ask for the recipe. In my work, maize gave me that etiquette. It reminded me to ask who had planted, who had watered, who had harvested before I made any recommendation. It reminded me to learn the local rites—the county fair, the Friday game, the church supper—so that my presence was not only official but also human. When I sat with farmers, I asked about seed choice, not only about policy. I asked about hail and soil texture and early frost—the vocabulary that makes a life legible to those who live it. Then I shared the vocabulary of my own formation—nixtamal, masa, comal, milpa—not as exotic artifacts but as tools, as techniques for nourishment and survival. We met in the shared kitchen of corn, and from there, we could build.

This is why naming our new 4-H program "Maize" was never cosmetic. It was a promise that the room itself would recognize heritage as instruction, not novelty. It was a way to say to youth and families: your knowledge travels; your language carries power; your work is legible here. Beyond that, the milpa rebukes extraction. It operates by reciprocity and balance. Corn grows tall, offering a ladder. Beans return nitrogen to the soil, offering sustenance. Squash spreads low, offering shade and moisture. Like people, communities, or even nations, no one thrives alone.

Translating this into public life means designing systems that refuse to consume people's energy without returning support. It means ensuring language or sign language interpreters are not an afterthought, that scheduling respects shift work, that meetings include childcare or stipends, that leadership development follows the logic of mentorship rather than gatekeeping. All of these are the essences of my DEIA practice.

This is because in true community practice, reciprocity looks like asking youth and families to co-design programs rather than fill out surveys after programs and decisions are already made. It looks like extending the courtesy of time—enough notice, enough repetition, enough patience—to those whose calendars are braided with obligations others do not see. It looks like celebrating wins in a way that honors the many hands involved, not only the faces at a podium.

Leading with humility is not about shrinking. It is about right-sizing the self in relation to the work, about keeping the ego from uprooting the field. Humility is a discipline when you are asked to speak for many, when every misstep risks confirming someone's worst assumptions. Maize taught me that humility and courage grow together. The stalk must be strong and also flexible. The roots must hold firm and also travel, seeking water where it can be found. To lead in that spirit is to move with steadiness and curiosity, to state clearly what you know and to admit plainly what you do not.

In my life, that humility (which I struggle with since my astrological sign is a Leo) meant acknowledging to rural Iowans that there were things about their traditions I was still learning, just as there were things about my own that I could teach. It meant asking for help without apology and offering it without condescension. It meant remembering that the outcome of any meeting is not only the policy drafted but the relationship cultivated.

But returning to K'i'ik', I hold this truth close: breath connects bodies to spirits, and communities to their sources of life. In meetings where tension thickened the air, I would literally attend to breath— slow mine, invite a pause, let a room exhale. Breath, as meditation research and studies have shown, changes the quality of a conversation. A small silence can become a blessing if it is respected. In a field, wind reveals the health of a crop; in a room, breath reveals the health of a dialogue. To breathe is to refuse panic and to steady the hand that is planting in uncertain weather.

B'alam (the Jaguar): The Kindling of Maize and Ujima

In 2014, Frank, a City Planner, Eliseo, an engineer from Iowa State University, and I were having lunch at a local Mexican restaurant that featured a large mural of an Aztec temple on the wall. I was trying to recruit two male Latino professionals to volunteer their time with 4-H, particularly in the fields of science, technology, engineering, and math (STEM). During our conversation, I shared a small anecdote about my eight-year-old daughter, Salome (my B'alam), when I asked her, "Why are you so good at math?" To my surprise, she responded confidently and without hesitation, "Because I am Maya."

When Eliseo heard the story, he said, "Let's do that!" When I asked what he meant, he reminded me that white Europeans aren't the only people who excel in STEM. He also made a statement that shifted my perspective on how STEM should be taught in our programs and public schools, highlighting how disconnected it can be from our identities and cultural roots as human beings and as part of our cultural heritage. His idea was simple: let's have youth explore STEM from a Mesoamerican indigenous and Latine perspective. For example, Frank added, we could highlight that the ancient Maya were not just astronomers or engineers; they were weavers of sacred knowledge. They tracked Venus with precision, built pyramids aligned to solstices, and developed a base-20 math system that included zero long before Europe caught up.

It is then that I realized that their science wasn't separate from agency or spirit. It was embedded in ceremony, cultures, and our different understanding of time. Today, when folks teach STEMP— Science, Technology, Engineering, Math through a Positive Youth Development lens (which adds the P), we often forget that STEM has always been cultural and always been spiritual. In our PYD programs, we don't just teach robotics or coding; we teach young people to see themselves as creators, as problem-solvers, as descendants of brilliance. When we center belonging, when we honor ancestral ways of knowing, we're not just preparing youth for careers—we're restoring the sacred balance between knowledge and purpose.

This is why and how, in 2015, we launched the first Culturally Based Youth Leadership Accelerator (CYLA). CYLA's were not programs in themselves; instead, they serve as launching pads for underrepresented and underserved youth into local 4-H Club learning communities. They were designed to utilize cultural strengths and culturally based narratives to introduce and strengthen the relationship between youth of color and county programs, introduce volunteers, staff, and faculty to culturally based leadership development work, and connect underrepresented youth to post-secondary education and resources available to them. The model was designed to ensure that youth of color were not isolated; instead, the two-and-a-half-day retreats served as on-ramps to full participation in local 4-H programs with increased cultural relevance and diversity.

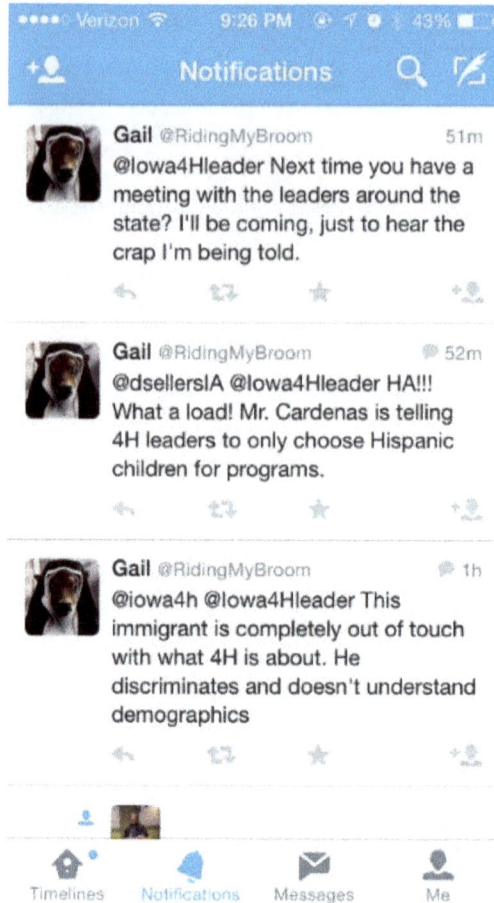

Messages to John-Paul accusing him of only caring about Latine youth

The programs were immensely successful, but too prosperous for some who began to rally against them, because, in their words, they were "anti-white," which is now the go-to argument for the cancellation of ethnic and gender studies curriculum in schools and universities by the "War on Woke" groups.

This was even though *all* youth (e.g., race, class, ethnicity, sexual orientation, etc) were welcome and encouraged to participate in the CYLAs. However, the complex reality about the "War on Woke" false narrative is that some white folks perceive programs like these, or gender and ethnic studies, as exclusionary because they challenge long-standing narratives that have centered whiteness as the default cultural and historical lens in American education. When curricula begin to foreground the experiences, histories, and epistemologies of marginalized communities, it can feel to some white folks (or males) like a displacement of their own identity or heritage. A discomfort that is often amplified by zero-sum thinking—the belief that elevating other voices necessarily diminishes their own.

Additionally, ethnic studies interrogate majoritarian systems of power, privilege, and racial hierarchy, which can provoke defensiveness or guilt, especially when whiteness is examined not just as a racial identity but as a social construct tied to institutional advantage. In politically charged environments, these feelings are sometimes weaponized into broader narratives of victimhood or censorship (e.g., DEI = racism), framing inclusion as exclusion. Something I will expound on later in this book.

8

DECENT TO XIBALBA: THE CONTEXT FOR DEIA IN IOWA 4-H (JOHN-PAUL)

As I begin this chapter, which I wrote with tears in my eyes, I want to gently but firmly invite the reader to lean in, even if what follows feels uncomfortable. This section focuses on my experiences with racism, sexism, and homophobia, highlighting painful experiences that emerged within Iowa Extension during my tenure, as they have in countless institutions across the country. I share these experiences not to tarnish 4-H but because I believe in the organization's promise with every fiber of my being. I have seen its ability to uplift youth, build community, and cultivate leadership. However, no beloved institution is immune to the forces of exclusion that shape our society. As someone who has dedicated a lifetime to advancing equity, I understand that "sunshine is the best remedy," as Kinich Ahau (the Sun God) symbolizes in this story. Naming what hurts is not an act of betrayal; it is an act of devotion. It is how we grow, how we heal, and how we ensure that 4-H can genuinely be a place where every young person feels a deep sense of belonging.

I am sharing these examples from my own experience because it is gentler but strategic and necessary. Throughout my years in Extension, I have interacted with hundreds—if not thousands—of individuals from minoritized communities (including women, LGBTQ+ individuals, and professionals of color) across the United States who work in Extension and 4-H programs. My interactions have taken place through various extension associations, national gatherings, and conferences such as Cambio de Colores, as well as national meetings hosted by organizations like the National Association of Extension 4-H Youth Development Professionals (NAE4-HYDP), the Extension Committee on Organization and Policy (ECOP), the Joint Council of Extension Professionals (JCEP), Epsilon Sigma Phi (ESP), and several other professional associations.

And before non-extension readers comment on it, yes Extension loves its acronyms – which may or may not be a way of testing loyalty, or the fidelity of new members (much like making me recite the 4-H Pledge at my interview), or simply culturally land locking new folks out of vital supports.

Whatever the reason, the voices of these stakeholders consistently share a common theme: when individuals from minoritized communities raise concerns about exclusion, bias, and inequitable practices within Extension and 4-H programs, their institutions often deflect accountability by blaming the messengers instead of addressing systemic barriers or examining whose voices are prioritized in decision-making, institutions may label these concerned stakeholders as "disruptive," "ungrateful," or "difficult to work with." As I highlighted in my scholarly article "Pet to Threat," which can be found in the appendix, this deflection not only silences legitimate critiques but also reinforces a culture where loyalty is measured by compliance rather than courage. In doing so, institutions safeguard the status quo and punish those who dare to speak truth to power—especially when that truth challenges deeply embedded norms surrounding race, class, language, and belonging. These gaps by leadership make it our collective responsibility to hold these institutions accountable and strive for a more just society.

This is why sharing our histories of oppression, and as oppressors, is so vital for learning, even when the history is hard to hear. This is the reason that history is not simply an organizational record—it is a compass for justice. It reveals the architecture of oppression and the resilience of those who resisted it, offering both warning and wisdom to future generations. Institutions like the Birmingham Civil Rights Institute, the Smithsonian institution I completed my national fellowship at, are not just repositories of memory—they are sanctuaries of truth. They hold the echoes of foot soldiers, freedom riders, and everyday people who dared to confront the machinery of segregation. To erase, white center, or sanitize these stories, as today's War on Woke is attempting to do, is to sever the roots of our collective conscience.

Learning from history demands that we look unflinchingly at the systems that produced suffering, not to dwell in despair, but to honor the courage it took to survive and transform them.

Today, the attacks on ethnic studies and museums like the National Museum of African American History and Culture are not just political maneuvers—they are acts of historical erasure. They target the very spaces where truth is curated, where complexity is embraced, and where young people—especially those from marginalized communities—can see themselves reflected in the arc of history. These efforts to defund, distort, or delegitimize the voices from the margins, whether they be women, LGBTQ+, or communities of color are attempts to flatten the narrative, to replace lived experience with myth. But history, especially the harrowing kind, refuses to be silenced. History lives in the soil of Birmingham, which was once nicknamed Bombingham, in the blood memory of ancestors, and in the sacred obligation of educators, curators, and storytellers to preserve the record intact. To defend history is to defend the possibility of a more honest, more just future.

But coming back to 4-H. Some people say that those who convert become the most passionate, and my journey with 4-H reflects that sentiment. I fell deeply in love with the program—its mission, its people, and the transformative potential it offers to youth who have never seen themselves represented in its spaces. My love for 4-H fueled my commitment to bring in new voices, new faces, and new energy. However, love does not mean silence. Despite my dedication, 4-H did not always embrace me—or the youth I aimed to include. Initially, some local community members, including individuals directly tied to 4-H and its land-grant extension service, actively resisted this pluralistic transformation.

To be abundantly clear, addressing these issues is not an attack on 4-H; it is an examination rooted in care and concern. When we love something, it's important to understand what can be improved to make it better.

With that said, I wish I could say my 4-H journey was free of racism, sexism, and homophobia. I wish I could tell you that everything was harmonious from the start, however that would not be true. Iowa 4-H, like any human institution, is a living contradiction—capable of both extraordinary good and deep harm. That is why, in the pages ahead, I will be brutally honest about my experiences. My intention is not to wound but to illuminate; not to condemn, it is to call forth the best of what 4-H can be. Acknowledging uncomfortable truths is the first step toward transformation.

However, to protect the privacy of those involved, especially the youth participants, I will change or obscure some names and details in the following examples. This is crucial, particularly since the media has covered most of these stories, as it can potentially cause additional harm.

The Lords of Xibalba: What I did not know did hurt me

In Maya cosmology, the Lords of Xibalba ruled the underworld not through brute force, but through invisibility and decay. They didn't announce themselves—they crept in through unswept corners, through small slights, apathy, fear, and primarily through silence. Each pair governed a specific affliction: blood sickness, swelling, skeletal wasting, or sudden death on forgotten roads. What you didn't see could hurt you. That was their power. In our institutions, too, harm often hides in plain sight—not in overt rejection, but in the quiet erosion of belonging, in the racist and sexist policies never questioned, in the "traditions" wrapped in fear. The Lords of Xibalba remind us: if we don't name what lurks beneath, it will name us.

The Token

It was only a few weeks after my first State Fair when I received a call from the U.S. Office of Civil Rights (OCR). They were wondering why Iowa 4-H hadn't responded to the findings from a federal equity review. I was surprised and asked, "What review?" I hadn't been informed by my own institution that OCR had conducted a review of Iowa 4-H and Extension due to a series of complaints about their services, or that I had been named as the contact person for Iowa Extension. The federal review found over 40 major deficiencies in hiring practices and services, many of which affected the 4-H program. Some examples of these deficiencies included:

1. Workforce Diversity & Hiring Gaps: ISUEO/4-H faced significant underrepresentation of racial/ethnic minorities and women in leadership, faculty, and county-level roles. Recruitment practices lacked reach and intentionality, and promotion/separation trends reflected systemic bias.

2. Training & Advancement Barriers: Staff received inconsistent civil rights training, particularly around ADA, Title VI, and Title IX. Minority employees had limited support for tenure-track advancement, and volunteers lacked guidance on inclusive outreach.

3. Policy & Compliance Shortfalls: The Affirmative Action Plan was incomplete and appeared not to have been looked at in decades. In addition, complaint procedures were unclear, and documentation practices remained insufficient. Staff often misunderstood that "all reasonable efforts" were required for equitable access.

4. Advisory Board Representation: Advisory councils and boards lacked racial and gender diversity. Recruitment efforts targeting minority communities were minimal, and barriers to participation persisted for underrepresented communities.

5. Program Access & Equity: Program delivery methods—especially in 4-H—created barriers for minority youth and volunteers. Scholarship access, club integration, and event participation showed signs of inequity. Outreach materials were rarely multilingual or culturally tailored.

6. Public Notification & Accessibility: Public-facing materials often omitted required nondiscrimination and disability access statements. There was no comprehensive plan for Limited English Proficiency (LEP) access. Migrant youth and disability

accommodations were poorly understood and rarely implemented by staff.

7. Data Collection & Impact Monitoring: Race, gender, and ethnicity data collection had been inconsistent, and in some cases appeared forged. ISUEO lacked systems to compare potential versus actual beneficiaries, which limited its ability to assess equity impact.

After becoming aware of the OCR review and the issues it cited, I approached leadership and human resources to discuss the matter. I inquired about how we should proceed to address these concerns. The chilling response I received was, "We hired you to fix it!" This made me believe I had been brought in as a "token" at 4-H, stepping into a role and spotlight I hadn't asked for. The conundrum is that my presence in 4-H was intended to signal progress on DEIA. Yet the exclusionary structure or attitudes around me had not changed.

It is here that I think the sociological definition of racial tokenism is helpful. Tokenism refers to the practice of making a performative or superficial effort to include individuals from underrepresented racial or ethnic groups. It often aims to create the appearance of diversity or equity without committing to meaningful inclusion or systemic change. In practice, it meant that I found myself as the only person of color in the room, particularly at the leadership level. I was expected to represent, alone, all underserved and marginalized 4-H communities while navigating a culture that had neither prepared nor been willing to hear diverse voices.

Furthermore, decisions impacting 4-H were frequently made without my input, yet I was paraded, especially at the national level, in brochures and meetings as proof of inclusion. The burden of visibility weighed heavily on me, especially as I witnessed talented youth from marginalized backgrounds being overlooked or excluded. It was not just about being hired; it was about being commodified, symbolized, and ultimately isolated in a system that had yet to commit to equity.

What made it more emotionally difficult for me was the tangibility of my hiring as a direct result of an equity review by the Office of Civil Rights. The timing was obvious. It was clear that my role was part of a corrective measure—a requirement following embarrassing findings that revealed systemic exclusion. While the federal review confirmed longstanding concerns expressed by minoritized staff and participants, it also created a significant and unattainable burden on my role. I wasn't just there to handle the DEIA work; I was there to, visibly, show that the institution had changed. But change hadn't truly happened; it had only been announced.

So, I found myself managing not only the responsibilities of the job but also the unspoken expectation to embody the solution to an entrenched systemic and structural problem, with very little power or support to create change genuinely. Moreover, I was now a messenger who was in danger of being shot for delivering a message that the institution may not like.

Now, tokenism is not an uncommon situation for minoritized leaders (see research article in the appendix). However, tokenism often leads to what researchers are calling the "Pet to threat" dynamic when it involves people of color and other minoritized groups in the workplace. Coined by Dr. Kecia M. Thomas, whom I had the honor of meeting as a Civil Rights FUSE Fellow at the Birmingham Civil Rights Institute, this phenomenon happens when a person of color, especially a black woman, is hired. She is often perceived as less significant, likable, adaptable, and non-threatening—a "pet" who reflects positively on the organization's diversity efforts. However, as she advances in her role, demonstrates expertise, and begins to challenge norms or assert her presence, the admiration turns into discomfort. Her confidence is now viewed as arrogant. Her leadership starts to threaten the status quo, and thus, she is labeled "threatening".

As with pet-to-threat dynamics, I was initially welcomed by extension as a symbol of progress and inclusion—a bilingual, culturally grounded leader whose presence signaled the organization's new commitment to diversity. I was praised for my ability to connect with marginalized youth, elevate underrepresented voices, and navigate complex community dynamics. However, as more underrepresented youth joined 4-H, I began to assert my vision more confidently—challenging exclusionary practices, advocating for inclusion, and confronting systemic inequities—the tone shifted. The same leadership that once celebrated my uniqueness grew uncomfortable with my push for structural change. My advocacy was seen as a disruption, and my confidence was viewed as defiance. Invitations declined, support faded, and I was no longer seen as an asset but as a threat to the status quo. The change was subtle but clear: I had shifted from pet to threat, not because I changed, but because I refused to stay in my place. Here are some examples, all of which happened in temporal proximity to each other, that illustrate my point.

La Feria and the Burning Cross

Each year during my time with Iowa 4-H, I would invite groups of non-traditional, urban, and diverse youth and their families to the state fair, especially those who hadn't previously had the chance to experience 4-H. In 2017, I invited a group primarily composed of Black and Latino youth and parents from Cedar Rapids and Waterloo. After visiting the 4-H building and pens, they also had the chance to enjoy the entire fair.

About 10 minutes after leaving us, one of the parents called my work cellphone and was in tears. She and the other parents were furious and wanted me to join them right away to report an alleged racist incident. When I got there, they pointed out a folding billboard featuring a Hereford cow, being shown by a white child wearing a 4-H shirt.

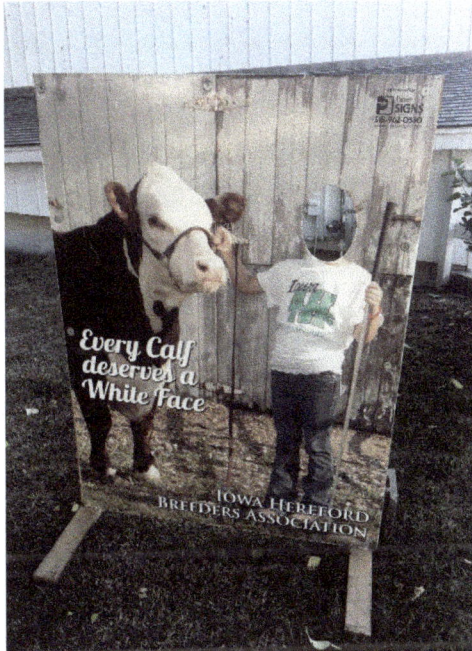

Sign: Every calf deserves a white face.
There was a cutout for kids to stick their faces through and take a memorable picture.

Like many fair and local tourism signs, there was a cutout for kids to stick their faces through and take a memorable picture. At the bottom of the sign, it read "Every calf deserves a white face," referencing the Hereford breed's distinctive white face, which contrasts with its typically reddish-brown body. This signature "red whiteface" pattern is a hallmark of the breed, making it easily recognizable to people with a livestock background.

However, the parents, who did not have ag backgrounds, had discovered the cutout sign after some of the youth of color started taking pictures of themselves and the sign. They took it as a racist message, stating that 4-H wasn't for kids of color.

While many readers will automatically jump to the conclusion that the sign itself was racist, I do not necessarily agree. This is because, from a cross-cultural communications standpoint, I think of the sign as a giant intercultural mix-up with the creators of the sign expressing one message: "We love and are proud of our 4-H and beautiful bovine friends", after all, Herefords are a very handsome breed. Thus, while I will talk about this incident as an example of racism, it is not the sign that I consider racist. I reserve that description for the respect and actions, or better said, the lack thereof, when the parents of the perspective, "diverse" or "urban" 4-Hers, presented their viewpoint.

In this, I cite two separate but interrelated responses to the complaint from influential 4-H stakeholders that illustrate my point. The first is the response from the Association, which not only denied that the sign was an issue but also complained directly to the senior leadership at extension that I had no authority to ask for the sign to be removed from the fair, which was wildly incorrect due to federal policy, which gives authority to the 4-H State Leader (me) to approve or deny use of the 4-H Clover and name. Furthermore, the fact that the association was more interested in preserving an old sign than welcoming youth of color still puzzles me to this day.

However, much more problematic was the response from leadership at my institution, which by then was led by three white straight men, who just kept on saying, "Just let it go." What they have never recognized is that "just let it go" also means, "just let them go" because what parent would let his or her child join an organization that does not care about their perspective, sensitivities, or belonging.

Social Media picture of alleged 4-H stakeholders in KKK garb

These feelings of being gaslighted increased a few weeks after the state fair incident, when I was driving to Creston, Iowa, to meet with local extension staff when my appointment was abruptly cancelled for an unspecified "emergency." Later, news outlets shared a photograph of several high school students wearing hoods, carrying guns, and burning a cross in an open field. The image spread rapidly on social media, and I discovered that four of the five youths had ties to Iowa 4-H. Seeing those symbols of hatred in my own community left me unsettled and searching for answers.

Hoping to understand what had happened, I reached out to extension leadership, only to learn they did not plan to investigate. I could not shake the feeling that this act might have been meant to intimidate me—after all, I had been traveling to Creston to address a related, sensitive matter. Yet without any formal inquiry, I could not prove my suspicions. I found myself caught between genuine concern and the absence of institutional support.

When I pressed further, my worries were dismissed as an "overreaction," a response that social scientists label "gaslighting." One senior leader even suggested that calling the students' actions racist reflected only my "personal opinion," likening the display to harmless "boys being boys." It was painful to hear such minimization, especially from someone in a position to foster accountability. After all, we were talking about white robes, burning crosses, and guns, which to me seem to be definitive of what a racist would wear.

While there are many other examples, the final one I will share is one from Ujima, the sister CYLA youth program to Maize, which I discussed earlier in the book. The Ujima three-day retreat, which was named after the seventh principle of Kwanzaa (meaning collective work and responsibility), focused on highlighting the history and lived experiences of black immigrant and African American youth in Iowa. The mini-conference was held at the Iowa 4-H camp, where it welcomed over 60 predominantly African American youth, as well as a significant number of African immigrants. This final group of youth became so excited about 4-H that they decided out of their own volition to translate the 4-H pledge into Arabic and post it to their social media, something that caught both great attention and something else.

For example, a group of 4-H youths from southcentral Iowa sent me social media posts of some former adult 4-H leaders, whom I will call Bob, Chris, and Brian, engaging in social media post conversations. The conversation starts with Bob's comment in response to the youth's post of the 4-H pledge.

❖ Bob: *"This would be fine if they were a Kuwait 4-H club, but they are an American 4-H Club. If they were going home to spread the concept of 4-H in the Middle East, this would be fine, but here, NO!! This is another example of University Political Correctness."*

❖ *To which Chris responded: The world is going to hell in a handbasket, and we're teaching our future generations to speak Arabic when they don't even respect our flag and our nation, and our country ...*"

❖ *This was followed by Brian, who posted: "What next? Making them wear burkas."*

❖ *To which Bob responds: I am surprised that they didn't say it kneeling.*

While I wish those alleged adult 4-H leaders had been held accountable, they were not. What links all these examples, and many more, is not the racism of the actions of 4-H-related individuals or groups. In my view, it is the lack of investigation or response by Extension officials, which I will label as a systemic form of institutional "gaslighting." The American Psychological Association defines racial gaslighting as a form of psychological manipulation in which individuals or institutions deny, distort, or dismiss the lived experiences of racism, causing people—especially those from marginalized communities—to question their own perceptions and realities.

Thus, in youth-serving organizations like 4-H, gaslighting can manifest when leaders respond to reports of discrimination with phrases like "That's not what they meant," or "We treat everyone the same here," or, in my case, "boys-will-be-boys", effectively silencing concerns and protecting the institution's image rather than addressing the harm. Such behavior not only invalidates the experiences of minoritized youth, families, and staff but also reinforces systemic inequities by deflecting accountability and eroding trust.

Over time, racial gaslighting within institutions and organizations undermines their stated commitments to inclusion, creating environments where equity is performative rather than practiced. As I look back at the many bias incidents I dealt with while at 4-H, one of the things that I realize is that, except for very few, they were inflicted and supported by adults, not the 4-H youth.

9

PYD AND KINICH AHAU: THE SUN GOD (JOHN-PAUL)

It is clear to me that 4-H, when infused with DEIA and PYD, is also the solution for many of the incidents in the previous chapter. This is because there is a rhythm to 4-H life in the heartland, and everywhere else, that feels both familiar and revolutionary. It's the rhythm of monthly club meetings (which are really learning communities, not clubs) in church basements and school cafeterias, of project talks and record books, of fair prep and community service. Still more than anything, it's the rhythm of generations, Iowa grandparents, parents, and youth all bound together by a shared commitment to growth, leadership, and community.

That's one of the things I love most about 4-H. It's not just a youth program—it's a generational promise. Kinich Ahau, the Maya sun god, offers a powerful metaphor for what 4-H was meant to be: a source of light, vitality, and sacred rhythm. Kinich Ahau didn't just illuminate the world—he governed its cycles, descending at midday to receive offerings and remind people that the sun's power was both cosmic and personal. Similarly, 4-H was designed to guide young people through the seasons of growth, leadership, and renewal. But when "tradition" hardens into gatekeeping, that light dims. Thus, to honor 4-H tradition is to restore the sacred balance—to ensure that every young person, regardless of background, can rise, shine, and be seen.

Across Iowa, where you'll find families where 4-H isn't just something you do—it's part of who you are. Where, a grandmother who once showed dairy cattle now mentors her granddaughter through a robotics project. Where, a father who learned parliamentary procedure as a club president and serves on the city council now watches his son lead their 4-H Club with the same gavel. These aren't isolated stories—they're woven into the fabric of Iowa's 1,490 active clubs, and they are genuinely a tradition to uphold. But they are also proof that Positive Youth Development (PYD) isn't just a framework—it's a gift.

This is because PYD teaches us that youth thrive when they experience connection, competence, and a sense of contribution.

In generational 4-H families, those experiences are passed down like heirlooms. Youth grow up watching adults model service, leadership, and resilience. They learn that their voice matters because they've seen it in action. And they carry those lessons into their own lives, often returning as volunteers, mentors, and leaders. But tradition alone isn't enough. If 4-H is going to live up to its promise, it must be more than a hand-me-down to diverse youth. It must be a space where every young person—regardless of their background—can find their own sense of belonging. That means honoring the generational legacy while allowing and nurturing new 4-H families to build their own. It means asking: Who's not here yet? And when we invite them to join us, how do we make sure they feel welcome?

We Were Succeeding, Perhaps That Was the Problem.

Between 2014 and 2018, Iowa 4-H made real strides in answering those questions. Club membership grew to over 23,000 youth in grades 4–12, with an additional 7,400 Clover Kids in grades K–3. That's a 9% increase in one year, driven mainly by diverse youth and clubs that did not look or feel traditional to many "traditional" 4-H stakeholders. However, while there was double-digit growth in the number of youth of color who joined Iowa 4-H, at its core, 4-H remained a predominantly white and rural organization, which is why I thought we were ok as related to backlash. Plus, while the club (learning community) structure itself was evolving, it still retained what was important. For example, in-school and after-school clubs expanded access for youth who couldn't attend traditional meetings, but they were still focused on being learning communities (clubs). Special interest clubs created space for niche passions and diverse peer groups. And youth-led initiatives gave members absolute ownership over their experience. This wasn't just programming—it was PYD in motion.

However, what I missed was that resistance and backlash wasn't just about numbers—it was about "who" was joining. Youth joining clubs that reflect their interests, their identities, and their communities. From livestock and baking to robotics and drones, as well as from English to Arabic, Bosnian, and Spanish, Iowa 4-H allowed youth and their families to explore, connect, and lead, something that felt threatening to some "traditional" 4-H

stakeholders

Ballet Folklorico dancer, member of 4-H

Additionally, between 2014 and 2018, we began embracing folkloric dance not only as a performance art but also as a powerful tool for youth leadership and cultural identity.

At statewide retreats like Maize and Ujima, youth choreographed and taught traditional dances rooted in Latin American, African, and Southeast Asian heritage, transforming 4-H spaces, including our Hall of Fame celebrations, into stages for identity, pride, and connection. These moments weren't side events; they were central to the experience.

Native drumming, especially by Meshkwahkihaki youth, and Mexican and Latin American dancers became a language of affirmation, allowing youth to say, "This is who I am, and I belong here." It reflected the heart of Positive Youth Development: giving young people the chance to lead with their whole selves, to build community through culture, and to feel seen not despite their heritage, but because of it.

Reverend Doctor Martin Luther King Jr. once said, "Power at its best is love implementing the demands of justice." In PYD, that power shows up in the way programs are built, led, and sustained by youth.

When a club makes space for an immigrant, an Arab, a queer, or transgender youth who's never felt safe in other settings, that's love. When a generational family welcomes a newcomer with open arms, that's justice. When youth are trusted to lead—not just participate—that's belonging. These are fundamental parts of growing a pluralistic democracy.

I saw this firsthand in counties where bilingual clubs thrived, where LGBTQ+ youth found affirmation, and where youth of color stepped into leadership roles. These weren't just feel-good stories—they were signs of a system moving toward equity. They were often led by volunteers who understood that tradition doesn't mean stagnation, it means stewardship. This mindset is how we bridge the gap, and how we can overcome the "traditional" mentality within 4-H.

Kukulkan: Starting new traditions

Kukulkan—known as Quetzalcoatl in Nahuatl and Mexica traditions—emerges in Maya cosmology as the divine embodiment of metamorphosis. He is the Feathered Serpent, a sacred bridge between sky and earth, spirit and matter. His form—part quetzal bird, part serpent—is not merely symbolic; it is a living metaphor for duality and change. The quetzal, Guatemala's national bird, evokes flight and freedom, while the serpent anchors us to the earth. Kukulkan is not just a symbol of transformation—he is the process of "becoming" itself.

That same spirit of transformation lives in the Iowa 4-H Hall of Fame. Each year, counties nominate individuals whose stewardship has shaped generations of youth. Many honorees come from families deeply rooted in 4-H—mentors, organizers, advocates who've poured decades of love into their communities. But the Hall of Fame doesn't just honor time served—it honors love. The kind of radical, inclusive love Dr. King spoke of. The kind that builds community, confronts injustice, and opens space for every voice - agape.

And that love is most visible in the quiet, everyday moments. A club leader staying late to help a youth finish their record book. A parent driving across town so their child can attend a meeting. A teen mentoring younger members through their first project talk. These acts may seem small, but they are the heartbeat of Positive Youth Development. They teach trust, leadership, and care—not through curriculum, but through relationship.

Belonging, in this context, isn't a slogan—it's a practice. It's cultivated through consistency, empathy, and shared purpose. It's what allows a young person to walk into a meeting and feel, deep in their bones, "This is my place." And it's what keeps them coming back—not just for the projects, but for the people.

Yet the work is never finished. Inclusion isn't a checkbox—it's a daily commitment. It requires reimagining how learning communities (clubs) recruit, how meetings are run, and how traditions are held. It means listening when youth say, "This space doesn't feel like mine," and responding not with defensiveness, but with love. Because in PYD, love is not passive. It's active. It's the force that turns a closed circle into an open door. It's what transforms generational legacy into generational justice. And it's what ensures that every young person—

whether their family has been in 4-H for five generations or they're the first ever—feels seen, valued, and at home.

So when I say I love 4-H, I mean I love 4-H's potential. I love 4-H's capacity to hold both tradition and transformation. I love how 4-H teaches youth to lead with empathy, to serve with purpose, and to build communities that reflect the best of who we are. This is the work of belonging. This is the work of love.

And it's the work that Iowa 4-H—through its clubs, families, and youth—is uniquely equipped to lead.

Everything else we call "tradition"—especially when it excludes or mandates conformity—is something else entirely. Because if 4-H is truly about empowering youth, then the measure of any tradition is whether it creates space for young people to teach themselves, to lead authentically, and to feel seen. Adults should never stand at the front—they should walk beside youth, offering support, not control. And when youth are trusted to shape their own learning, belonging isn't a goal—it's the natural outcome. And our pluralistic democracy is stronger for it.

10

FEDERAL CAREER EMPLOYEE PERSPECTIVE: OBAMA TO TRUMP TRANSITIONS (LISA)

As a career federal employee, some transitions occurred -every two years, whether for the mid-term or the regular elections. Initially, it was something I had not experienced in any other position. You would just get acquainted with some political appointee staff, and then they would be off to assist with campaigning. Serving as a USDA federal career employee under Secretary Vilsack for eight years was unique and not an experience shared by other federal career employees.

NIFA as an agency under USDA 'grew up' during Vilsack's tenure and experienced growing pains from how to pronounce the agency's name, whose role was what, what responsibilities best fit under what roles, creating a strategic plan that aligned with USDA's priorities and just hiring and filling positions from those at the senior executive service (SES) level to division director to national program leader to all the supportive positions as program specialists and assistants. Organizationally, NIFA navigated finding its niche to support education, extension, and research funding, which complemented and enhanced the overall USDA's vision.

The stability of the same agency leader ensured clarity, direction, transparency, and authenticity for all USDA agencies, as well as a collaborative approach with other federal agencies. It also meant that there was continuity of key initiatives for the Obama administration that covered more than one four-year term. This was evident in initiatives that crossed federal agencies. Where USDA sought to be a partner such example efforts as the bullying initiative by Department of Education, efforts to support military child, youth and family programs, Science engagement and education for youth fostered by the Office of Science and Technology Policy (OSTEP), Dept. of Justice's Office of Juvenile Justice and Delinquency Programs (OJJDP) to support afterschool feeding programs, and the First Lady Michelle Obama's Let's Move, an initiative for childhood obesity.

Secretary Vilsack and Department of Education Secretary Arne Duncan both came to the 2011 National 4-H Conference. They did a Q&A session with 4-H'ers, which showed the closeness and collaborative nature of these two agencies, Ag and Ed. Topics they addressed were education, community service, and health and nutrition. In Secretary Vilsack's remarks, he asked 4-H youth to reach out to their friends, family and peers in their communities if they are at risk of dropping out of school. He shared his personal story about when he answered the call to public service. His experience in helping to raise funds to build an athletic complex in his small Iowa town led to his eventual election as mayor, Iowa State Senator, Governor of Iowa, and his subsequent appointment by President Obama to U.S. Secretary of Agriculture.

The Secretary asked the 4-Hers to use their pledge of head, heart, hands, and health to help guide them to success. The heart, said Vilsack, represents a commitment to the voice of youth, and he encouraged kids to hold a youth roundtable about issues that are important to them and their communities. Vilsack's call to public service was one that resonated for myself, and I sincerely hoped inspired those 4-H youth in attendance to mobilize social change for issues that affect them then and now. It was and still is important for youth to see how they too might answer such a public service call, to also be a role model for those younger.

Early on, Secretary Vilsack laid out a path for civil rights for USDA Employees. I still have my copy of the Civil Rights document, which was signed and distributed to staff. To me, it speaks volumes as to why it was such an honor to serve at the USDA.

Here's what it said…

As Secretary of Agriculture, I fully support the U.S. Department of Agriculture's (USDA) civil rights, equal employment opportunity, and diversity policies and programs. Improving civil rights throughout USDA is one of my top priorities, and by pursuing this goal together in a transparent and ethical manner, we can lead the way in making USDA a model organization.

The success of today's "People's Department" requires the steadfast support and commitment of every USDA employee. We will have zero tolerance for any form of discrimination or reprisal. There exists no reason to discriminate based on race, color, religion, national origin, age, sex, sexual orientation, disability, marital or familial status, political beliefs, parental status, receipt of public assistance, or protected genetic information. Our policy at USDA is simply to understand that there will be zero tolerance for any form of discrimination. This standard is applicable to every employee at USDA and to every action taken at USDA.

To realize our vision of a modern workforce working in a modern workplace, USDA must become a model department of tolerance and inclusion. Only then will we live up to President Lincoln's description of USDA as "The People's Department." This is my commitment to you, and I expect every employee to demonstrate respect for and adherence to USDA civil rights, equal employment opportunity, and diversity policies.

To this end, accountability is key. USDA employees will be held accountable for doing their part to ensure that all USDA applicants, customers, constituents, and stakeholders, as well as other USDA employees are provided equal access to the opportunities, programs, and services available through "The People's Department." Accordingly, I am counting on all senior leaders, managers, and supervisors to model appropriate behavior and to lead by example.

We must all strive to create an inclusive environment in which every employee· is respected, trusted, and valued. Let us continue to cultivate and reap the benefits of a diverse CSDA workforce that is rich in talent, ideas, background, and experience. The USDA mission depends on it.

So, as a career employee, those eight years coincided with the access, equity, and opportunity, the evergreen 4-H theme, which had resonated so well with USDA's vision.

With the Trump administration's arrival, it was the first time for me at NIFA that I experienced preparing for a transition. To assist with an administration transition, a 'book' is put together to help the transition landing team. These are the folks who come in ahead of the actual appointment of the secretary and key deputy, and other administrator positions. As I wasn't familiar with the process, I prepared materials when asked, noting any challenges, issues, concerns, or trends that they would need to be aware of, which, of course, was amplified by the Director and other key NIFA staff.

There was less interaction with the landing team, and from what I gathered, there was less communication and little desire to get acquainted. I will admit that in my role, I was several steps removed from this process. So, the 4-H HQ team continued the efforts initiated under the previous administration, as we had not been told to cease doing them. This included the theme of access, equity, and accountability.

There are two key memories I have once Secretary Perdue was appointed. One was the challenge issued to USDA employees to name the Secretary's office space, a glassed-in enclosure which had been called the 'Cage'. I believe the winning entry was "Front Porch" with rocking chairs placed to convey a homey space.

The second memory was when I met Secretary Perdue in person at the National 4-H Congress, a national 4-H event held in Atlanta, GA, during the Thanksgiving weekend, Nov. 25, 20217. He was to speak, and I was tasked with working with his communication team on developing talking points for his address to the 4-H youth and adults in attendance. Secretary Perdue had been the governor of Georgia, so he was well acquainted with the Georgia 4-H Program and extension personnel. He was 'at home' and came across that way to all in attendance. His keywords were "You are the next generation of advocates for American Agriculture". That was the only time I was physically around him.

11

BACKLASH: THE TITLE IX STORM IN IOWA AND FROM OBAMA TO TRUMP (JOHN-PAUL)

This chapter unfolds amid a storm – Huracán. It is not just about policy shifts or political backlash against gay, lesbian, bi, and transgender kids for daring to be proud of who they are. It is about all of us, especially those from marginalized groups, caught in the cruelty of these politics of power. It is about what happens when institutions are tested, when belonging is threatened, and when love must become a force strong enough to withstand the political winds – but it is also about when institutions abandon their values and principles because they prioritize politics.

From the Obama administration's support for LGBTQ+ youth through Federal Title IX policies to the Trump administration's deliberate dismantling of those protections, Iowa's 4-H program became a reflection of a national conflict. The withdrawal of Title IX guidance, the bureaucratic pressure to exclude LGBTQ+ inclusion, and the personal consequences I faced as Iowa's 4-H Leader—all of it felt like Huracán had arrived. Not as myth, but as a hardship. Not as punishment, but as the chaos that happens when power tries to erase truth. In Maya cosmology, Huracán is not just the god of storms— they are the divine force of upheaval and creation. Known as UK'ux Kaj, the Heart of Sky, Huracán called forth the earth from the primordial sea and later unleashed a biblical flood that wiped out the first flawed human beings.

Huracán, in English, hurricane, is the god whose swirling motion brought about transformation through destruction, the churn. In the Popol Vuh, Huracán's storm is not necessarily a punishment—it is also a cauterization, a necessary rupture that paves the way for renewal. Today, I believe that we as a nation can decide where this renewal ends. Will it be a pluralistic democracy or something much worse? It's up to us, but only if we take a stance, because in times like these, inaction is a privilege, a statement, and a form of action in itself, siding with those who want to go back in time to the proverbial "again".

The Churn

In the aftermath of the 2016 election, the Trump administration initiated a coordinated backlash against LGBTQ+ youth inclusion. The attack targeted longstanding youth organizations as battlegrounds in a broader culture war, turning administrative tools into signals of "moral panic." Moral panic is a sociological concept describing widespread, often exaggerated fear that an individual, group, or behavior threatens the perceived "traditional" societal values and stability. Coined by Stanley Cohen, it involves creating "folk devils"— marginalized groups depicted as dangerous—and is amplified by media and moral entrepreneurs pushing for control or punishment.

For example, after we realized the proposed guidance, which was simply a copy-and-paste of the Guidance that National 4-H and NIFA had released (see in the appendix), we started receiving a lot of feedback and correspondence. Over the next week, we received 1,576 comments on the guidance, with seventy-five percent of the responses opposing it. However, as we reviewed the comments, we found that most appeared to come from a standard template. Later, we discovered that multiple national anti-LGBTQ+ organizations had been mobilized to respond and had been instructed to claim they were Iowa 4-H stakeholders.

My primary concern from the comments was centered around this false moral notion that anyone (especially a 4-H leader) from the LGBTQ+IA+ community was automatically a groomer, predator, or child molester. While I was troubled by the responses, I did my homework and examined the research closely. Additionally, because we were at an academic institution, and value science and research, I contacted faculty who specialize in this field. Many of my conversations took place with Iowa State faculty, and I also collaborated with faculty at the University of Iowa (including medical school faculty at the University of Iowa Hospitals and Clinics), Purdue, the University of California, and even reached out to several national health, psychological, and medical associations.

In conversation, after conversations, and article after article, I learned the same things. Specifically, that being gay or transgender does not make anyone a sexual predator. Sexual orientation and gender identity describe who someone loves or how they understand their gender, not whether they engage in coercive or criminal behavior. Decades of criminology and public health research show ***no elevated rates of sexual offending among LGBTQ+ people compared with the general population***. In fact, most sexual abuse is perpetrated by individuals known to the victim—often within families or trusted networks—and overwhelmingly by men who identify as heterosexual. Predatory behavior correlates with factors like power and access, prior offenses, antisocial traits, substance misuse, and situational opportunity, none of which are determined by being gay or transgender.

This included statements and studies from major medical and psychological organizations, and government institutes (before the Trump administration removed them from online archives), such as the National Institute of Health, which consistently affirmed that LGBTQ+ identity is not a risk factor for sexual violence. Thus, to me, conflating LGBTQ+ identity with predation was and is a harmful stereotype that stigmatizes innocent people, deters victims from reporting, and misdirects prevention resources away from actual risk indicators.

Therefore, I looked critically into comments such as the one entered by an alleged 4-H leader in Storm Lake, IA (who, when googled, actually lived in Arkansas):

"Truthful biology. Homosexuality is a Psycho sexual malady which prevents natural inclinations for procreation. It is a form of cultural suicide taken to its extreme conclusion. $H is about husbandry of natural procreative results. Ther is bsoluitel no credible evidence Homosexuality exiusts except in humans who can chose their sex partners and prefferences"

Based on these issues, I began to realize that anti-LBGTQ+ hate groups had hijacked our guidance review process, and that their goal was not to support 4-H youth, but to exclude LGBTQ+ youth, families, staff, and leaders from 4-H. Something that at the time was illegal in Iowa and against existing federal policy (since Title IX was not yet fully rescinded).

Additionally, because LGBTQ+ youth face higher risks of harassment and assault and are more often targets than perpetrators, I decided that strengthening all our safety measures related to behaviors and environments was the best approach. For example, thorough background checks, a policy of no adults alone with children, evidence-based risk assessments, strong supervision and staffing ratios, trauma-informed training, clear reporting pathways, and swift, fair responses to misconduct. Therefore, thanks to this approach, all policies and procedures got strengthened but remained inclusive and non-discriminatory to protect everyone's civil rights while also enhancing safety outcomes by encouraging reporting, building trust, and focusing on the behaviors that truly predict harm.

However, it is not lost on me that, across schools and extracurricular spaces, debates over bathrooms, pronouns, and club access escalated into public campaigns that pressured institutions to strip inclusive Guidance, curtail programming, and cast routine youth development work as ideologically suspect. The federal rescission of transgender student protections served as both a legal pretext and a political cue, emboldening local efforts to challenge Gay-Straight Alliances (GSAs), library literacy events, and national youth organizations such as GLSEN, the Trevor Project, and PFLAG.

Even mainstream programs like Girl Scouts of the USA and YMCA youth initiatives faced scrutiny for affirming trans and queer participation. At the same time, controversies in K–12 sports were elevated into archetypes used to justify sweeping restrictions. Within 4-H, these dynamics converged symbolically and operationally: public pressure to remove LGBTQ-affirming materials signaled a shift in oversight, and leadership changes in key state programs chilled innovation and narrowed the space for staff to pursue inclusion without fear. Federal administrative moves—such as relocating USDA research and grant offices—disrupted extension systems that supported county-level youth work, delaying awards and destabilizing partnerships critical to inclusive initiatives. The cumulative effect was not a single legal dismantling, but a sustained constriction of practice: slower grants, heightened scrutiny, and politicized narratives that made it increasingly difficult for youth programs to fulfill their developmental mission while fully welcoming LGBTQ+ participants.

It was in that context that I received a letter from a 4-H youth who was transitioning in northern Iowa, expressing the following:

"My name is [Earl], I am 16, and I've been part of a 4-H club in north central Iowa for two years. However, once I started to transition, I stopped feeling safe in 4-H. Some of the 4-H leaders kept misgendering me on purpose, even after I asked them to stop, and one told me that talking about my identity was 'too political' for 4-H. When I asked to use the boys' bathroom, instead of the girls I was told that I could not, then I was told that I should wait until I'm older to be open about it; it was like I wasn't allowed to exist yet. I started dreading meetings— my stomach would knot up, and I would throw up. I eventually stopped going to 4-H because I was scared of being humiliated again. I thought 4-H was supposed to be about leadership and belonging for everyone, but it felt like I was being pushed out just for being me."

As Iowa's 4-H Leader, an organization serving some 120,000 youth, I could not rely solely on one youth's lived experiences but also needed data to guide our inclusion efforts. However, on this matter, the research and polling numbers were plentiful and devastating. The 2016 Iowa Youth Survey revealed that LGBTQ+-identifying students across the state were facing dramatically higher rates of bullying, harassment, and emotional distress than their heterosexual and cisgender peers. More than half of LGBTQ+ youth reported being verbally abused at school, and many described feeling unsafe simply because of their identity. Rates of depression and suicidal ideation were especially elevated among transgender and nonbinary students. These findings weren't just troubling; they were urgent. They confirmed what we were seeing in our clubs: young people bracing for rejection, navigating fear, and searching for spaces where they could be themselves.

National data from the same period reinforced these patterns. GLSEN's 2017 National School Climate Survey, which included over 23,000 LGBTQ+ middle and high school students, found that 70% had experienced verbal harassment, 28% had been physically harassed, and 12% had been assaulted because of their sexual orientation or gender identity. These hostile environments had measurable academic consequences: LGBTQ+ students in unsupportive schools were more likely to skip class, earn lower grades, and feel disconnected from their learning communities. The survey also showed the protective power of inclusive policies—students in schools with GSAs, LGBTQ+-inclusive curricula, and comprehensive anti-bullying policies reported significantly better well-being and educational outcomes.

In that same vein, the Human Rights Campaign's 2017 LGBTQ+ Youth Report, based on responses from over 12,000 youth ages 13–17, painted an equally stark picture. Only 26% of LGBTQ+ youth felt safe in their classrooms, and just 5% believed their teachers were adequately trained to support them. Mental health disparities were also pronounced: 28% of LGBTQ+ youth—and 40% of transgender youth—reported feeling depressed most or all of the time in the previous month. Many cited fear of rejection, lack of family support, and unsafe school environments as major stressors.

The report also highlighted the consequences of institutional neglect. For example, transgender youth denied access to gender-affirming bathrooms were 45% more likely to attempt suicide.

Even broader longitudinal studies, like the Williams Institute's Generations Study, confirmed that younger LGBTQ+ adults (ages 18–34), at the time, were experiencing higher levels of minority stress, internalized stigma, and mental health challenges than older cohorts.

These findings underscore the long-term impact of exclusion and the importance of affirming youth programs during adolescence.

Taken together, these surveys formed a sobering mosaic and hardened my views on supporting LGBTQ+ youth in my 4-H program. This is especially true because, in 2016 and 2017, LGBTQ+ youth in Iowa and across the country were navigating a landscape of heightened vulnerability—marked by policy rollbacks, cultural backlash, and especially institutional silence. The data didn't just validate our inclusion efforts in Iowa 4-H; it demanded them. In a climate where visibility came with risk, our commitment to individual civil rights and belonging was not just bold—it was necessary. These studies made the stakes impossible to ignore. When we said, "you belong," we weren't offering comfort. We were offering lifelines.

However, the Trump administration's posture toward federal bureaucracy—what Steve Bannon called "the deconstruction of the administrative state"—wasn't just ideological. It became an operational weapon. In 2018, USDA political leadership began pressuring parts of the 4-H system to remove LGBTQ+-inclusive materials from state and federal program websites. The push was subtle, bureaucratic, and deeply chilling. In Iowa, where we had posted proposed Guidance aligned with the Obama-era Title IX interpretation, the pressure came swiftly. I was asked to retract our guidance documents by the same USDA that initially approved them. Due to the well-being consequences for our LGBTQ+ 4-Hers, and based on state law, I refused to comply with the federal USDA order.

That refusal cost me my position as Iowa's 4-H Leader.

In my letter of refusal, I officially stated the following to USDA:

"It is in times like these that I look at our shared law, policy, ideals, and value statements to see what they say. Thus, after review of Iowa Code § 216, which explicitly protects sexual orientation and gender identity, and since it does not

144

reconcile with the orders by your office to not protect LGBTQ+ youth from discrimination or harm. Furthermore, as I look at the vitriol in many of the enclosed responses to our request to feedback on the Guidance, I cite that the responses, including and especially from some who claim to be 4-H leaders or volunteers, are not only spurious, but threatening, and possibly discriminatory responses, thus have they become the "why" in the needs arguments for the Guidance. My resolve is now stronger than ever, that we as Iowa State University Extension and Outreach have a role and responsibility in creating a safe, welcoming, and discrimination-free environment for all our 4-Hers."

Political agents within the USDA, such as its Chief of Staff, who gained attention mainly for her role in the Trump and Agriculture Secretary Sonny Perdue administration's USDA transition, seem to have shared my response with far-right and Christian nationalist groups like WorldNetDaily (WND), the Liberty Council, ACT, the Daily Stormer Book Club, and the American Guard. This included my professional and personal contact details (what people call doxing), which led to threats, including death threats, endangering my family and me.

As the national media reported, in early 2018, internal pressure from appointed USDA officials catalyzed a quiet but forceful campaign to remove LGBTQ+-inclusive Guidance from state 4-H programs. It is during that time that the chief of staff to Agriculture Secretary Sonny Perdue contacted the National Institute of Food and Agriculture (NIFA) leadership multiple times, urging them to rescind the newly posted inclusion materials. She also forcefully threatened State 4-H leaders, including me, from around the US, stating that all LGBTQ+ Guidance must be removed from all land-grant university websites.

It is notable that former NIFA director Sonny Ramaswamy later confirmed receiving direct requests from Green and expressed regret for complying. Although USDA publicly framed the Guidance as unofficial and locally determined, internal communications revealed a coordinated effort to enforce its removal in states like Iowa, Idaho, California, and New York—undermining the autonomy of state extension systems and signaling a shift toward centralized political oversight of the 4-H program.

This appears to be when my refusal to violate existing state civil rights law was also communicated to political players in Iowa, including, but not limited to, the Governor, the Board of Regents, and leadership at Iowa State Extension, urging for my removal. I am also aware that there was a conversation between the Governor's office, the Board of Regents, and Iowa State, where the Governor's office was pressuring for my removal. However, those communications mainly remained a black box to me. That said, the effect was a reversal by extension leadership: leaders who had at first been supportive of the Guidance soon turned on the Guidance and me.

In a termination letter that was provided to the Des Moines Register before I received it later the same day. John Lawrence, the then vice president of extension and outreach, wrote that he had "decided to make a change in the leadership of the 4-H Youth Development Program." And that "Your letter of intent states that your position serves at the pleasure of the administration," therefore, "At this time, I have decided to exercise that provision and terminate your employment ... effective immediately," There was no conversation about the national recognitions or awards that I had just (within the month) received, my excellent performance reviews, or the increasing number of youth in the Iowa 4-H program. All that followed was a police escort off campus.

As I drove home that day, my memories were filled with what had started on February 22, 2017—not the Iowa weather, or what happened to me. But the political atmosphere. That day, the federal Guidance protecting transgender students under Title IX was rescinded by the Trump administration. It was a quiet bureaucratic move, but for those of us working in youth development, it thundered. In Iowa's 4-H, we had spent years building a culture of belonging— one where every young person, regardless of identity, could walk into a meeting and feel safe, affirmed, and empowered. In hindsight, that Obama-era LGBTQ+ supportive federal guidance had been more than a national policy; it was a promise to our youth. And even though Iowa's civil rights were still affirmatively protected for LGBTQ+ youth (something that changed in July 2025), with the federal removal, the ground beneath us shifted.

The "War on Woke" Reaches Iowa

Simultaneously, in Iowa, my skepticism about the removal of LGBTQ+ guidance prompted my abrupt ouster, reinforcing the perception that USDA's actions were not merely bureaucratic but ideologically driven. Together, these developments illustrated how early-MAGA federal political actors leveraged institutional levers to reshape youth program policy, narrowing the space for equity and belonging under the guise of administrative neutrality. These are now the hallmarks of the "War on Woke".

Eventually, resistance began to grow. For example, hundreds of Iowa State University students, faculty, and staff, joined by other extension and 4-H stakeholders, signed a petition to reinstate me. The Human Rights Campaign demanded records related to what it called an attack on LGBTQ+ youth, and more than 100 federal legislators sent a letter to Secretary Perdue, calling the USDA's actions "inappropriate overreach" and "detrimental to current and future LGBTQ+ participants".

This pushback against the new federal tactic, a tactic that is now a staple approach in the trump administration, included Senator Chuck Grassley, a Republican from Iowa, who publicly stated, "Common sense tells me that for 100 years … 4-H has been operating as a very competent organization, and I don't know of any federal interference in the past. So why would you have it in this particular case?" Back then, even he, a conservative republican, recognized the intrusion as unprecedented.

But by then the damage was done. My removals sent a message: *inclusion was conditional on being straight.* And that message echoed far beyond Iowa, and past 2019 to today, for it is interesting to think about these events in today's "War on Woke" context. That backlash wasn't just institutional; it was national and ideological. It also foreshadows what is happening in today's anti-LBGTQ+, anti-woke, and anti-DEIA efforts.

As all this was happening, Conservative and Christian nationalist groups celebrated the reversal of protections in Iowa 4-H, framing it as a victory for "traditional" values. The Family Research Council, which labeled LGBTQ+ inclusion as "indoctrination," had long opposed including sexual orientation in nondiscrimination policies in 4-H. Thus, in this matter and in Iowa, their influence on government policy and people's civil rights was no longer peripheral; it was central, especially with the, at the time, incoming Iowa Governor Raynolds and her Board of Regents. The administration's broader war on DEIA was already underway, and 4-H, Lisa, and I were some of its first primary public victims, but we would not be the last.

By 2025, this trend would become much more robust and mature, accelerating with President Trump's declaration in a joint session of Congress, *"We have ended the tyranny of so-called diversity, equity, and inclusion policies all across the entire federal government and, indeed, the private sector and our military. Our country will be woke no longer."* His executive orders targeted Ivy League universities, dismissed federal contractors, pressured agencies to investigate companies with DEIA policies, and demanded certification that nonprofits did not engage in "radical gender ideology." Soon after, on July 1, 2025, the Iowa legislature officially removed gender identity protections from its Civil Rights Act, becoming the first state to strip a previously protected class from its anti-discrimination laws.

12

THE WAR ON PUBLIC SERVANTS: NATIONAL INSTITUTE OF FOOD AND AGRICULTURE (JOHN-PAUL)

At the same time, another storm was brewing nationally. In 2019, USDA relocated the National Institute of Food and Agriculture (NIFA)—the federal partner for extension and many 4-H grants—from Washington, D.C., to the Kansas City area. The move was framed as a cost-saving measure, but insiders knew better. Surveys showed that around 70% of NIFA employees wouldn't relocate, and the resulting attrition gutted institutional capacity. Like today's attacks on public agencies such as the USDA and the Department of Education, agency grant processing slowed. Studies were postponed; civil rights investigations were truncated. Millions in funding hung in limbo. For 4-H, which relies on extension infrastructure to deliver programming, the impact was immediate and profound.

From my perspective in Iowa, the relocation did not seem logistical; it appeared ideological. After all, I attended undergraduate college at a Catholic University, St Mary's in Leavenworth, KS, which is not far from Kansas City, and I can tell you that while Kansas City is diverse, it is not D.C. diverse. So, it seemed more aligned with the administration's larger effort to de-diversify programs, punish civil servants, and weaken federal scientific capacity, especially in areas like climate, nutrition, and DEIA that challenge political orthodoxy. Staff saw efforts to suppress inconvenient research, and senior officials promoted the move as a way to cut government headcount. However, for those of us in the field, it felt like sabotage.

And yet, amid the turbulence, some things held. The Cooperative Extension System continued to receive Smith-Lever Section 3(b)–(c) capacity grants. Total extension appropriations even rose from FY2017 to FY2019. The statutory scaffolding remained intact, a testament to the bipartisan support for land-grant institutions and the enduring value of youth development. However, funding alone couldn't shield 4-H and other youth-serving organizations from the cultural clash unfolding beneath the surface, the same cultural clash that would become a central point of the MAGA movement that elected Donald Trump to a second term.

This is because the Tea Party's post-2009 rise had already reshaped Republican conservatism, channeling grassroots anger and white grievance through local chapters and pushing the party toward more hardline positions on women's rights, LGBTQ+, immigration, redistribution, and federal authority. Scholars like Kimberlé Crensha, Katherine Stewart, Theda Skocpol, Vanessa Williamson, and now us, documented how these networks normalized skepticism of federal bureaucracy while defending earned benefits—a paradox that Trumpism would later weaponize. MAGA consolidated that energy, anchoring it in white evangelical support and a promise to upend liberal cultural gains.

White Christian nationalism, which is an ideology fusing Christianity with American civic life, supplied the cultural logic. By definition, Christian nationalists are associated with nativism, patriarchy, and heteronormativity, and strongly correlated with support for Trump. Academic studies linked it to tolerance for hierarchical social orders and opposition to LGBTQ+ protections— patterns that aligned with the administration's cultural war policy priorities. In 4-H, these pressures translated into real consequences: Guidance removed, leadership ousted, confidence in inclusion undermined.

I remember sitting with LGBTQ+ youth leaders at an event hosted by Iowa Safe Schools after my removal, listening as they processed what had happened. Some were angry. Some were scared. All were disillusioned. They had believed in the promise of 4-H—not just as a program, but as a movement. They had seen it as a place where democracy could be practiced, where pluralism could be lived. And now, they were watching that promise fracture. But they didn't give up. They organized. They spoke out. They reminded their communities that 4-H was bigger than any one administration, any one policy, any one leader. They carried the torch forward, even as the winds threatened to extinguish it.

Joining them nationally, the President and CEO of the National 4-H Council continued to affirm the importance of diversity in agriculture. As one of her communications states: "4-H has a unique ability to create opportunity for all youth… That's why 4-H is investing in agricultural education and career readiness for young people from all backgrounds and communities". She was joined by Dr. Nia Imani Fields, Extension Assistant Director and Maryland 4-H Program Leader, who wrote, "We believe that when we build a more inclusive, diverse, and equitable organization, all 4-H members will excel in social mobility and communities will thrive". These voices remind us that politics do not define the soul of 4-H—it is determined by purpose.

For me, the transition from Obama to Trump was not just a political shift—it was a spiritual Huracán. It forced me to confront the limits of institutional courage, the fragility of progress, and the cost of authenticity. It reminded me that belonging is not a given—it is a practice. And that practice must be renewed, even when it is punished. Oh, yes, and that I can also be Huracán, the churn if you will. After all, I am Ts'unu'um, the hummingbird, and I live in liminality.

13

THE TEST
(LISA)

2015 was a pivotal year for inclusion as a 4-H priority both nationally and at the state level. 4-H re-affirmed the evergreen theme of Access, Equity and Opportunity within the newly revitalized National 4-H Strategic 2020 to 2025 Plan, ECOP 4-H Committee set a Goal to reach more youth that reflected the demographics by 2025 and then in the next year or so, Program Leaders Working Group (PLWG) chartered the Vulnerable Populations or what is known now as the Access, Equity and Opportunity Working Group.

State 4-H programs were identifying how they would reflect the demographics of their state and what best practices were needed to engage in targeted outreach efforts. Enrollment management discussions led to what data to collect and how to standardize and operationalize the definitions used within the 4-H program for data quality and accountability. This meant looking at how to define participation from what had been considered as the 'club model' for individuals to the broader group enrollment participation levels. It harkened to the discussion of what is the 'dosage and duration' for 4-H's Positive Youth Development theory, which Oregon State was working on to refine for use within all states. The 4-H PYD Theory elevated the 100+ year old 4-H program to a new level, making it evidence-based and reflecting the research base, the translation of science into practice.

Questions started to emerge in 2016 and 2017 on how to support those targeted groups, primarily how to provide guidance and best practices for working with LGBTQ+ youth. In October of 2017, 4-H Headquarters held a DY4-H e-Academy on Diversity and Inclusion that had 10 sessions on how to engage our diverse youth, "The Role of Diversity and Inclusion in Positive Youth Development" as an online professional development series. As outlined, the purpose of the e-academy was to be an in-depth, targeted online professional development series designed for 4-H and other youth development professionals. The focus was to promote diversity and inclusion throughout 4-H's programs and increase the awareness of social issues that affect youth development.

Outcomes were:

1. Participants will understand how culture, diversity, inclusion, and intersectionality play a role in youth development.

2. Participants will understand how race relations and social justice affect youth.

3. Participants will be introduced to methods on how to make 4-H programs inclusive to all minorities.

The Target Audience was:

- Field-level 4-H youth development professionals

- State-level 4-H youth development professionals

- Youth development professionals from partner organizations

These ten one-hour live interactive webinar-style presentations were on the following topics and pulled together extension professionals:

- The Role of Diversity and Inclusion in Positive Youth Development: Keynote

- Social Justice and Activism

- LGBT Youth

- Disabled Youth

- Race Relations

- Latino Youth

- Tribal Youth

- Homeless Youth

- Civility & Civil Discourse

- Intersectionality & Inclusion

Questions during 2016 to 2017 were also being asked by states on how to address demographics-related issues and ES-237 around youth's identification beyond biological sex for data collection and enrollment. There were concerns circulating amongst the state 4-H program leaders' regional groups, particularly in the west. One state was in the process of initiating guidance on how to work with LGBTQ+I youth, to ensure they were emotionally, mentally, and physically safe, as were other youth who participated. Drawing upon the research and evidence-based on the extension land-grant system, this guidance was initially presented to the Program Leaders Working Group in 2017.

Similar to the work to develop the 4-H Guiding Principles, there was a group of extension professionals as well as 4-H National HQ and National 4-H Council representatives who reviewed, revised, and presented this draft to the 4-H system. This process of writing a draft and delivering it to the system was the process that validated most 4-H fact sheets for use in the extension system. States would then adopt or adapt as appropriate for their use. The PLWG representative shared the draft with the 4-H ECOP Committee, who were to review and request affirmation from ECOP as a best practice document. This final draft document was also shared internally by 4-H HQ staff within NIFA's Civil Rights office and subsequently with key USDA Civil Rights legal representatives.

By this point in time, it was early 2018. Though a White House administration change had occurred, which also meant a change within USDA, however, this shift was only beginning to register in how the various USDA agencies would conduct business and handle programs. Things do move slowly within the federal government, and this was particularly true during Trump's first term, due to the slowness in confirming political appointments. My team and I were verbally told that 'no one wanted to get ahead of this administration.'

Yet, monthly, my team and I were being asked or emailed about how much time it would take for the review of the draft to be considered 'done' and could be distributed to the states. Informally, the draft was shared by the initial lead state. At least eight months went by, and now it is the beginning of 2018. State 4-H program leaders expressed their concerns as they were being pressured for such guidance by their staff. There had been no word from the USDA legal point person, which, as I later found out, was due to both the severe illness in the fall and the subsequent death of the individual who had been engaged with the review.

At the 2018 National Meeting for Program Leaders, an announcement was made that the LGBTQ+ guidance would be published 'soon. About a month earlier, a national program leader and I had determined that the recourse was to obtain approval from the ECOP 4-H Committee, based on a recommendation from the PLWG, which also took place in February. Prior programmatic guidance had been handled by 4-H HQ national program leaders for other fact sheets related to 4-H, as well as the 4-H Guidelines. So, following previous precedent, the team under my direction proceeded to publish the document on the website. I may have even commented to a national program leader, What's the worst that could happen by publishing? We would only be asked to take it down, right? Famous last words as I reflect on those days.

While I was attending a USDA Foreign Agricultural Service workshop training in Islamabad, Pakistan, the LGBTQ+I Guidance was published in early March. An email was sent out to the state 4-H program leader listserv, and state 4-H program leaders began sharing the guidance with their state and county extension 4-H professionals.

Within less than two days of the guidance being published, there were targeted emails and letters going to the Secretary of Agriculture's office. These letters were written to express how these 4-H families would no longer be part of 4-H - two examples follow of the emails received.

I shared the first email that came to my attention with my USDA legal point of contact.

Email Texts

"......I am writing this letter to let you know that I will no longer be serving in a leadership capacity for 4H. My children will also not be participating in your

organization. This is a heartbreaking decision for our family to make. We have greatly enjoyed our last year in 4H. It has been such a positive experience for my children. My husband and I have loved the growth we have seen in our children's confidence and leadership skills; however, the recent release of 4H's policy regarding gender expression and inclusion (4H Guidance for Inclusion of All Gender Identities, Gender Expressions, Sexual Orientations, and Sexes- March 2018) is something that our family cannot support.

I served in public education for over ten years before homeschooling my children. I worked as a special education case manager for students in an alternative high school, many of whom struggled with gender identity issues. I have both a bachelor's and a master's degree in education, spending years studying children's growth and development. I am a published educational author who has spent much of my career focusing on how to include students with disabilities and those with other learning and social challenges. I believe that each child is unique and deserves to be welcomed and to feel safe.

With that said, this policy does not make my children feel safe. It also violates the First Amendment rights of our family. I will address the individual points within the policy with which I disagree.

- *First and foremost, this policy violates mine and my children's rights under the First Amendment. The statement, "4H, including all paid and volunteer personnel, as well as youth members, will use pronouns and names consistent with a transgender or intersex individual's gender identity," directly restricts our speech and asks us to assert things we do not believe to be true because of our faith. Believing that God creates us in His own image as male and female is not hate speech. When you create an environment in which my family is discriminated against because we refuse to use and subscribe to specific terms and vocabulary that go against our religious beliefs, you are infringing on our rights. I could care less how someone looks or the decisions they make about their identity, but I refuse to be forced into lockstep with preapproved vocabulary and prescribed interpersonal communications. There can be a*

*middle ground between respecting an individual's choices and not
compromising your own personal religious beliefs. The specificity of this
policy in its mandates towards individual's responses leaves little room for
this. 4H has now created a hostile environment for myself and my
children*

- *The following statement is not in line with federal law: "As is
consistently recognized in civil rights cases, the desire to accommodate
others' discomfort cannot justify a practice that singles out and
disadvantages a particular class of individuals." Federal law does not
include gender identity as a protected class under the Civil Rights Act of
1964. Additionally, in October 2017, the Department of Justice and
the Attorney General released a memo clarifying that gender identity is
not covered specifically under Title VII of the Civil Rights Act. You are
creating your policy under the umbrella of anti-discrimination by cherry-
picking court cases and disputes while ignoring the law and guidance
from the federal government. My right to not have my speech restricted,
whether it is related to my religious beliefs or not, is not a 'discomfort'. It
is protected by the First Amendment of the United States Constitution.
I would encourage 4H to review guidance from the Department of Justice
regarding the situations under which speech is not protected by the First
Amendment. Not using a pronoun or a name that someone requests is
not included on the list.*

- *Despite the specificity of what myself and my children are required to say
and do, this policy provides no guidelines to assure me or my children
that they will be safe from people taking advantage of this policy to act
inappropriately. Without any requirements for documentation, be it
medical, legal, or other, you are putting children at risk of exposing them
to people who could have ill intentions. How will you protect against
someone, be it a child or an adult leader, who says they identify with the
opposite sex to gain access to a child in the most vulnerable of places (i.e.
a restroom, cabin, etc.)? If you do not believe this is a real threat, then I*

encourage the leaders of 4H to spend some time with law enforcement and see the lengths to which sexual predators and child molesters go to in order to commit their crimes. The danger of this is real, and you have provided no guidelines to help children feel safe.

- *It is a shame that the National 4-H program has decided to create an environment in which my family no longer feels welcome. In addition to our departure, every leader from our club is stepping down and not continuing with 4H, as well as at least half of our club's members. I will be contacting our lawmakers, as well as federal agencies, to express my displeasure with your policy. What a disappointment from such a promising program for future leaders. "*

There appeared to be a targeted letter-writing campaign, as evidenced by an inadvertent email exchange shared where the first emailer says to another and cc'd me on...

"......The following statement directly resulted in our leaving: "As is consistently recognized in civil rights cases, the desire to accommodate others' discomfort cannot justify a practice that singles out and disadvantages a particular class of individuals." In October 2017, the Department of Justice and the Attorney General released a memo clarifying that gender identity is not covered specifically under Title VII of the Civil Rights Act. You are ignoring the law and guidance from the federal government with this policy.

The 'discomfort' you speak of directly affects children in their most vulnerable situation, while at sleep-away camp. A child away from a parent in a camp scenario should have the security in knowing that their best interests are being looked after. Requiring no documentation, medical, legal or otherwise, opens a door for anyone with ill intent to access a child at their most vulnerable. For example, an 18-year old male could now have access to an 8-year old female camper simply because he says he is a female. A 9-year old boy could find himself in the showers alongside a 17-year old girl because she states she is a male. A 50-year old male camp counselor, now identifying as a female, could sleep in the girls' cabin and have full access to the girls while they are sleeping in a closed room. The idea that their 'rights' supersede the right of children to feel safe and secure is unacceptable.

Creating this environment within the 4-H community no longer allows me to feel comfortable promoting 4-H as a wonderful vehicle for children."

It wasn't until later, after forwarding the first text to NIFA's Office of General Counsel point of contact, that things began to happen. I recall being on the metro platform at the end of the day, being asked how to pull down the guidance. I had neither access nor control, yet by 10 pm that evening, the guidance was removed.

The next day, others and I were brought in to discuss what had happened. It was at that point in time that emails received by the now deceased legal counsel were shared, to which I had only previously had a verbal conversation nearly a year before. Then, there was a meeting with key Perdue administration staff that I, the NIFA Director and a Deputy NIFA Director, were involved with, where basically we were chastised for the guidance having been published. They did not want to hear how or why the guidance was published. I heard later that they were seeking 'heads to roll'. I figured then that they wanted mine.

It was nearly time for the National 4-H Conference, in which my staff was handling the sensitive issue of a youth who, it was disclosed to us, identified as LGBTQ, would be in attendance. This was a 'test' for how to handle lodging at the National 4-H Center. Yet I was told not to attend specific National 4-H Conference events. I had always been the point of contact for the House and Senate Ag Committee youth briefings, along with other key NIFA staff. I began to feel ostracized and isolated.

Meanwhile, I and others at NIFA received training as middle managers related to gender identity. One of my dear colleagues was undergoing the process of transitioning. For me, this wasn't a case of 'those people', it was someone I respected, admired, whose resiliency and courage were to be protected and defended.

To continue with the restrictions, I and my staff were asked in mid-April in an email:

".. After reassessing the ongoing sensitivities around social issues pertaining to 4-H, I am asking that NIFA's 4-H staff should not pursue and stop with immediate effect until further notice any activities such as webinars, templates development, developing guidances, entering into conversations on behalf of NIFA or USDA, conducting media training etc on topics such as Race, gender and faith issues, Shooting sports, Animal welfare and rights and possibly any additional topics with similar or related sensitivities for which you might request a clarification or prior permission.

I ask that you communicate this expectation to your entire staff as soon as possible."

To which I had each of them read/review and initial the document. I was later told that it was not necessary to have to read and initialize.

As the folk idiom goes, 'when it rains, it pours', well, another Civil Rights same-sex issue popped up in April 2018 from the South Dakota State University (SDSU) 4-H Program based on an exchange initiated by then Representative Noem and Secretary Perdue in November 2017.

There had been a previous review and request for the legal opinion on this matter in 2010, when the then SDSU extension director sought out a legal opinion from USDA. Here's what was shared then on the matter…

"To summarize the attached information, USDA Deputy General Council XXX affirmed that sex-exclusive or sex-segregated rodeo contests are inconsistent with Title IX. Recipients who operate USDA-funded 4-H rodeo events must

conduct events in a manner that allows qualified participants to compete without regard to sex." - documentation from 1979 to Dr. Mary Nell Greenwood, Acting

Here's an excerpt from the letter to Senator Thune… April 2010 for a letter initially sent in May 2009 from Senator Thune's office ….

"Concerning the issue of sex-separate events in 4-H rodeo contests. You are seeking an update on the status of USDA's legal opinion on the issue of whether such sex-separate events violate Title IX of the Civil Rights Amendments of 1972 (Title IX), which prohibits discrimination on the basis of sex in education and training programs. Your letter was referred to this office for response.

As you are aware, the Director of the National Institute of Food and Agriculture (NIFA), formerly the Cooperative State Research, Education, and Extension Service (CSREES), USDA, requested a legal opinion from the Office of the General Counsel (OGC), USDA, on whether sex-separate rodeo contests held by 4-H clubs violate Title IX. This request was prompted by a request for guidance on this issue to NIFA from South Dakota State University. OGC has reviewed its prior opinion from 1979 and all recent Title IX case law. Based on this review, OGC has determined that the prior legal opinion (see enclosure) is still valid law and remains the position of USDA. It remains our opinion that sex-exclusive or sex-segregated rodeo contests are inconsistent with Title IX and its implementing regulations. We recommend that recipients who operate USDA-funded 4-H rodeo events ensure that those events are conducted in a manner that allows qualified participants to compete without regard to sex.

I hope that you will find this information helpful. Please feel free to contact me if we can provide additional information on this matter.

Documentation provided from 1979 then explained why there was no change in the opinion in 2010:

"….As we understand from the information you provided, some, but not all, local 4-H rodeos are conducted on a sex-· segregated or sex-exclusive basis. For example, calf roping, bull riding, and bareback riding may be for boys only, and goat tying, barrel racing, and pole bending may be for girls only. In certain events,

strength and running speed are important in successful performance, and generally, boys have the advantage. In other events, the horse's speed is a significant factor in the contest, and the generally lighter weight of the girls gives them an advantage. However, most events require agility, hand/eye coordination or riding skill; and neither sex has any general advantage....

It is our opinion that sex-exclusive or sex-segregated rodeo contests are inconsistent with Title IX and the implementing regulation. 7 CFR Part 15a. The general rule applicable to athletic events is that exclusion, separation and different treatment on the basis of sex are precluded. 7 CFR 15a.41(a)....

It appears that having sex exclusive contests is based in part upon traditional roles and the presumed interest ·of· boy and girl rodeo contestants and in part upon the general physical attributes (strength, weight, etc.) that tend. To give one sex ·an advantage over the other. These stereotypical differences do not justify the exclusion of either boys or girls from participating in any of the rodeo events. Just because most girls may be disinterested in the bull riding event or not strong enough to compete successfully does not mean that some girls are not interested and fully capable of performing respectably or successfully in such events. Similarly, there appears to be no compelling reason for excluding boys from those events which have traditionally been limited to girls.

In conclusion, we recommend that rodeo contests sponsored by 4-H be operated in a manner that permits participation without regard to sex."

During my 4-H career, which spans from 1979, when the opinion was shared, all 4-H rodeo events were 'open' to all, at least in the states where I worked.

However, in 2017, Kristi Noem wrote Secretary Perdue regarding the issue in November 2017.

In her letter, she explained:

"Dear Secretary Perdue,

4-H A Dei Love Story:
How Positive Youth Development Became a Battleground for Democracy

Rodeo is a sport that contains diverse contests. The outcomes of these contests are heavily dependent both on the skill of the contestants and, in many instances, the inherent differences between the sexes. Whether it is barrel racing or calf roping, the differences between the male and female competitors can create unfair advantages.

To that end, a number of my constituents have expressed concern to me that the U.S. Department of Agriculture's legal opinion from 1972 is advantaging some competitors over others in an otherwise fair sport.

Over the years, the organization spread across the nation. With the passage of the Smith-Lever Act and the creation of the Cooperative Extension System, youth across the nation gained the opportunity to increase their knowledge of agriculture and C skills.

In South Dakota, the 4-H organization is affiliated with many youth rodeo events. As you know, 4-H is the nation's largest youth program. The organization has a rich history dating back over a hundred years. Since its founding, 4-H has encouraged participation by both sexes.

As a mother who has had three children participate in the program and volunteered for over 16 years, I respectfully request that your department to conduct a review of its legal opinion on the issue of whether such sex-separate events violate Title IX of the Civil Rights Amendments of 1972. Specifically, whether Title IX requires youth rodeos operated in cooperation with 4-H not to be sex-segregated or sex-exclusive, I believe, upon review, you will find that rodeo deserves an exemption.

Thank you for your time. I look forward to your response. "

In the news article, it was shared that Secretary Perdue wrote in response that it would withhold action while the U.S. Department of Education conducted a broader review of Title IX regulations. The Secretary further confirmed that, "It would also not be appropriate for the USDA to take action against the traditional structure of South Dakota's 4-H rodeos while this review is ongoing. 4-H may organize its rodeos in South Dakota as it always has."

I received phone calls and requests to speak on the topic yet of course deferred to NIFA's Director and Deputy Directors. As I had received a copy of the original legal opinion rendered in 1979, as well as the 2010 version, I felt caught between a rock and a hard place. Apparently, it was a state-specific issue, as no other state came forward to request a change in youth's participation in sex-specific rode events.

You know, sometimes competition drives the conversation as well as prize money and awards.

I recall that in my first extension position, this initial ruling meant we no longer held a 4-H Fair Queen contest and instead had a Fair Queen and Fair King contest.

The emails, the ones on the LGBTQ guidance and the Rodeo – Gender Identity, that I shared earlier in the book, were ones I, as a federal career employee, was not allowed to respond to. Now, what I would say is that there is a concentrated effort to use selective pieces from the First Amendment as a weapon, rather than as a tool for respect for all. Respecting all rights for me is the frame of reference as well as a choice. 4-H is a choice one makes to belong to, with values and beliefs that adhere to the foundation of 4-H as an ideal. Once 4-H begins to feel like it is exclusionary or only for certain groups, then it is no longer an ideal nor reflective of Positive Youth Development.

All this was to say that April was a firestorm month, and then in May, I knew I would be losing a 4-H HQ national program leader who perhaps saw the handwriting on the wall. The 4-H HQ team all went out for a brief off-site retreat to celebrate and say 'goodbye'. The next day, I was handed a letter informing me that I was being written up for insubordination. I was told to read it and 'sign' that I had read it. That was how my Friday morning started.

I was planning to be out of the office for two weeks on leave, as my youngest son was graduating from law school and my high school was honoring me as a distinguished alumna. Two celebrations that were soon to be marred. Still, I had to track down that Friday and request an extension so I could handle all the paperwork for my hearing. I had to hold it together in the office, not show any emotion, and act as if it were a typical workday. Swallowing my emotions helped me get through the next few months and probably these past few years.

In June, I had my hearing, and I tried to outline that I was not insubordinate, as none of my superiors told me not to publish. I tried to outline that it was a misunderstanding, and if I had been aware of all the details as outlined, I would have made a different decision. Now, looking back, I didn't explain what that different decision was that I would have made, and now, I don't believe there was or ought to be a 'different decision'. It was more like I was trying to, again, as a woman, placate those in power. I also noted that the punishment was excessive, a two-week, unpaid suspension, as it was a first-time offense, which typically merited a letter of reprimand and was not even listed as the offense to be administered. I did 'grieve' the punishment and prepared additional documents. Yet, that did not stop the process of being sent a letter while on my two-week, unpaid suspension, that I was to be removed as division director and be placed in another position at NIFA. I remember calling using my personal cell to a few extension professionals to let them know what was happening by leaving voice mail messages. When I returned to the office, I was told by one of my staff that I was to be watched to make sure I didn't take anything that I shouldn't. Imagine you are sitting at a desk and going through all your work for nearly a decade. I had to sort through what was relevant to someone who would step in yet also consider what was 'mine' to keep.

When I went to my 'new' space that day, I was treated with suspicion and hostility as someone had told them I was throwing my staff under the bus and blaming them. This wasn't said to me directly; it was communicated by others who were hearing rumors. In the next year in my new position, I actually had people stop by my office and ask how I got the position since it had not been advertised. I was blamed for NIFA being moved out of the District of Columbia and had a few other staff members imply that I was the reason for the targeting of NIFA by our agency's administration.

In my last year at NIFA, I was scrutinized for any work I did that might resemble 4-H. Though I did all the work for a USDA FAS PYD presentation in Mexico, I was not allowed to travel to present because there was concern that it would look like I was being 'successful'.

I reached out to keep in touch with some state 4-H program leaders and had 'crickets' as a response. Yet, the staff I had at 4-H HQ were still supportive and kept in touch. As NIFA was being pushed out of the District of Columbia, I worked to create an opportunity to work with youth engagement in agriculture within USAID and with USDA FAS. I was able to connect with a project in the country of Georgia on extension programming. I began to feel the opportunity to pivot. However, I was told by the NIFA Director that I would have to 'go to Kansas City'. That meant I had to redo my paperwork, and I went to Kansas City only to find out after 3 days there that those promises were not universally agreed upon. By my first week there, I was told travel was being scrutinized and that my work was to assist in getting the money out the door. So, I tendered my retirement notice and was able to retire in less than a week from USDA NIFA on Oct. 11, 2019.

Writing this chapter has meant remembering what transpired, and reflecting on that time period, I would say that I was in some state of shock, yet understood that some sought to 'punish' someone, anyone, for the "embarrassment" caused to USDA for the publication of guidance, as well as the desire to show they were responsive to their constituency. There was, however, no acknowledgement of the harm that was being done for the sharp reversals on either access, equity, and opportunity.

My identity was shaped and framed by 4-H, from my parents' meeting to my career as an extension professional, with its twists. Underneath it all was my deep love for 4-H. Suddenly, I no longer had an identity. I had been shunned, perhaps perceived as having turned my back on 4-H by some who didn't know the story, as I was no longer in my role as "Head Clover". And, there were others who wanted to distance themselves as they saw me as being a pariah, fear that I would infect them. It was like watching one's life play out on a stage while you were sitting in the audience. For me, my survival mode was where I reached back to the other pillars in my life, my faith and family, to get me through. My newly graduated law school student son offered me 'advice' and my mom provided me with emotional support. I found my cadre of support through my yoga community, from other fellow federal career employees from other agencies outside of NIFA, and it was through the support of this emerging community that I built a life without 4-H as my ballast. Later while living through the isolation of COVID, I connected with an on-line, one-year spiritual academy which paired me with a group that was primarily composed of female pastors and quarterly sessions that provided a spiritual rhythm to my then disrupted life.

This loss of 4-H identity, with such an abruptness like my dad's sudden death on the day of 4-H Officers' training, where I had to scramble, find others to assist, yet still face the ultimate loss of life of a loved one, was and still is for me a process in grief, where there are moments that trigger a visceral response, a welling of tears.

Do No Harm, Do Good, Stay in Love with God

I grew up and worshiped in a practicing Christian home. I learned early on and tried to adhere to John Wesley's three simple rules for a Christ-like life: Do No Harm, Do Good, and Stay in Love with God. The Three Simple Rules:

1. Do No Harm: This means avoiding actions and even inaction that could cause destruction or harm to others, including extending this principle to care for the environment and systems of oppression.

2. Do Good: This principle encourages acts of kindness, charity, and service toward others, ensuring you don't become isolated but instead actively bring God's grace and goodness to the world.

3. Stay in Love with God: This rule calls for consistent action in one's relationship with God, emphasizing the importance of spiritual disciplines or "ordinances" such as prayer, Bible study, and worship.

My favorite Bible verse is from Philippians 4:13 to which leaned on heavily the words throughout my career, as the first female 4-H Agent where I devoured readings from Norman Vincent Peale and Catherine Marshall, as this verse *"I can do all things through Christ Jesus who strengthens me"* which is preceded in Phil 4:10 (paraphrased) as *"...I have learned to be content in whatever the circumstances".*

For me, my faith meant to be open, to welcome all, to have an open heart and mind. It is also why I write this love story to 4-H. 4-H to me embodies all, is welcoming and open to all, with an open head, heart, hands, and health - the four H's of the 4-H Pledge.

John-Paul and I have discussed how writing this book served as a catharsis, often bringing tears, once we began to write. Both of us have had to wrestle with storytelling. In my mind, I have rationally and logically outlined what happened when, but in my heart, I have felt the memories that have surfaced and poured out of me. I didn't want to hurt 4-H, as it wasn't 4-H that hurt me. 4-H was taken away from me, which shook my foundation. 4-H is and always has been a core part of me; it's in my DNA and lives in my soul. Opening up to let the long-buried pain of that loss surface, I feel a kinship, much like John-Paul shares in the next chapter —one heart, one soul—because that is what 4-H means to me. I "bleed green," and as I shed tears, I know they represent a cleansing, clearing the way for more love to fully emerge. In 2024, I was inducted into the National 4-H Hall of Fame, which felt like a small piece of my heart was being restored ——a return home to myself, to my soul and to 4-H.

14

THE PRICE OF PRINCIPLE
(JOHN-PAUL)

There's a Maya phrase I carry with me: jun k'u'x, jun ch'ulel—
one heart, one soul. It's not a romantic expression, but it conveys the
idea of Agape, a sacred love. This form of love binds people across
generations, through struggles, and throughout transformations. In
this chapter, love was what held me together. When the political
climate shifted and Title IX protections were stripped away, and when
the pressure to erase LGBTQ+ youth from Iowa's 4-H program
intensified, I found myself without a roadmap. What I did have was
jun k'u'x, jun ch'ulel—a deep, ancestral understanding that love is not
passive. It's fierce like Balam, the Jaguar. It shelters, resists, and
rebuilds.

While I recognize that I wasn't raised in 4-H, I didn't inherit it
through family tradition or grow up attending county fairs. My
connection to the 4-H program came later through conversion, rather
than through legacy. However, that does not change how I feel about
4-H to this day. I honestly believe that if we focus on belonging, equity,
and youth voice, 4-H could become more than just a nostalgic
institution — it could be a powerful force for democratic pluralism
worldwide.

However, I also recognize the high cost of disobedience to the Trump administration and MAGA, a price that most are still unwilling to pay. As a professional, I became untouchable for many years. Institutions that had celebrated my leadership stopped responding to my calls. Staff and colleagues, I mentored, distanced themselves, afraid of being associated with me or the controversy. Even my allies in the LGBTQ+ community told me I had gone "too far" or that I should have known better than to challenge a system that wasn't ready to change, which always made me raise an eyebrow. Some others did not support me because I was straight and a person of color and thus not part of the "community."

Friendships faded, not in dramatic confrontations, but in silence. Invitations stopped coming, and I found myself sitting alone at home. Texts went unanswered. I watched as people I had supported, celebrated, and stood beside quietly step away. Some did so out of fear. Others did so out of convenience or politics. And a few, I suspect, out of disappointment that I hadn't played the game better. That I hadn't found a way to "keep my job" while "doing the work." Unemployment brought its own kind of stigma to my life. I wasn't just jobless—I had a scarlet letter. Not only had I been fired, but the world knew before I did. I was a whistleblower, a traitor. As HR professionals say, in the employment sector, reputation is a currency. Mine had been irreconcilably devalued, if not completely cancelled.

Furthermore, in the eyes of many 4-H stakeholders, I was the one who had "made trouble," even though the guidance stemmed from USDA. The one who had "brought politics into youth work." The one who had refused to compromise, even though compromise would have meant sacrificing LGBTQ+ youth to the altar of politics and hate. Then came death threats for me and my family.

There were many days I couldn't get out of bed. Not because I regretted my choices, but because I felt erased, silenced, and betrayed by an institution I had given everything to. Per my job description, I had poured my heart into building programs that made young people feel seen. And now, I was invisible.

The loneliness was suffocating. Not just the absence of work, but the lack of affirmation. Of being told, "You mattered." Of being reminded, "You made a difference." And yet, in that silence, something else began to emerge, a more profound clarity. A spiritual maturity where I started to understand that belonging isn't just something we should offer to others, it's something we must claim for ourselves, even when the world tells us we don't deserve it. It is then that I returned to my roots—not institutional ones, but ancestral ones. To my Maya spirituality, my amazing wife, my family, and especially to my commitment to social justice, human and civil rights. Thus, I began to examine the ethics of relational accountability, especially that of radical love (agape). Agape (pronounced ah-GAH-pay) is a Greek word that refers to the highest form of love: selfless, unconditional, and sacrificial. It's not driven by attraction, obligation, or sentimentality, but by a willful commitment to the well-being of others.

I remembered that justice isn't transactional. That love for one's neighbor is inclusive, disruptive, and unapologetic, and that it does not expect reward. Many times, it's even punished. But it's still worth choosing.

Ts'unu'um; Crossing the thresholds between worlds

This is when I returned to graduate school, thanks in significant part to a GoFundMe page created for me by some amazing folks who were proud of me for standing up, and a $5,000 scholarship from a prominent local LGBTQ+ leader. When I began to pursue my Ph.D. in Educational Leadership and Policy, it wasn't a career move—it was a search for understanding. To the frustration of some of my outstanding University of Iowa faculty, I wasn't seeking the tenured professor or researcher status, or even the professional credentials. I was seeking clarity. Clarity about how racism, homophobia, sexism, and so many other evils reside and maneuver in our educational institutions. After years of frontline DEIA work, I began to understand that the forces pushing back were not personal or only driven by "bad people". That there is such a thing, as Bonilla Silva, a seminal scholar on race, puts it – "Racism, without racists." There are systemic, structural, and invisible maintainers of prejudice and exclusion – and I needed the language, the theory, and the validation that only a PhD. from a Research 1 University can provide, especially the historical depth to name what happens to diversity, equity, inclusion, and accessibility, and why they rarely become realized in our institutions.

My doctoral journey became archaeology of the mind, a deep excavation of racism and oppression—not just as interpersonal bias, but as embedded architecture. I studied how policies masquerade as neutrality, how data can be weaponized to obscure inequity, and how institutions perform allyship while quietly reproducing harm. I traced the lineage of backlash: from Reconstruction to the Southern Strategy, from school desegregation to the dismantling of affirmative action, to today's "War on Woke". I learned that resistance to equity is not new—it is cyclical, adaptive, and often cloaked in civility.

But what gripped me most was the pattern of institutional resistance to DEIA. Not the overt hostility, but the subtler forms: the strategic delays, the procedural deflections, the cowardness of inaction, the calls for "balance" that silence marginalized voices. I began to specialize in this terrain—mapping how organizations respond when equity becomes inconvenient, when belonging demands transformation rather than celebration. I saw how backlash operates not just through policy, but also through culture: through the fear of disruption, through nostalgia for exclusion, and through the myth of meritocracy.

This work was not abstract for me. It is still personal, because I have felt the cost of principled resistance—been fired, isolated, and mischaracterized as a "transvestite child molesting predator" for standing with youth who dared to demand to go to a bathroom that they felt comfortable in. But my Ph.D. gave me more than theory. It gave me a framework to understand that what happened to me was not an anomaly—it was a pattern. And that pattern must be named, disrupted, and eliminated. Today, I use what I learned to help institutions move beyond performative DEIA. To challenge leaders to confront their own passivity, which is within itself a form of resistance, and to reckon with the ways they protect power under the guise of process. I bring data, history, and lived experience into the room—and I refuse to leave my values at the door.

Thus, for me, going back to school was not a retreat. It was a return to the kindling to rekindle my internal fire. It is a fire that I fully intend to keep burning until I am called to the spirits.

This is when this dysgraphic boy began writing. Not just to process the pain, but to preserve the truth. Document what it means to be cast out for doing what's right. To name the high cost of institutional courage and regain control over the truth. The stories in this memoir became a lifeline—a way to reclaim narrative, stitch together the fragments of a story others tried to erase, and slowly, new connections formed. Not with the institutions that had abandoned me, but with people who had lived similar truths. Youth workers and librarians who had been pushed out for affirming queer kids. Diversity professionals who are now considered anti-American. Educators who had been silenced for teaching the history of African Americans in school. Artists who had lost funding for challenging dominant narratives. We found each other in the margins. And in those margins, we built something sacred, so I dedicated this book to you: the first, the whistleblower, and the brave – we need more of you.

In simple words, being fired from 4-H didn't break me. But it did change me. It stripped away my Pollyannaish illusions that good always wins. It revealed to me the concept of institutional betrayal and exposed the fragility of institutional allyship. It forced me to confront "Who I am" when my job stops. While I still grieve for what I lost— my career progression, my retirement nest egg, and the programs I led (especially Maize and Ujima), which were immediately dismantled when I left, and many of my colleagues who chose silence over solidarity— I also celebrate what remains: the truth. The legacy of resistance. The quiet, persistent flame of radical love.

15

I AM JUST A FOOT SOLDIER, BUT WE SHALL OVERCOME (JOHN-PAUL)

I learned the cost of resistance not through theory but through experience. When I stood up for LGBTQ+ youth, bilingual inclusion, and youth-led equity in 4-H, I wasn't just promoting policy—I was confronting power. Because of that, I was fired, branded a threat, and left to face the isolation that arises when institutions prioritize comfort over courage. But more importantly, I found my north star. Through the Birmingham Civil Rights Institute, I learned that the price we pay for justice is not new. As a National Civil Rights FUSE Fellow, I attended a ceremony at the 16th Street Baptist Church honoring the mother of one of the girls killed in the 1963 Church bombing. I listened to elders who, as children, had dogs and fire hoses turned on them by Bull Connor. Their stories didn't just echo mine—they clarified it. Resistance, they showed me, isn't a detour; sometimes it's the only way forward.

As Dr. Martin Luther King Jr. wrote in his letter from the Birmingham Jail in 1963, confined to a narrow cell for leading nonviolent protests against segregation, a cell I sometimes used to clean when the museum closed.

"I cannot sit idly by in Atlanta and not be concerned about what happens in Birmingham. Injustice anywhere is a threat to justice everywhere. We are caught in an inescapable network of mutuality, tied in a single garment of destiny. Whatever affects one directly affects all indirectly. Never again can we afford to live with the narrow, provincial "outside agitator" idea. Anyone who lives inside the United States can never be considered an outsider anywhere within its bounds." – Dr Martin Luther King

His words, which were smuggled out of jail on scraps of paper, were not just a defense of civil disobedience; they were a moral command. That line has become a compass for me.

In 4-H, I saw young people whose destinies were being denied—because of who they loved, the language they spoke, the color of their skin. To stand with them was not charity. It was mutuality. I was, as Dr. Bettina Love says in her books, a "conspirator". My own humanity and integrity were bound up with theirs.

The Reverend Doctor also recognized that civil disobedience isn't lawless; it's a higher form of lawfulness. "One has not only a legal but a moral responsibility to obey just laws," he wrote. "Conversely, one has a moral responsibility to disobey unjust laws." I didn't break laws in 4-H, but I broke the organizational silence that protects institutions, even when it's objectively wrong. I was a whistleblower, a public servant, which in this case meant I broke the unwritten organizational rule of institutional neutrality. I refused to pretend that exclusion was moderation. And in saying "no," I practiced a form of organizational civil disobedience—refusing to perpetuate harm, even when it cost me my position, my community, and my family's sense of safety.

The young people I served understood this intuitively; they knew that justice was not abstract. It was about whether they could speak

Spanish in their clubs without shame. Whether they could come out as queer without fear. Whether they could lead—not just participate—in shaping their own futures. When I stood beside them, I was not leading—I was following their courage. And that, too, is part of the legacy King left us. "Human progress never rolls in on wheels of inevitability," he wrote. "It comes through the tireless efforts of men willing to be co-workers with God." I believe the youth are those co-workers. They are prophets in sneakers, truth-tellers in hoodies. And when we silence them, we betray not just them; we betray the future.

This is why, when I returned to graduate school to pursue my Ph.D. in Educational Leadership and Policy, it wasn't a career move—it was a reckoning. I wasn't seeking credentials. I was seeking clarity. After years of frontline DEIA work—building bilingual youth programs, defending LGBTQ+ inclusion, and confronting institutional inertia—I knew that the forces pushing back weren't just personal. They were structural. And I needed the language, the theory, and the historical depth to name them fully.

Doctor Chaisson-Cardenas: Please call me Dr DEIA

My doctoral journey was not merely academic—it was an excavation. I unearthed racism and oppression not as isolated acts of bias, but as structural design. I studied how neutrality in policy can mask inequity, how data can be weaponized to obscure harm, and how institutions perform allyship while quietly sustaining injustice. I traced the lineage of backlash—from Reconstruction to the Southern Strategy, from desegregation to the erosion of affirmative action—and came to understand that resistance to equity is not new. It is cyclical, adaptive, and often dressed in civility. *See the scholarly Article in the appendix.*

However, what gripped me most—and ultimately shaped my dissertation—was the institutional resistance to inclusion. Not the overt hostility, but the quieter sabotage: strategic delays, procedural deflections, and calls for "balance" that silence marginalized voices. I began to specialize in this terrain, mapping how organizations respond when equity demands transformation rather than celebration. I saw how backlash operates not only through policy, but through culture— through "tradition," fear of disruption, nostalgia for exclusion, and the myth of meritocracy.

This work is not theoretical for me. It's lived. I am a war survivor, uprooted and replanted by immigration. I've paid the price of principled resistance—fired, isolated, mischaracterized for standing with youth who dared to demand more. My Ph.D. gave me more than language; it gave me a framework to understand that what happened to me was not an exception—it was a pattern. And patterns like that must be named, disrupted, and dismantled.

Among the most insidious tactics I encountered was racial gaslighting: the subtle dismissal of lived experience, the reframing of truth as exaggeration. When people of color speak out, they're met with phrases like "You're being divisive" or "Let's not make this about race." These responses deflect accountability and place emotional burdens on those raising concerns. Over time, they erode trust, isolate advocates, and reinforce the status quo. Racial gaslighting doesn't just deny reality—it punishes truth-tellers.

Today, I use my scholarship to help institutions move beyond performative DEIA. I challenge them to confront their resistance, to reckon with the ways they protect power under the guise of process. I bring data, history, civil rights law, and lived experience into the room—and I refuse to leave my values at the door.

Returning to school was not a retreat. It was a rekindling. Agape— the fierce, redemptive love at the heart of Dr. King's movement—

became my compass. Not sentimental love, but the kind that refuses to hate, even when hatred is earned. However, I've wrestled with this deeply every day I watch the news.

When I lost my job, when colleagues turned away, when friends disappeared, I felt grief. I felt rage. But I also found clarity. I was not called to retaliate. I was called to love more fiercely. To love the youth who were watching. To love the institutions, I hoped to transform. Even to love those who harmed me—not passively, but with conviction that they, too, could change.

With that said, Dr. King warned us about the "moderate" who prefers order over justice. That warning echoes across every institution that values stability more than truth. In 4-H, I saw this often: leaders who said, "We support inclusion, but not like this." Colleagues who whispered, "You're moving too fast." Administrators who urged, "Let's wait until the backlash dies down." But youth cannot wait. Their lives are unfolding now. Their need for belonging is urgent—not just eventually.

This lesson is especially important in today's MAGA era, as institutions that once pledged to uphold equity quietly pull back. Under pressure from the so-called "war on woke," many abandon their principles—not because of legal issues, but due to a lack of moral conviction. The irony is clear: these setbacks often go against constitutional protections, yet few leaders oppose the current trend. Instead, they opt for silence, restructuring, or neutrality, hoping to avoid conflict.

But this is not just a political moment—it is a moral test. Institutions must decide whether their commitments were ever real. As they retreat, the cost is borne by the most vulnerable: students, workers, and communities whose dignity becomes negotiable. The "War on Woke" may be unconstitutional, but more urgently, it is unjust. Those who know better must speak—not just to defend programs, but to protect civil rights.

Extremism or a Commitment to Justice?

Dr. King reframed extremism, asking: "Will we be extremists for hate or for love?" I, too, have been called to be an agape extremist. For insisting that queer youth deserve safety. For refusing to compromise on human dignity. For believing that belonging is non-negotiable. If that is extremism, I accept it. Because I believe, as King did, that "the arc of the moral universe is long, but it bends toward justice"—and we are called to help bend it.

Yes, resistance has a cost. I've paid it in isolation, grief, with my retirement savings, and the loss of institutional trust. But I've gained clarity of purpose, a community of truth-tellers, and a spiritual grounding that reminds me: love is not weak—it is revolutionary. And youth, when trusted and empowered, can lead us toward a more just and joyful world.

I write this not to mourn what was lost, but to affirm what remains: the spirit of agape, the power of civil disobedience, the courage to resist, and the belief that fierce, principled love is our most radical force.

My love for PYD and 4-H endures because 4-H is more than a youth program—it is a moral blueprint for pluralistic democracy. Rooted in positive youth development, it teaches not just leadership, but belonging. It affirms that every child, regardless of identity or background, deserves a seat at the table and a voice in shaping the future. It cultivates empathy, civic responsibility, and collective care—reminding us that we are, indeed, our brother's keeper.

In an era where division is marketed as strength and difference weaponized for gain, 4-H offers a counter-narrative: radical inclusion and shared purpose. It prepares youth not just to navigate complexity, but to embrace it. It insists that democracy thrives not on uniformity, but on the courageous work of living together across lines of difference. Through service, dialogue, and leadership, young people learn that justice is not inherited—it is built.

If we are to uphold the promise of pluralistic democracy, we must invest in spaces that teach youth how to care, how to listen, and how to act. 4-H is one of those spaces. It is not perfect, but it is powerful. And when it centers on belonging, equity, and love, it becomes a training ground for the kind of citizens our future demands. Youth development is not peripheral—it is foundational because the health of our democracy depends on whether we raise a generation that knows how to care for one another.

16

A THANK YOU AND A RECOMMENDATION

"Until justice rolls down like water and righteousness like a mighty stream." "True peace is not merely the absence of tension: it is the presence of justice." "We must learn that passively to accept an unjust system is to cooperate with that system, and thereby to become a participant in its evil."

— *Reverend Doctor Martin Luther King, Jr*

A note for Public Servants and DEIA Leaders: I'm speaking to you now—especially if you've felt the slow, corrosive sting of being silenced or "canceled." I'm also reaching out to anyone who hasn't experienced this but wants to understand what it truly does to someone who served in good faith.

Hear me: erasure is uglier than the headlines can ever depict. It's not just about losing a job but also the livelihood for you and your family. It's also the ongoing devaluation that follows—the unanswered calls, the invitations that cease, the coworkers and mentees who pull back because proximity has become a political risk. Having to sell your house and move far away, to live in exile from your previous life. It is your life turned into a warning.

I know this place. I stood with LGBTQ+ youth during the first battles of the War on Woke and paid for it. Institutions that once celebrated my work stopped returning my calls. Allies whispered that I'd "gone too far." Organized groups tried to get me fired each time I got a new position or contract. They even showed up at my dissertation defense, attempting to disrupt the proceedings. My family and I received credible death threats. There were mornings I couldn't get out of bed—not from regret, but from feeling invisible in the place I had poured my life into.

But my story is not an outlier. It sits inside a current national pattern: credential revocations, threatened licenses, frozen DEIA funding, rebranded equity offices, suspended commentators, curated outrage at museums, and the sidelining of science, doctors, inspectors, and statisticians. When librarians, referees, and reporters are threatened, institutions learn to prune curricula, cancel speakers, and warn staff to "avoid controversy." That lesson moves fast—from D.C. to your local school board, your university, your county fair.

While I turned my grief into work, I went back to school, found language and theory that named structural exclusion, and leaned into community. That pathway needs to be rebuilt for others, and you can be part of it. Here are concrete ways to stand with someone who's been canceled by the War on Woke:

- Stay in touch consistently. A single message is helpful, but regular contact is what breaks isolation, especially after months pass.

- Offer practical support. Help with references, portfolio reviews, introductions, or fundraising. Small acts open doors.

- Validate their experience. Do not privatize or gaslight the harm; name it, believe it, and listen without redirecting to convenience or politics.

- Protect opportunities. Invite them to speak, to consult, to teach—actions that restore economic and professional footing.

- Build community care. Host referral circles, mentoring pods, or mutual aid funds that redistribute risk across a network.

- Advocate publicly. When institutions try to discipline truth-tellers, use your voice and privilege to push back—write op-eds, sign petitions, call decision-makers.

- Help them reclaim narrative. Offer to co-author statements, edit applications, or craft CVs that center the work rather than the controversy.

- Hold space for grief. Rebuilding is not only professional; it's emotional. Encourage therapy, spiritual practices, and time for rest without pressure to "perform resilience."

Why does this matter? It's not just about personal cost; the price of standing by my principles was real—professional exile, grief, and a loss of income. But silence harms our young people far more. I found clarity of purpose, a community of truth-tellers, and a spiritual grounding that affirms love as a revolutionary act. I still believe in positive youth development and in 4-H as a moral classroom for pluralistic democracy. I say this now as Vice President of Diversity, Equity, and Inclusion at one of the largest community colleges in the country, where cancellation is not only a distant memory but a current risk, especially now as we publish this book.

Therefore, I firmly believe that standing up for youth, for truth, for democracy, and for belonging is a moral obligation worth any sacrifice. If doing so means sacrificing comfort, status, or even personal or professional safety, I am willing to pay that price again. The alternative is watching our human and civil rights and freedoms deteriorate and vanish. This, to me, is unacceptable. Having witnessed this decline in Guatemala, I am determined that it must not happen here, so we cannot afford to remain silent or passive in the face of such threats.

But no one should have to pay for sharing agape, bravery, and commitment to pluralistic democratic principles alone. If you know someone who has been canceled, please reach out. Help them rebuild emotionally and professionally. Show up when others walk away. Because having a scarlet letter is one of the loneliest, most disruptive states a person can be in, your steady presence can make the difference between erasure and a renewed life, especially since that scarlet letter was earned on the arch towards justice.

17

DO NO HARM

At the age of 13, I went through catechism led in a Sunday School class taught by a relative, Daisy McPheeters in a small country church in Industry, Kansas. As a small child, I attended church weekly and sometimes even mid-week where there was even a tent revival where one preacher spoke of hell, fire and brimstone. Later, there were times in worship for altar calls for folks to profess their faith and be blest. For me, faith was so intertwined with our daily lives on the farm. It was so natural to speak with God, to ask questions, and to see God in 'everything' - in the cows that we cared for, in the ground and the growing crops, in the weather, and in each other. Caring for others was elemental despite differences. I do recall wondering why there wasn't an 'umbrella' church for all those who loved the Lord. And I did not understand the differences between and within denominations nor understood the differences between Catholics and Protestants. In fact, I recall telling this kid that I was not a pro-test-ant which was a word I had not heard before. I told him I was an "EUB'er", an Evangelical United Brethren. My catechism classes were unique as it was during that time that the EUB and Methodist church united to become the United Methodist. I learned about Jacob Albright, Phillip Otterbein, Charles and John Wesley, two who spoke German primarily and the other two spoke English. For me, it was the methods, the practices that spoke to me, to learn, to discern, to question, to be curious, while adhering to practices and the 3 previously mentioned principles, *Do No Harm, Do Good, and Stay in Love with God through practices.*

Now, for me, these three principles sound like a 'learn-by-doing' approach which reflects why 4-H resonates in my head, heart, health and hands. Do No Harm implies for me that all are welcome, the tent is large, and all may fit underneath. Much like my desire as a small child to have a 'universal' church where all belong, all fit. There is only inclusion, no exclusion of who can be 'under the tent'.

I took to heart Do No Harm even as an extension professional. There were times when the rules and regulations that I had to follow and administer didn't make sense to me. I learned that they were often put in place to correct something someone else did yet in the process created potential harm for someone else. For example, I had a 4-H youth who wanted to apply for National 4-H Congress after having attended National 4-H Conference as a delegate. I read the rules and saw nothing that prohibited their participation in both so submitted their application. I was told it was an 'unwritten' rule in a phone call, yet I challenged that 'unwritten' rule as I saw that as a 'harm' and pushed back, so the application was allowed. Another case involved a 4-H'er who was taking education college classes as a member of the county 4-H meats judging team which had placed 1st in state competition. There was a rule that said they couldn't judge at national competitions if they were taking college classes. I challenged this rule as those education courses were not courses that would create an unfair advantage in meats judging. The final decision was left up to the meats judging coaches on this youth's participation and though the ruling didn't allow the youth's scores to count, the ruling was subsequently changed for the future. Rules and regulations are by nature exclusionary. They don't allow for the 'tent' to be large enough for all to participate. Rules and regulations are meant typically to set boundaries, to set up how to administer, how and if any punishment needs to be administered, to find or point out who to blame without regard to the situation or circumstances. We are all humans, and mistakes or errors in judgment might not have been intentional. Key point is that word "Intent." If one intends to circumvent a rule just because they don't like it, or seeks to avoid consequences for one's actions, then their actions speak toward an intent that may harm. I would note that as a PYD professional, the pre-frontal cortex is not 'fully formed' until age 25 so there needs to be 'grace' for those 'younger' and opportunities for those 'older' to process how to help those 'younger' learn from and experience positive risk taking. I know that I benefited from this type of 'grace' through my 4-H experiences and in my career until I 'grew' into my adulthood.

I work hard to acknowledge and accept consequences for my actions. I practice forgiveness when I know that someone else's actions were not intended to create harm. I'm not sure that reflects that I have 'turned the cheek' or let others 'win'. It does mean that I do not however forget how others and I've been treated. It falls more under 'forgive yet do not forget'. I too like John-Paul do not like bullies. I find in my own way how to stand up, speak up and show up, to Do No Harm.

Publishing LGBTQ+ guidance was to ensure 4-H Did NO Harm. From a researcher's evidence-based Positive Youth Development background, the guidance is rational, logical and translates science into practice which is my adherence to my extension worker's creed. I swallow and reflect though on what the cost was and still is to practice Do No Harm, to create for all a sense of belonging, to embrace and engage with those for whom I've never met and may not. This is my legacy, my way to pay it forward for all those who preceded me and who I hope will follow, to ensure that 4-H is open to all. It is to ensure there is a broad tent where 4-H provides a PYD safe place, as shelter and shade. As a generational 4-H'er, one whose family was steeped in 4-H and Cooperative Extension, and for whom 4-H provided lifelong connections, created skillful competencies, and enhanced my capacity to share with and with tears flowing down my cheeks, I love 4-H with my whole heart, hands, health and head... I say it again, I "bleed green."

Photo of Heart Wall
4-H Project: White fence with various colored hearts

Gathering Voices

We, John-Paul and Lisa, love 4-H. Individually, we shared our voices, yet we are not alone.

There are many others who love 4-H and other positive youth development programs, and they have experiences to share. We want to uplift those who came before us in this journey to ensure that 4-H and all positive youth development programs are accessible to everyone. Some navigated challenges as 4-H became 'integrated' in different states, with programming conducted by and with 1862s, 1890s, and 1994s. We want to give a shout-out to the voices of those who continue to push forward, ensuring fewer exclusions, greater accessibility, and more opportunities for all youth. We invite you to share your efforts in your own voices.

Voices matter. Love overcomes hate. Youth must be heard. 4-H and other positive youth development programs are the tools. Let's keep working to ensure that life, love, and laughter are available to everyone.

Love to ALL

Dear friends, let us love one another, for love comes from God. Everyone who loves has been born of God and knows God. 8 Whoever does not love does not know God, because God is love…..11 Dear friends, since God so loved us, we also ought to love one another. 12 No one has ever seen God; but if we love one another, God lives in us and his love is made complete in us.

– 1st John 4: 71-8; 11-12 NIV –

Please, share Your DEI PYD Love Story Please share your love stories. We'd love to hear them. Here are some starter questions to help you reflect on your story and find ways to keep working toward a brighter future.

- What has been your most loving, rewarding experience in expanding the reach of DEIA in your Positive Youth Development Work?

Challenges Faced for DEIA-PYD

- What has been your greatest challenge regarding expanding DEIA principles?
- How did you respond to those challenges? Would you do anything differently? Why? Or why not?

DEI and PYD – Future Desires, Concerns

- What are your concerns about the future of DEI and its impact on positive youth development?
- What are your desires for the future of DEI in relation to positive youth development?
- How can you bring those desires to life? Who can you work with to bring those desires to life?

4-H A Dei Love Story:
How Positive Youth Development Became a Battleground for Democracy

Please scan QR or go to 4-HLove.org to see and tell your "DEIA Love for 4-H Story"

APPENDICES

USDA 🍀

United States	National Institute	
Department of	of Food	4-H National
Agriculture	and Agriculture	Headquarters

This national guidance document has been adopted from a document created by a Western Region Program Leaders Workgroup (Katherine E. Soule, James Lindstrom, Sarah Chvilicek, and Jean Glowacki). It has been approved by the National 4-H Program Leaders Working Group and 4-H National Headquarters.

4-H Guidance for Inclusion of Individuals of All Gender Identities, Gender Expressions, Sexual Orientations, and Sexes

As the nation's largest youth development program, 4-H engages millions of people from all areas of the country to provide opportunities for youth to learn life skills, confidence, and compassion. The 4-H Program is committed to being inclusive and welcoming of all forms of diversity. This 4-H Program guidance was developed to guide 4-H Programs around the country on how to be inclusive for individuals of all gender identities, gender expressions, sexual orientations, and sexes. These guidelines shall serve as guidance for all members of 4-H communities, including staff, faculty, youth members, adult volunteers, families, and other community members.

As noted by the United States Department of Agriculture: "The use of the 4-H Name and Emblem is defined through 7 Code of Federal Regulations (CFR) 8...The U.S. Congress has legislated responsibility for the proper management of the 4-H Name and Emblem to the Secretary of Agriculture...The Secretary of Agriculture has delegated that authority to 4-H National Headquarters in the Division of Youth and 4-H, housed at USDA's National Institute of Food and Agriculture (NIFA)."[1] The USDA prohibits discrimination of any individual based on gender identity, gender expression, sexual orientation, and/or sex.[2] These guidelines summarize recommendations to 4-H Programs regarding inclusion of individuals of all gender identities, gender expressions, sexual orientations, and sexes.

Terminology
Sexual orientation refers to who an individual is attracted to (generally based on gender identities). A person who is a *lesbian* is a woman who is attracted to women. A person who is *gay* is a man who is attracted to men. A person who is *bisexual* is a person who is attracted to two genders (most commonly men and women). A person who is *polysexual* is a person who is attracted to others regardless of sex, gender identity, gender expression, or sexual orientation.

Gender expression refers to an individual's presentation of gender to others, including their dress, grooming, speech, mannerisms, and other factors.

Sex is a medical term referring to a combination of physiological attributes, including chromosomes, gonads, hormones, sex and reproductive organs, as well as secondary sex characteristics. Most commonly, individuals are assigned to be either male or female at birth.

Intersex describes those individuals who are born with physiological attributes that include a combination of male and female anatomy, which may include chromosomes, gonads, hormones, or sex and reproductive organs. There are countless ways physiological attributes might vary. One example, is an individual may have male-typical anatomy externally while having mostly female-typical anatomy internally.

---

[1] USDA, 2017. *4-H Name and Emblem*
[2] USDA, 2015. *And Justice for All*
The 4-H Youth Development Program is the youth outreach program from the land-grant institutions' Cooperative Extension Services, and the U.S. Department of Agriculture (USDA). USDA is an equal opportunity provider and employer. March 2018.

4-H A Dei Love Story:
How Positive Youth Development Became a Battleground for Democracy

Sex assigned at birth refers to a person's sex designation as recorded on their birth certificate. Generally, a medical professional or guardian designates either "male" or "female" sex after examining a newborn infant's genitalia.

Gender identity describes a person's internal sense of gender. A person's gender identity may or may not match the person's sex assigned at birth. Some common gender identities include: man, woman, gender neutral, transgender man, transgender woman, and gender non-binary.

Transgender describes a person whose gender identity is different than the sex they were assigned at birth. A *transgender male* describes a person who identifies as male but was assigned female sex at birth. A *transgender female* describes a person who identifies as female but was assigned male sex at birth.

Gender transition describes the process in which a person asserts the sex that corresponds to their gender identity rather than the sex assigned at birth. A person in gender transition may (or may not) alter their dress/grooming habits, change their name, or use pronouns that are consistent with their gender identity. A person may begin gender transition at any point in their life, and gender transition may happen over a short or extended duration of time.

Guidance for Inclusion

4-H shall not segregate or otherwise distinguish individuals on the basis of their sex, gender identity, gender expression, or sexual orientation, in any 4-H activities or the application of any 4-H rule.[3] This guidance is consistent with courts' and other agencies' interpretations of Federal laws prohibiting sex discrimination,[4] as well as research-based and emerging best practices[5] for positive youth development. When an individual (youth or adult) notifies 4-H administration (at the county/parrish/local, and/or state level as appropriate) that the individual will assert a gender identity that differs from previous representations or records, 4-H will begin treating the individual consistent with the individual's gender identity. There is no medical diagnosis or treatment requirement that individuals (youth or adult) must meet as a prerequisite to being treated consistent with their gender identity.[6] Because transgender and intersex individuals often are unable to obtain identification documents that reflect their gender identity (e.g., due to restrictions imposed by state or local law in their place of birth or residence),[7] requiring individuals to produce such identification documents in

---

[3] USDA, 2015. *And Justice for All*

[4] *See, e.g., Price Waterhouse v. Hopkins*, 490 U.S. 228 (1989); *Oncale v. Sundowner Offshore Servs. Inc.*, 523 U.S. 75, 79 (1998); *G.G. v. Gloucester Cnty. Sch. Bd.*, No. 15-2056, 2016 WL 1567467, at *8 (4th Cir. Apr. 19, 2016); *Glenn v. Brumby*, 663 F.3d 1312, 1317 (11th Cir. 2011); *Smith v. City of Salem*, 378 F.3d 566, 572-75 (6th Cir. 2004); *Rosa v. Park W. Bank & Trust Co.*, 214 F.3d 213, 215–16 (1st Cir. 2000); *Schwenk v. Hartford*, 204 F.3d 1187, 1201–02 (9th Cir. 2000); *Schroer v. Billington*, 577 F. Supp. 2d 293, 306-08 (D.D.C. 2008); *Macy v. Dep't of Justice*, Appeal No. 012012082 (U.S. Equal Emp't Opportunity Comm'n Apr. 20, 2012). *See also* U.S. Dep't of Labor (USDOL), Training and Employment Guidance Letter No. 37-14, *Update on Complying with Nondiscrimination Requirements: Discrimination Based on Gender Identity, Gender Expression and Sex Stereotyping are Prohibited Forms of Sex Discrimination in the Workforce Development System (2015)*; USDOL, Job Corps, Directive, Job Corps Program Instruction Notice No. 14-31, *Ensuring Equal Access for Transgender Applicants and Students to the Job Corps Program (May 1, 2015)*; DOJ, Memorandum from the Attorney General, *Treatment of Transgender Employment Discrimination Claims Under Title VII of the Civil Rights Act of 1964 (2014)*; USDOL, Office of Federal Contract Compliance Programs, Directive 2014-02, *Gender Identity and Sex Discrimination (2014)*.

[5] *See, e.g., The New York State Education Department (2015)*; GLSEN (2016); *California School Boards Association (2014)*; *Massachusetts Board of Elementary and Secondary Education (2015)*; *Connecticut Safe Schools Coalition (2012)*; *Schools in Transition: A Guide to Supporting Transgender Students in k-12 Schools*; Trevor Project, American Foundation for Suicide Prevention, the American School Counselor Association, and the National Association of School Psychologists.

[6] *See Lusardi v. Dep't of the Army*, Appeal No. 0120133395 at 9 (U.S. Equal Emp't Opportunity Comm'n Apr. 1, 2015) ("An agency may not condition access to facilities—or to other terms, conditions, or privileges of employment—on the completion of certain medical steps that the agency itself has unilaterally determined will somehow prove the bona fides of the individual's gender identity.").

[7] *See G.G.*, 2016 WL 1567467, at *1 n.1 (noting that medical authorities "do not permit sex reassignment surgery The 4-H Youth Development Program is the youth outreach program from the land-grant institutions' Cooperative Extension Services, and the U.S. Department of Agriculture (USDA). USDA is an equal opportunity provider and employer. March 2018.

order to treat them consistent with their gender identity may have the practical effect of limiting or denying individuals equal access to an educational program or activity.

As is consistently recognized in civil rights cases, the desire to accommodate others' discomfort cannot justify a practice that singles out and disadvantages a particular class of individuals.[8] The USDA has identified the following as protected classes: gender identity, gender expression, sex, and sexual orientation.[9] 4-H shall ensure nondiscrimination to provide transgender and intersex individuals equal access to programs and activities even in circumstances in which staff, faculty, youth members, adult volunteers, families, other community members, and/or a youth members' own guardian raise objections or concerns. Likewise, 4-H shall provide individuals of all gender expressions and sexual orientations equal access to programs and activities. 4-H shall not discipline individuals or exclude them from participating in activities for appearing or behaving in a manner that is consistent with their gender identity or in a manner that does not conform to stereotypical notions of masculinity or femininity (e.g., in uniform or other attire requirements, at dances, or at recognition ceremonies).[10]

Safe and Nondiscriminatory Environment

4-H has a responsibility to provide a safe and nondiscriminatory environment for all individuals. Harassment based on an individual's sex, gender identity, gender expression, or sexual orientation shall be prohibited.[11] If harassment creates a hostile environment, 4-H shall take prompt and effective steps to end the harassment, prevent its recurrence, and, as appropriate, remedy its effects. 4-H 's failure to treat individuals consistent with their gender identity may create or contribute to a hostile environment. For a more detailed discussion of Title IX requirements related to sex-based harassment, see guidance documents from ED's Office for Civil Rights (OCR) that are specific to this topic.[12]

Identification Documents, Names, and Pronouns

4-H shall treat individuals consistent with their gender identity even if their program records or identification documents indicate a different sex. 4-H, including all paid and volunteer personnel, as well as youth members, will use pronouns and names consistent with a transgender or intersex

---

for persons who are under the legal age of majority").

[8] 34 C.F.R. § 106.31(b)(4); see G.G., 2016 WL 1567467, at *8 & n.10 (affirming that individuals have legitimate and important privacy interests and noting that these interests do not inherently conflict with nondiscrimination principles); Cruzan v. Special Sch. Dist. No. 1, 294 F.3d 981, 984 (8th Cir. 2002) (rejecting claim that allowing a transgender woman "merely [to be] present in the women's faculty restroom" created a hostile environment); Glenn, 663 F.3d at 1321 (defendant's proffered justification that "other women might object to [the plaintiff]'s restroom use" was "wholly irrelevant"). See also Palmore v. Sidoti, 466 U.S. 429, 433 (1984) ("Private biases may be outside the reach of the law, but the law cannot, directly or indirectly, give them effect."); City of Cleburne v. Cleburne Living Ctr., 473 U.S. 432, 448 (1985) (recognizing that "mere negative attitudes, or fear . . . are not permissible bases for" government action).

[9] USDA, 2015, And Justice for All.

[10] See 34 C.F.R. §§ 106.31(a), 106.31(b)(4). See also, In re Downey Unified Sch. Dist., CA, supra n. 9; In re Cent. Piedmont Cmty. Coll., NC, supra n. 11.

[11] See, e.g., Resolution Agreement, In re Downey Unified Sch. Dist., CA, OCR Case No. 09-12-1095 (Oct. 8, 2014) (agreement to address harassment of transgender student, including allegations that peers continued to call her by her former name, shared pictures of her prior to her transition, and frequently asked questions about her anatomy and sexuality); Consent Decree, Doe v. Anoka-Hennepin Sch. Dist. No. 11, MN (D. Minn. Mar. 1, 2012), (consent decree to address sex-based harassment, including based on nonconformity with gender stereotypes); Resolution Agreement, In re Tehachapi Unified Sch. Dist., CA, OCR Case No. 09-11-1031 (June 30, 2011), (agreement to address sexual and gender-based harassment, including harassment based on nonconformity with gender stereotypes). See also Lusardi, Appeal No. 0120133395, at *15 ("Persistent failure to use the employee's correct name and pronoun may constitute unlawful, sex-based harassment if such conduct is either severe or pervasive enough to create a hostile work environment").

[12] See, e.g., OCR, Revised Sexual Harassment Guidance: Harassment of Students by School Employees, Other Students, or Third Parties (2001); OCR, Dear Colleague Letter: Harassment and Bullying (Oct. 26, 2010); OCR, Dear Colleague Letter: Sexual Violence (Apr. 4, 2011); OCR, Questions and Answers on Title IX and Sexual Violence (Apr. 29, 2014).

The 4-H Youth Development Program is the youth outreach program from the land-grant institutions' Cooperative Extension Services, and the U.S. Department of Agriculture (USDA). USDA is an equal opportunity provider and employer. March 2018.

individual's gender identity. [13]

Sex-Segregated Activities and Facilities

Title IX's implementing regulations permit 4-H to provide sex-segregated restrooms, locker rooms, shower facilities, housing, and athletic teams, as well as single-sex classes under certain circumstances. [14] If 4-H provides sex-segregated activities and facilities, transgender and intersex individuals shall be allowed to participate in such activities and access such facilities consistent with their gender identity. [15] 4-H shall not segregate individuals from activities and facilities on the basis of gender expression or sexual orientation.

Restrooms and Locker Rooms. 4-H may provide separate facilities on the basis of sex, but should allow transgender and intersex individuals' access to such facilities consistent with their gender identity. [16] 4-H shall not require transgender or intersex individuals to use facilities inconsistent with their gender identity or to use single-user facilities when other individuals are not required to do so. 4-H shall not require individuals to use single-user facilities based on gender expression or sexual orientation when other individuals are not required to use single-user facilities. 4-H may make individual-user options available to all individuals who voluntarily seek additional privacy. [17]

Athletics. Title IX regulations permit 4-H to operate or sponsor sex-segregated athletics teams (such as Special Interest [SPIN] Soccer Clubs) when selection for such teams is based upon competitive skill or when the activity involved is a contact sport. [18] 4-H shall not, however, adopt or adhere to requirements that rely on overly broad generalizations or stereotypes about the differences between transgender or intersex individuals and other individuals of the same sex (*i.e.*, the same gender identity) or others' discomfort with transgender or intersex individuals. [19] 4-H shall not segregate individuals' participation based on their gender expression or sexual orientation and should allow individuals to participate on team with others of the same gender identity. The USDA does not prohibit age-appropriate, tailored requirements based on sound, current, and research-based medical knowledge about the impact of the individuals' participation on the competitive fairness or physical safety of the sport. [20]

Single-Sex Classes. Although separating individuals by sex in classes and activities is generally

---

[13] *See, e.g., Resolution Agreement, In re Cent. Piedmont Cmty. Coll., NC, OCR Case No. 11-14-2265 (Aug. 13, 2015)* (agreement to use a transgender student's preferred   name and gender and change the student's official record to reflect a name change).

[14] 34 C.F.R. §§ 106.32, 106.33, 106.34, 106.41(b).

[15] *See* 34 C.F.R. § 106.31.

[16] 34 C.F.R. § 106.33.

[17] *See, e.g.,* Resolution Agreement, *In re Township High Sch. Dist. 211, IL, OCR Case No. 05-14-1055 (Dec. 2, 2015),* (agreement to provide any student who requests   additional privacy "access to a reasonable alternative, such as assignment of a student locker in near proximity to the office of a teacher or coach; use of another private area (such as a restroom stall) within the public area; use of a nearby private area (such as a single-use facility); or a separate schedule of use.").

[18] 34 C.F.R. § 106.41(b). Nothing in Title IX prohibits schools from offering coeducational athletic opportunities.

[19] 34 C.F.R. § 106.6(b), (c). An interscholastic athletic association is subject to Title IX if (1) the association receives Federal financial assistance or (2) its members are recipients of Federal financial assistance and have ceded controlling authority over portions of their athletic program to the association. Where an athletic association is covered by Title IX, a school's obligations regarding transgender athletes apply with equal force to the association.

[20] The National Collegiate Athletic Association (NCAA), for example, reported that in developing its policy for participation by transgender students in college athletics, it consulted with medical experts, athletics officials, affected students, and a consensus report entitled *On the Team: Equal Opportunity for Transgender Student Athletes (2010)* by Dr. Pat Griffin & Helen J. Carroll (*On the Team*). *See NCAA Office of Inclusion, NCAA Inclusion of Transgender Student-Athletes 2, 30-31 (2011),* (citing *On the Team*). The *On the   Team* report noted that policies that may be appropriate at the college level may "be unfair and too complicated   for [the high school] level of competition." *On the Team* at 26. After engaging in similar processes, some state interscholastic athletics associations have adopted policies for participation by transgender students in high school   athletics that they determined were age-appropriate.

The 4-H Youth Development Program is the youth outreach program from the land-grant institutions' Cooperative Extension Services, and the U.S. Department of Agriculture (USDA). USDA is an equal opportunity provider and employer. March 2018.

prohibited, 4-H may offer single-sex classes and activities under certain circumstances.[21] When offering such classes and activities, 4-H shall allow transgender and intersex 4-H participants to participate consistent with their gender identity. 4-H shall not segregate individuals based on their gender expression or sexual orientation.

Housing and Overnight Accommodations. 4-H may provide separate housing on the basis of sex.[22] In such cases, 4-H shall allow transgender and intersex individuals to access housing consistent with their gender identity. 4-H shall not require transgender or intersex individuals to stay in single-occupancy accommodations or to disclose personal information when not required of other individuals. 4-H shall not require individuals to stay in single-occupancy accomodations based on gender expression or sexual orientation or to disclose personal information when not required of other individuals. 4-H may honor individuals' voluntary requests for single-occupancy accommodations.[23]

Privacy and Program Records
4-H collects as little personally idenfitaible information (PII) as possible, collecting only that information that is necessary to conduct 4-H. 4-H may maintain records with birth name and sex assigned at birth, if there is a legitimate programmatic need, but such records shall be kept confidential. As 4-H is a national program, privacy policies vary according to federal, state, university policies, and other contractual agreements.

Protecting transgender and intersex individuals' privacy is critical to ensuring they are treated consistent with their gender identity. 4-H shall take reasonable steps to protect individuals' privacy related to their transgender or intersex status, including protectingtheir birth name or sex assigned at birth.[24] Additionally, nonconsensual disclosure of personally identifiable information, such as an individual's birth name or sex assigned at birth, could be harmful to or invade the privacy of transgender and intersex individuals.

Disclosure of Personal Information. PII from an individual's program records must be kept confidential. PII records shall only be disclosed to 4-H personnel who have been determined to have a legitimate programmatic need for the information.[25] Even if an individual has disclosed that they are transgender or intersex to some members of 4-H community, 4-H shall not disclose PII from program records to others (including 4-H personnel), who do not have a legitimate programmatic need for the information. Even if an individual has disclosed their sexual orientation to some members of the 4-H community, 4-H shall not disclose this information to others.

Disclosure of Directory Information. 4-H may disclose appropriately designated directory information from an individual's program record to approved 4-H personnel (including club leaders) if disclosure would not be considered harmful or an invasion of privacy.[26] Directory information may include an individual's name, telephone number, date of birth, honors and awards, and dates of attendance.[27] To protect youth safety, 4-H must not disclose youth addresses unless necessary and may only disclose youth addresses to approved 4-H personnel. 4-H officials shall not designate individuals' sex, including transgender or intersex status, or sexual orientation as directory information because doing so could be harmful or an

---

[21] 34 C.F.R. § 106.34(a), (b). Schools may also separate students by sex in physical education classes during participation in contact sports. *Id.* § 106.34(a)(1).

[22] 20 U.S.C. § 1686; 34 C.F.R. § 106.32.

[23] *See, e.g.,* Resolution Agreement, *In re Arcadia Unified. Sch. Dist.,* CA, OCR Case No. 09-12-1020, DOJ Case No. 169-12C-70, (July 24, 2013), www.justice.gov/sites/default/files/crt/legacy/2013/07/26/arcadiaagree.pdf (agreement to provide access to single-sex overnight events consistent with students' gender identity, but allowing students to request access to private facilities).

[24] 34 C.F.R. § 106.31(b)(7).

[25] 20 U.S.C. § 1232g(b)(1)(A); 34 C.F.R. § 99.31(a)(1).

[26] 34 C.F.R. §§ 99.3, 99.31(a)(11), 99.37.

[27] 20 U.S.C. § 1232g(a)(5)(A); 34 C.F.R. § 99.3.

The 4-H Youth Development Program is the youth outreach program from the land-grant institutions' Cooperative Extension Services, and the U.S. Department of Agriculture (USDA). USDA is an equal opportunity provider and employer. March 2018

invasion of privacy.[28]

Amendment or Correction of Participant Records. 4-H may receive requests (from youth, adults, and/or parent/guardian) to correct an individual's enrollment records to make the records consistent with the individual's gender identity. Updating a transgender or intersex individual's enrollment records to reflect the individual's gender identity and new name (if applicable) helps to protect privacy and ensure that 4-H consistently use appropriate names and pronouns.

- 4-H shall respond to the request of an individual (youth or adult) to amend information in the individual's enrollment records that is inaccurate, misleading, or in violation of the individual's privacy rights. 4-H shall correct names and gender identities in participant records to be consistent with a transgender or intersex individual's gender identity.[29]

- 4-H shall respond to a request to amend information related to an individual's transgender or intersex status consistent with its general practices for amending other individual's records.[30] If the individual (or a youth members' guardians) complain about 4-H's handling of such a request, 4-H shall promptly and equitably resolve the complaint.[31]

---

[28] Letter from FPCO to Institutions of Postsecondary Education 3 (Sept. 2009).

[29] See, e.g., Resolution Agreement, In re Cent. Piedmont Cmty. Coll., NC, OCR Case No. 11-14-2265 (Aug. 13, 2015), (agreement to use a transgender student's preferred name and gender and change the student's official record to reflect a name change).

[30] See 34 C.F.R. § 106.31(b)(4).

[31] 34 C.F.R. § 106.8(b).

The 4-H Youth Development Program is the youth outreach program from the land-grant institutions' Cooperative Extension Services, and the U.S. Department of Agriculture (USDA). USDA is an equal opportunity provider and employer. March 2018.

Research Note:
The DEIA Paradox:
A scholarly perspective, "Tokens"
and "Pet to Threat":

"Democratic pluralism is the idea that democracy works best when multiple interest groups compete and collaborate. It prevents the concentration of power and ensures that diverse voices are represented in policymaking."

— *Michael P. Auerbach, in Democracy: The Pluralist Perspective*

The best Positive Youth Development (PYD) leaders, including youth leaders, professionals, and volunteers, are, by definition and in action, the grassroots drivers of diversity, equity, inclusion, and accessibility (DEIA) transformation. This is especially true in 4-H, where they don't just support young people—they co-create equitable ecosystems where youth of all identities can lead, belong, and thrive.

Every mentoring session, accommodation, youth-led initiative, and trauma-informed practice serves as a direct action against systemic exclusion. PYD professionals implement DEIA every day: they amplify marginalized voices, challenge adultism, and develop culturally responsive programs that mirror the lived realities of rural, youth of color, immigrant and migrant youth, and those who may have a disability.

Their work is not peripheral to DEIA—it is its core. In fact, many DEIA frameworks adopt PYD's relational, strengths-based approach to inclusion. Recognizing PYD and 4-H workers means honoring justice architects who build it from the ground up with radical love, ancestral wisdom, and youth-powered vision.

At a time when democracy is struggling both locally and globally, Positive Youth Development is essential. It may be our best chance to cultivate a society where individuals can experience a true "sense of belonging," supported by respect for diverse cultures, identities, and especially for Human and Civil Rights – in simple words, a pluralistic democracy. Having dedicated my life to advancing equity, I firmly believe that democratic pluralism is not merely a political ideal; it is a practical approach to creating a better, more inclusive nation and society where people from various backgrounds can live, love, play, and work together.

The international stakes are equally high, so Positive Youth Development (PYD) also has a role there. In regions where democracy is fragile or under threat, such as my home country of Guatemala, pluralism presents a path forward. It offers a way to resist authoritarianism, heal historical wounds, and build coalitions across lines of race, ethnicity, gender, spirituality, and belief. This is because, in pluralistic democracies, where multiple identities, beliefs, and traditions coexist, the health of the system depends not on uniformity but on the ethical engagement of difference.

This is where DEIA—Diversity, Equity, Inclusion, and Accessibility (DEIA) resides, not as indoctrination or policy checklist, but as a liberatory and democratic imperative. This is because diversity acknowledges the full spectrum of human identity and experience. Whether it be racial, cultural, gendered, neurodiverse, or more, it is essential to the public sphere. Equity, in contrast, ensures that systemic barriers are dismantled so that all individuals can participate meaningfully. Inclusion transforms institutions to empower marginalized voices, while Accessibility guarantees that physical, digital, and social spaces are navigable by all. Together, DEIA creates the conditions and strategies for civilized conflict, where disagreement is not suppressed but negotiated—a hallmark of pluralistic democracy.

This means that professionals such as educators, youth workers, and institutional leaders involved in Diversity, Equity, Inclusion, and Accessibility (DEIA) efforts are not simply implementing programs or policies; they are fostering an environment where democratic pluralism can thrive in our clubs, communities, countries, and across the world, as stated in the 4-H pledge. By recognizing and affirming the full spectrum of identities and experiences among youth, programs, and organizations, DEIA practitioners embody pluralism as a lived ethic.

This approach values diversity as a source of strength, promotes belonging through intentional design, and ensures that historically marginalized voices contribute to collective decision-making. Their efforts transform institutions from gatekeepers into gateways, where civic engagement is nurtured, enabling young people to navigate complexity with empathy and purpose. In this way, DEIA professionals act as architects of pluralistic democracy, creating systems where inclusion is a fundamental principle rather than an afterthought in shared governance.

The escalating "war on woke" led by the MAGA movement has weaponized white resentment in a broad backlash against Diversity, Equity, Inclusion, and Accessibility (DEIA), particularly targeting the professionals and community members who advocate for these values. This campaign is fueled by narratives of cultural loss and economic displacement, portraying DEIA as a threat to "traditional" hierarchies and merit-based ideals. This perspective overlooks the substantial evidence that historical, structural, and systemic inequities persist in our society and its institutions.

I draw on my previous scholarly work, which examines how individuals, organizations, and institutions— including the U.S. Supreme Court—resist efforts related to diversity, equity, inclusion, and accessibility (DEIA) and condone the backlash against those who advocate for it, particularly individuals from minoritized groups. This section also addresses the human costs faced by DEIA practitioners, and by corollary, PYD and 4-H leaders who strive daily to foster a "sense of belonging."

But before we proceed, let's clarify some terms. Dass and Parker (1999) described "diversity resistance" as a stance taken by organizations marked by inertia, silence, defiance, and sometimes manipulation. This resistance actively and strategically opposes DEIA-focused changes. In higher education, Thomas and Plaut (2008) defined diversity resistance as "a range of practices and behaviors within and by organizations that interfere, intentionally or unintentionally, with the use of diversity as an opportunity for learning and effectiveness." Similarly, Burke and Black (1997) introduced the term "diversity backlash" to describe any form of resistance—overt or covert—that dominant groups in society display toward policies, programs, and initiatives aimed at increasing the hiring and advancement of marginalized employees.

By examining these definitions, I emphasize the distinction between DEIA resistance and backlash. Specifically, resistance focuses on obstructing DEIA-oriented change. At the same time, backlash not only resists such change but also seeks to diminish, discredit, demonize, or punish those who are perceived or labeled as advocates for DEIA initiatives. Notably, this definition of backlash can extend beyond mere lack of awareness to encompass more harmful attitudes, such as racism, structural racism, homophobia, and sexism. For example, a situation that illustrates DEIA backlash is when a DEIA professional attempts to implement DEIA-oriented change within an organization and subsequently faces repercussions, such as being dismissed, demonized, reassigned, demoted, or even fired for fulfilling their role.

In 2013, Dr. Kecia M. Thomas introduced the term "Pet to Threat" to describe a form of organizational resistance and backlash that particularly affects Black women and other women of color. Her research found that these individuals are often celebrated early in their careers but quickly viewed as threats when they assert their leadership or challenge workplace norms. This phrase has since become an important framework for understanding racial and gender bias in professional environments. This essay explores similar dynamics faced by Diversity, Equity, Inclusion, and Accessibility (DEIA) professionals, who often experience increased backlash due to the intersection of their gender and racial identities with the misrepresentation of their DEIA work.

The book also delves into the compounded effects of anti-DEIA efforts, especially when minoritized professionals are hired as racial tokens. "Tokenism" refers to the superficial inclusion of individuals from marginalized racial or ethnic groups—often aimed at creating the illusion of diversity without addressing systemic inequities or empowering meaningful participation. In practice, tokenism reduces people to commodities or symbols of performative representation, rather than recognizing their full humanity, expertise, and lived experiences.

For DEIA professionals, this dynamic poses a significant challenge, as they are often the first individuals (e.g., the first woman or the first Latino) to occupy and work within a particular space. While they strive to build inclusive systems rooted in equity and belonging, they frequently encounter resistance from institutions that treat diversity as a marketing strategy rather than a genuine commitment to structural change.

Tokenism not only undermines trust but also isolates those who are expected to "represent" entire communities, placing emotional and professional burdens on individuals while shielding organizations from deeper accountability. In pluralistic democracies, true inclusion requires more than mere visibility or performative actions—it necessitates genuine transformation.

Ironically, this book was written during a time when white grievance was prevalent, notably exemplified by the "Make America Great Again" (MAGA) movement. Through a Critical Race Theory lens, this movement reflects a yearning for a past when white dominance faced less resistance. The ambiguous term "again" evokes memories of segregation and exclusion for communities of color. Critics argue that it serves as a racial dog whistle, tapping into backlash against civil rights progress and demographic changes while subtly reinforcing resistance to equity and inclusion. Furthermore, MAGA builds upon the racial messaging of the Southern Strategy, which emerged in the 1960s to attract white voters by opposing civil rights advancements. Like the Southern Strategy's use of coded terms—often referred to as "dog whistles"—such as "communism," "law and order," and "states' rights," MAGA invokes nostalgia linked to past racial, gender, and religious hierarchies. However, while the Southern Strategy was focused regionally, MAGA nationalized these appeals, engaging in racial grievance politics and resisting demographic change under the guise of "restoring greatness."

It is important to note that the "War on Woke" has been implemented through various executive orders, Department of Justice memos, and the weaponization of federal Civil Rights offices. A significant example is Presidential Executive Order 13985 (2025), which mandates the end of "all discriminatory programs," categorizing "illegal" diversity, equity, inclusion, and accessibility (DEIA) initiatives within 60 days of the order's signing. Although this order raises fundamental constitutional questions, it has created confusion and fear among many DEIA professionals and advocates.

As a result, thousands of DEIA professionals have left the field or been laid off due to the termination of DEIA programs at local, state, and national levels. Conservative media have described this situation as "The War on Woke," a political campaign that blames "Diversity, Equity, Inclusion, and Accessibility hires" for various societal issues, from excessive government spending to airplane crashes. This perspective promotes a majoritarian mindset that devalues women, people of color, and other marginalized communities, including women, LGBTQ+ individuals, and those with disabilities. It portrays these individuals and their views as radical, biased, less qualified, and less American than white men, exemplifying what literature identifies as white or male privilege.

In this context, the book juxtaposes MAGA's "War on Woke" and other prejudicial frameworks with DEIA (Diversity, Equity, Inclusion, and Accessibility) leaders, who represent the longest-standing and most consistent DEIA-related interventions in business and academic institutions across the United States. In simpler terms, DEIA and, by corollary, PYD and 4-H professionals act as the "miners' canary" in relation to DEIA efforts. Importantly, unlike other standard roles—such as superintendents, CEOs, faculty, and comptrollers—which are typically valued within most organizational structures, DEIA professionals remain significantly undervalued and inadequately studied in research related to business, government, non-profit, and education sectors. Thus, to understand the role of DEIA professionals from a historical perspective, it is essential to acknowledge the sociopolitical forces, including societal resistance and backlash against the human and civil rights of marginalized populations (e.g., Jim Crow laws, slavery, racial deportations such as operation wetback), that have shaped this organizational position.

It is notable that many core DEIA (Diversity, Equity, Inclusion, and Accessibility) strategies, often negatively labeled as "anti-woke," have a long history of success. Movements such as ethnic and gender studies, Affirmative Action, school desegregation, LGBTQ+ rights, Title IX, the Americans with Disabilities Act (ADA), the Individuals with Disabilities Education Act (IDEA), and Section 504 illustrate this success. However, this progress often leads to backlash, as white grievance politics such as MAGA frequently promote a zero-sum narrative. This false and restrictive MAGA narrative suggests that the achievements of diverse and marginalized groups are a direct threat to the so-called "God-given rights" of the majority.

Board v. Brown: The roots of DEIA

For several decades following the Brown v. Board of Education (1954) decision, professionals dedicated to DEIA faced significant institutional resistance. Still, they ultimately succeeded in hiring and promoting white women—who are often seen as the primary beneficiaries of these programs—as well as individuals of color. This progress was instrumental in shaping the Civil Rights and Feminist movements, which in turn helped advance the passage of the Americans with Disabilities Act (ADA). Whereby the DEIA framework was extended to include the "A" for accessibility, promoting rights for people with disabilities.

By the early 1980s, DEIA professionals, then known as Affirmative Action (AA) and Equal Employment Opportunity (EEO) Officers, had made significant strides in encouraging institutions to hire and admit diverse populations. However, similar to today, the political landscape underwent substantial shifts during the Reagan administration. This shift was analogous to, but less intense than, the current MAGA movement, and it altered the federal government's approach to equity and inclusion. Following Ronald Reagan's election, a nationwide backlash against DEIA initiatives emerged. For instance, the Reagan administration weakened the Equal Employment Opportunity (EEO) and Affirmative Action (AA) systems by supporting legal challenges centered on claims of "reverse discrimination" and criticizing "politically correct language." Additionally, they restricted the enforcement powers of federal anti-discrimination agencies.

One significant example of resistance to Diversity, Equity, Inclusion, and Access (DEIA) during this period was the 1978 Bakke Supreme Court decision regarding affirmative action. This ruling had a profound impact on efforts to promote educational diversity and inclusion, marking a notable shift in the interpretation of equal opportunity under the law. It favored a colorblind (anti-classification) approach to discrimination over a race- and gender-sensitive (anti-subordination) perspective.

While the Bakke decision is often examined in the context of higher education, it also had important implications for pre-K-12 schools, businesses, and government agencies. For instance, the case of Parents Involved in Community Schools v. Seattle School District No. 1 (2007) effectively ended voluntary desegregation plans across the United States, ruling them discriminatory against white students and parents.

These actions exemplify a form of macro-level resistance to DEIA. This resistance can be traced back to what Edelman (1988) referred to as the "political spectacle," which emerged from the forces driving the Southern Strategy. In U.S. politics, the Southern Strategy is an electoral approach used by the Republican Party to secure support from white voters in the South by appealing to notions of white victimhood and opposing the equal status of African Americans and other marginalized groups, including Native Americans, LGBTQ+ individuals, people with disabilities, Latine communities, and women.

It is also crucial to note that the first approach, known as the colorblind or anti-classification constitutional perspective, prioritizes individual rights as the "primary measure of inequality." This perspective views the world through an ahistorical lens, undermining the original restorative intent of antidiscrimination laws. By contrasting the colorblind approach with race or gender-sensitive (antisubordination) methods, we can underscore the neglect of the rights of marginalized groups and the potential for restorative, group-based remedies to address historical racial inequities. As Kennedy (2013) points out, colorblindness in the law is appealing to businesses and educational institutions because it provides a "clear rule" that is "vivid and simple." More importantly, colorblind and anti-classification approaches do not require reparations for past injustices.

As a political concept, colorblindness promotes the misleading yet widely accepted notion of universal equal opportunity, all while ignoring the historical and systemic forces that have created inequality. For example, colorblindness overlooks the socio-structural, political, and economic history of oppression that benefited white men, and by extension, white women, in the United States. This perspective fails to recognize the generational advantages that these individuals have received—and continue to receive—from slavery, colonialism, and ongoing white supremacy. Ultimately, colorblind approaches dilute the reality of racism by stripping away the historical and contextual factors tied to white power and supremacy. This allows white individuals to maintain a false sense of "racial innocence" (Baldwin, 1998) while promoting a belief in meritocracy and equal opportunity.

Another way to illustrate this situation is to examine the backlash labeled "reverse discrimination," which was promoted by the Reagan administration. This backlash threatened the existence of the Equal Employment Opportunity (EEO) and Affirmative Action (AA) programs, which many institutions relied on to ensure diversity in their

212

workforces. At that time, much like today, it prompted institutions to alter or discontinue their Diversity, Equity, Inclusion, and Accessibility (DEIA) programs due to fears of government intervention. Moreover, in the current anti-woke climate, DEIA professionals began to conceal their identities or adapt by integrating into other areas of organizational management, such as human resources, recruitment, marketing, and targeted minority programs. This strategy ultimately failed and ironically contributed to the emergence of today's DEIA roles.

Over time, however, the original corporate and institutional programs designed to combat discrimination and promote inclusion became diluted and dispersed. For example, research conducted by Kelly and Dobbin in 1998 traced the evolution of diversity and inclusion programs from their roots in antidiscrimination practices to contemporary diversity management approaches. They noted a transition from a focus on structural reform, affirmative action, equal opportunity, and the experiences of historically excluded groups— elements that constitute the "Equity and Inclusion" (EI) within diversity, equity, and inclusion—to a more performative and superficial understanding of diversity. As a result, the federal backlash against equity and inclusion efforts shifted public discourse on diversity from a race- and gender-sensitive anti-subordination compliance framework to one focused on anti-classification and the colorblind, or white-centered, perspective of organizational effectiveness. This change in rhetoric is exemplified by the rhetoric of the current occupant of the White House and some members of the Supreme Court.

Moreover, the concept of colorblindness in the legal system has allowed current anti-DEIA efforts to regain support in educational institutions following the Brown v. Board of Education decision. Today's MAGA "war on woke" advocates have intensified anti-classification or colorblind legal approaches, sparking a national and international political backlash that is redefining the history, experiences, and identities of minoritized groups as radical, anti-American, anti-white, and even perverted—particularly regarding LGBTQ+ individuals and communities of color. As a result, these groups are not merely perceived as individuals or ideas but are seen as symbols of entire value systems (e.g., "War on woke") that must be punished or eradicated.

An illustrative example can be found in an internal memo from the U.S. Department of Justice (DOJ), released on May 19, 2025. This memo instructs DOJ Civil Rights staff to use the False Claims Act (31 U.S.C. § 3729 et seq.) to dismantle and penalize DEIA (Diversity, Equity, Inclusion, and Accessibility) programs, even in states where such practices are required by law.

Another example is a memo dated July 29, 2025, from U.S. Attorney General Pamela Bondi. This memo categorizes all DEIA initiatives—such as cultural competence training, cultural centers, diversity statements, minority-owned business preferences, and even the requirement for work experience with language or racial minorities—as inherently suspect of discrimination.

Why focus on DEIA, PYD, and 4-H professionals of color?

In past research, I explored how Diversity, Equity, Inclusion, and Accessibility (DEIA) professionals of color often have different work and life experiences compared to their white counterparts. This distinction is important because educational institutions and businesses frequently aim to "perform" diversity to satisfy diverse and pro-DEIA stakeholders. Many achieve this by recruiting DEIA professionals from marginalized communities to serve as "tokens" or commodities in their public relations efforts.

214

This performative approach means that a significant number of DEIA professionals come from groups such as people of color, immigrants, LGBTQ+ individuals, women, and people with disabilities—identities that can expose them to the same racial and oppressive dynamics they are typically hired to address. As a result, DEIA professionals may become particularly vulnerable to the harmful practice of corrosive code-switching or professional masking to avoid retaliation or backlash. Corrosive code switching or racial masking refers to the psychological and behavioral adaptation employees of marginalized backgrounds make to conceal aspects of their identity to navigate predominantly male, heteronormative, white, or racially biased workplace cultures. It often involves suppressing cultural expressions, altering speech patterns (code-switching), or downplaying experiences of racism to avoid being perceived as "difficult," "unprofessional," or "not a cultural fit." This masking is a survival strategy born from systemic inequities and microaggressions.

However, while it may help individuals avoid immediate harm, it exacts a steep toll on mental health, authenticity, and long-term engagement. For organizational leaders, recognizing racial masking is crucial to creating truly inclusive environments—ones where psychological safety, cultural affirmation, and racial equity are not just aspirational, but deeply embedded in everyday practice.

Furthermore, these vulnerabilities exist within a societal context where simply being an employee of color or belonging to another marginalized group (such as women, LGBTQ+ individuals, or persons with disabilities) can be challenging, particularly in predominantly white or majoritarian institutions. For instance, research on faculty of color at colleges and universities has shown that they often receive lower teaching evaluations from students, experience slower advancement in promotions, and face more adverse treatment compared to similarly positioned white faculty members.

Even in executive leadership roles, administrators of color and women often face challenges that their white counterparts do not. They are frequently allowed to lead only in more difficult circumstances, face increased scrutiny, and, over time, receive less recognition and prestige, even when they succeed. This trend is especially noticeable when leaders from marginalized groups advocate for inclusion and equity, which are essential aspects of the roles of DEIA professionals.

For example, I refer you to a 2016 article in the Harvard Business Review, where Hekman and Johnson introduced the concept of the "Diversity Penalty." Building on that work, in 2017, they teamed up with researchers from the University of Colorado for a larger study that further confirmed this phenomenon. Their findings were later supported by another study that examined why the upper ranks of leadership are mainly composed of white men. This combined research showed that gaps in race and gender-based status and power still exist, partly because ethnic minority and female leaders are often discouraged from engaging in behaviors that promote diversity. In summary, all managers faced harsher judgments if they hired individuals who resembled themselves, except for white male managers. These patterns of marginalization continue as organizations seek new leadership.

Beyond that, research in business and higher education highlights the disproportionate costs associated with promoting Diversity, Equity, Inclusion, and Accessibility (DEIA), particularly affecting professionals of color and women. One illustrative example is the Glass Cliff phenomenon. According to the Oxford Dictionary of Human Resource Management (2019, 3rd ed.), the Glass Cliff refers to "a senior job in which the risks of failure are high and visible, to which a woman or a member of a minority group is appointed because the likelihood of failure is significant, potentially jeopardizing their career prospects." Most studies on the Glass Cliff, which contrasts with the "Savior Effect" typically experienced by white males, primarily focus on women. However, recent articles indicate that this dynamic also affects leaders of color across various fields.

In this context, I argue that DEIA professionals, particularly those of color in youth organizations and educational institutions, face heightened vulnerability to institutional backlash against DEIA initiatives. Given the challenging nature of working at the intersections of multiple and often conflicting narratives, these professionals may experience significant resistance, as documented in the "Pet to threat" and antiracism literature. This resistance can lead to real consequences, including loss of prestige, stress, burnout, shortened professional tenures, and health issues.

The negative career and personal impacts on DEIA professionals from marginalized groups highlight the need for both DEIA advocates and organizational leaders to better understand the systemic and institutional forces that influence their effectiveness and well-being. For example, if the environments in which DEIA professionals—especially those of color—operate render them ineffective, disposable, or unwell, it will be challenging, if not impossible, for our nation, communities, businesses, or educational institutions to thrive in cultivating a pluralistic democracy.

It is in that light that current research highlights why many professionals of color and individuals from other marginalized groups engage in code-switching (masking) as a strategy to fit in, survive, or mitigate harm. This situation is particularly challenging for Diversity, Equity, Inclusion, and Accessibility (DEIA) professionals. Due to the nature of their roles, they often find themselves in a constant state of tension, being perceived either as saviors or threats—sometimes both—by their organizations and institutions. This conflicting position creates dissonance in their roles, which can gradually constrain, corrode, and even harm DEIA professionals over time.

We intentionally use the term "savior" to underscore a contradiction whereby organizations may express a desire to promote diversity without making the necessary changes to their policies, practices, and culture to eliminate oppressive behaviors. A clear example of this dynamic occurs when educational institutions and businesses focus on diversity by recruiting and hiring professionals from underrepresented groups—such as people of color, immigrants, LGBTQ+ individuals, and women—without providing the essential tools, support, funding, or authority needed to implement real organizational change. This situation becomes particularly damaging when DEIA professionals from marginalized communities also face the same racial and oppressive dynamics they are hired to address.

Sadly, many organizational leaders often overlook the long-term harm that corrosive dynamics can inflict on their institutions. This is because, from a civil rights and equity standpoint, the roles of Diversity, Equity, Inclusion, and Accessibility (DEIA) professionals parallel those of financial or legal comptrollers. Both aim to identify and challenge undesirable practices—such as harassment, exclusion, oppression, or discrimination—that could lead to illegal actions or transactions by the organization and its stakeholders. However, unlike financial and legal comptrollers, who are typically regarded as essential checks and balances within an organization, DEIA professionals are often perceived as "extra," "less important," or even negatively. This perception makes DEIA positions vulnerable to shifts in organizational leadership opinions and political affiliations, a phenomenon referred to by Thomas as "Pet to threat" dynamics.

An illustration of this "Pet to threat" dynamic occurs when a DEIA professional is engaged to assist with "performative" initiatives or events. For example, after the Black Lives Matter movement, many organizations highlighted the images and profiles of DEIA professionals to showcase their newfound commitment to diversity, portraying them as organizational saviors and expecting positive, high-visibility changes from them. However, this perception tends to change when the DEIA professional advocates for or implements genuine diversity-related changes, such as antiracist or anti-sexist policies. At this point, existing power dynamics within the organization may feel threatened, disrupting the status quo of "how we have always done it." Consequently, the DEIA professional may be labeled as a rogue, overly passionate, problematic, or a non-team player, leading to a backlash against DEIA efforts (refer to pet-to-threat research). Furthermore, studies have shown that this dynamic is intensified when the DEIA professional is a person of color or belongs to another marginalized group, such as women or LGBTQ+ individuals.

My aim with this supplemental research note has been to help readers contextualize many of the issues discussed in the book and to provide a connection to the research and practice literature, which are also deeply connected to the dignity and well-being of the individuals involved in this work. I also hope it will help the reader deconstruct the systemic issues related to DEIA in PYD and 4-H, as illustrated throughout this book.

REFERENCES LIST

4-H History Preservation. (2010). The history of the National 4 H Camp, 1927–1956.4-hhistorypreservation

Act of Aug. 30, 1890 (Second Morrill Act), ch. 841, 26 Stat. 417 (1890).govinfo+1

Agger, B. (1991). Critical Theory, Poststructuralism, Postmodernism: Their Sociological Relevance. Annual review of sociology, 17(1), 105-131. doi:10.1146/annurev.so.17.080191.000541

Ahmed, S. (2007). "'You end up doing the document rather than doing the doing': Diversity, race equality and the politics of documentation." Ethnic and Racial Studies 30(4): 590–609.

Ahmed, S. (2018). Rocking the Boat: Women of Colour as Diversity Workers. Cham, Cham: Springer International Publishing: 331–348.

Alexander, M. (2012). The new Jim Crow: mass incarceration in the age of colorblindness. New York

American Indian Higher Education Consortium. (n.d.). Land grant.aihec

Ancheta, A. (2006). "Civil Rights, Education Research, and the Courts." Educational Researcher 35(1): 26–29.

Ancheta, A. (2008). "The School Desegregation Cases and the Uncertain Future of Racial Equality: Science and Constitutional Fact Finding in Equal Protection Analysis." Ohio State Law Journal 69: 1115–1321.

Ancheta, A. N. (2002). Constitutional law and race-conscious policies in K-12 education / Angelo Ancheta. New York, NY, New York, NY: ERIC Clearinghouse on Urban Education.

Ancheta, A. N. (2008). "A Constitutional Analysis of Parents Involved in Community Schools v. Seattle School District No. 1 and Voluntary School Integration Policies." Rutgers Race & the Law Review 10(1): 297–339.

Anderson, C. (2016). White rage: the unspoken truth of our racial divide / Carol Anderson. New York, NY, New York, NY: Bloomsbury USA, an imprint of Bloomsbury Publishing Plc.

Anderson, J. D. (1988). The education of Blacks in the South, 1860–1935. University of North Carolina Press.

Angelo, N. A. (2008). The School Desegregation Cases and the Uncertain Future of Racial Equality: Science and Constitutional Fact Finding in Equal Protection Analysis. Ohio State Law Journal, 69, 1115-1321.

Angus, L. (2012). "Teaching within and against the circle of privilege: reforming teachers, reforming schools." J EDUC POLICY 27(2): 231-251.

Arnold, M, Ferrari, T, Editors "Positive Youth Development Integrating Research and Practice" July 8, 2025, Springer Publisher

Aruguete, M. S., et al. (2017). "The Effects of Professors' Race and Clothing Style on Student Evaluations." The Journal of Negro Education 86(4): 494–502.

Arum, R. & I. R. Beattie (2000). The structure of schooling: readings in the sociology of education / [compiled by] Richard Arum and Irenee R. Beattie. Boston: McGraw-Hill.

Auerbach, M. P. (2021). Democracy: The pluralist perspective. EBSCO Research Starters. https://about.ebsco.com/research-starters/religion-and-philosophy/democracy-pluralist-perspective

Bailey, L. H., & Bailey, E. Z. (1915). The country-life movement in the United States. Macmillan.

Baldwin, J. (1998). The Fire Next Time. In James Baldwin: Collected Essays (pp. 722). New York: Library of America

Baldwin, J. (1998). The Fire Next Time. James Baldwin: Collected Essays. New York, Library of America 722.

Baltimore, Md., Boulder, Colo.: University Press of Colorado.

Barlow, K. & E. Dunbar (2010). "Race, Class, and Whiteness in Gifted and Talented Identification: A Case Study." Berkeley Review of Education 1(1): 63–85.

Barnes, M. B. & M. S. Moses (2021). "Racial Misdirection: How Anti-affirmative Action Crusaders Use Distraction and Spectacle to Promote Incomplete Conceptions of Merit and Perpetuate Racial Inequality." Educational policy (Los Altos, Calif.) 35(2): 323–346.

Barnhardt, C. L., Phillips, C. W., Young, R. L., & Sheets, J. E. (2017). The Administration of Diversity and Equity on Campuses and Its Relationships to Serving Undocumented Immigrant Students. Journal of Diversity in Higher Education, 10(1), 1-10. doi:10.1037/a0040025

Bartholet, E. (1986). "The radical nature of the Reagan administration's assault on affirmative action." Harvard Blackletter Journal 3: 37–45.

Bastedo, M. N. (2012). The organization of higher education : managing colleges for a new era / edited by Michael N. Bastedo. Baltimore: Baltimore : Johns Hopkins University Press.

Bell, D. (1987). Moreover, we are not saved: the elusive quest for racial justice / Derrick Bell. New York, New York: Basic Books.

Bell, D. (2004). Silent covenants: Brown v. Board of Education and the unfulfilled hopes for racial reform / by Derrick Bell. New York, New York: Oxford University Press.

Bell, D. (2005). The Derrick Bell reader / edited by Richard Delgado and Jean Stefancic. New York, New York: New York University Press.

Bennett, C. I. (2001). History of education and the role of multicultural education. In J. A. Banks & C. A. McGee Banks (Eds.), Handbook of research on multicultural education (pp. 29–44). Jossey-Bass.

Besley, T. (2013). Social Education and Mental Hygiene: Foucault, disciplinary technologies and the moral constitution of youth. Educational Philosophy and Theory, 34(4), 419-433. doi:10.1111/j.1469-5812.2002.tb00517.x

Bonds, A., & Inwood, J. (2016). Beyond white privilege: Geographies of white supremacy and settler colonialism. Progress in human geography, 40(6), 715-733. doi:10.1177/0309132515613166

Bonilla-Silva, E. (1997). Rethinking Racism: Toward a Structural Interpretation. American Sociological Review, 62(3), 465-480. doi:10.2307/2657316

Bonilla-Silva, E. (2018). Racism without racists : color-blind racism and the persistence of racial inequality in America / Eduardo Bonilla-Silva (Fifth edition.. ed.). Lanham: Lanham : Rowman & Littlefield.

Bourdieu, P. (1992). An invitation to reflexive sociology / Pierre Bourdieu and Loïc J.D. Wacquant. Chicago: Chicago : University of Chicago Press.

Briggs, L., Krasny, M., & Stedman, R. C., (2019). Exploring youth development through an environmental education program for rural indigenous women. Journal of Environmental Education, 50(1), 37–51. https://doi.org/10.1080/00958964.2018.1502137

Bureau of International Labor Affairs. (2017). Guatemala, Findings, Child Labor. Washington DC.

Burke, M. (2018). Colorblind Racism. Newark, Newark: Polity Press.

Burke, M. A. (2012). "Discursive Fault Lines: Reproducing White Habitus in a Racially Diverse Community." Critical Sociology 38(5): 645–668.

Cabezas Gamarra, C. G. (2020). Structural Racism and the Explanation of Durable Racial Inequality. In: ProQuest Dissertations Publishing.

Cacho, L. (2014). "The Presumption of White Innocence." American Quarterly 66(4): 1085–1090.

Camp John Hope FFA–FCCLA Center. (n.d.). History.campjohnhope

Campbell, T. M. (1936). The movable school goes to the Negro farmer. Tuskegee Institute Press.archive

Capoccia, G., & Kelemen, R. D. (2007). The Study of Critical Junctures: Theory, Narrative, and Counterfactuals in Historical Institutionalism. World Pol, 59(3), 341-369. doi:10.1017/S0043887100020852

Cardin: Martin Luther King Jr. Led a Movement Guided by Peace and Compassion that Challenged the Forces of Hate and Intolerance. MENA Report, (2020)

Carleton, S. (2011). Colonizing minds: public education, the "textbook Indian," and settler colonialism in British Columbia, 1920-1970. BC studies(169), 101.

Carroll, K., et al. (2019). "Minority Public Administrators: Managing Organizational Demands While Acting as an Advocate." American review of public administration 49(7): 810-824.

Carter, J. S., et al. (2019). "Veiled Threats: Colorblind Frames and Group Threat in Affirmative Action Discourse." Social Problems 66(4): 503–518.

Castagno, A. E. (2013). Multicultural Education and the Protection of Whiteness. American Journal of Education, 120(1), 101. doi:10.1086/673121

Castagno, A. E. (2014). Educated in Whiteness: good intentions and Diversity in schools / Angelina E. Castagno. Minneapolis: University of Minnesota Press.

Chapman, T. K. (2013). "You cannot erase race! Using CRT to explain the presence of race and racism in majority white suburban schools." DISCOURSE-ABINGDON 34(4): 611–627.

Chavez-Haroldson, M. T. (2020). LatinX Diversity Officers in Higher Education: Capacitating Cultural Values

Cherry, M. (2021). The Case for Rage: Why Anger Is Essential to Antiracist Struggle. New York, New York: Oxford University Press.

Chow, R. M., et al. (2021). "Fighting Backlash to Racial Equity Efforts." MIT Sloan management review 62(4): 25–31.

CIA. (2019). Guatemala Profile. Retrieved from CIA World Factbook - Guatemala website: https://www.cia.gov/library/publications/the-world-factbook/geos/gt.html

Congressional Research Service. (2022). 1994 land grant universities: Background and selected issues.congress

Conrad, A. H., & Meyer, J. R. (1958). The Economics of Slavery in the Ante Bellum South. The Journal of Political Economy, 66(2), 95-130. Retrieved from https://www.jstor.org/stable/1827270

Cook, A. and C. Glass (2013). "Glass Cliffs and Organizational Saviors: Barriers to Minority Leadership in Work Organizations?" Social problems (Berkeley, Calif.) 60(2): 168–187.

Crenshaw, K., et al. (2019). Seeing race again: countering colorblindness across the disciplines / edited by Kimberlé Williams Crenshaw, Luke Charles Harris, Daniel Martinez HoSang, and George Lipsitz. Oakland, California, Oakland, California: University of California Press.

Cross, C. F. (1999). Land-grant colleges and the struggle for community. University Press of Florida.

Crozier, G. (2001). "Excluded parents: the deracialisation of parental involvement." Race, ethnicity, and education 4(4): 329–341.

Danbom, D. B. (1991). The Resisted Revolution: Urban America and the Industrialization of Agriculture, 1900–1930. Iowa State University Press.

Darden, E. C. & E. Cavendish (2012). "Achieving Resource Equity Within a Single School District: Erasing the Opportunity Gap By Examining School Board Decisions." Education and Urban Society 44(1): 61–82.

DasGupta, A. A. (2019). Navigating the Racialized Neoliberal Gaze: Asian American Women Diversity, Equity, and Inclusion Professionals in US Higher Education, ProQuest Dissertations Publishing.

Dass, P. and B. Parker (1999). "Strategies for Managing Human Resource Diversity: From Resistance to Learning." The Academy of Management executive (1993) 13(2): 68-80.

Delgado, M. Y. and T. Ozuna Allen (2019). "Case Studies of Women of Color Leading Community Colleges in Texas: Navigating the Leadership Pipeline through Mentoring and Culture." Community college journal of research and practice 43(10-11): 718-729.

Delgado, R. (1999). When equality ends: stories about race and resistance. Boulder, Colo., Westview Press.

Delgado, R., & Stefancic, J. (2000). Critical race theory : the cutting edge (2nd ed.). Philadelphia: Temple University Press.

Derald Sue, et al. (2011). "Racial Dialogues: Challenges Faculty of Color Face in the Classroom." Cultural Divers Ethnic Minor Psychol 17(3): 331–340.

DiAngelo, R. J. (2018). White fragility: why it is so hard for White people to talk about racism / Robin DiAngelo. Boston: Beacon Press.

Díez-Martín, E., Díez-de-Castro, E., & Vázquez-Sánchez, A. (2018). Refocusing isomorphism to explain organizational legitimacy: A new approach.

DiMaggio, P., & Powell, W. (1983). The Iron Cage Revisited: Institutional Isomorphism and Collective Rationality in

Dixon, C. (2014). Another politics: talking across today's transformative movements / Chris Dixon; with a foreword by Angela Y. Davis. Oakland, California, Oakland, California: University of California Press.

Dobbin, F., et al. (2015). "Rage against the Iron Cage: The Varied Effects of Bureaucratic Personnel Reforms on Diversity." Am Social Rev 80(5): 1014-1044.

Donnor, J. K. (2012). "Whose Compelling Interest? The Ending of Desegregation and the Affirming of Racial Inequality in Education." EDUC URBAN SOC 44(5): 535–552.

Dovidio, J. F., & Gaertner, S. L. (1986). Prejudice, discrimination, and racism / edited by John F. Dovidio and Samuel L. Gaertner. Orlando: Orlando : Academic Press.

Edelman, L., Fuller, S., & Maradrita, I. (2001). Diversity Rhetoric and the Managerialization of Law 1. American Journal of Sociology, 106(6), 1589-1641. doi:10.1086/321303

Edelman, M. J. (1988). Constructing the political spectacle / Murray Edelman. Chicago, Chicago: University of Chicago Press.

Editorial: Drake University responded to racism with spirit, unity. https://www.desmoinesregister.com/story/opinion/editorials/2018 /11/21/editorial-drake-university-responded-racism-spirit-unity/2071528002/

Emerson, M. O., Smith, C., & Sikkink, D. (1999). Equal in Christ, but Not in the World: White Conservative Protestants and Explanations of Black-White Inequality. Social problems (Berkeley, Calif.), 46(3), 398-417. doi:10.1525/sp.1999.46.3.03x0252r

Fernández Calonge, S. (2017). Witches across time: The image of the witch in Katherine Howe's The physick book of Deliverance Dane (2012). https://core.ac.uk/download/211108835.pdf

Ferrantino, A. (2015). Diversity professionals' perception of role, implicit bias, and microaggression in institutions of higher education. S. M. Perry, ProQuest Dissertations Publishing.

Foucault, M., Martin, L. H., Gutman, H., & Hutton, P. H. (1988). Technologies of the self : a seminar with Michel Foucault / edited by Luther H. Martin, Huck Gutman, Patrick H. Hutton. Amherst: Amherst : University of Massachusetts Press.

Foundation, C., (2015). Clinton foundation. Retrieved from About us website: https://www.clintonfoundation.org/clinton-global-initiative/commitments/4-h-central-america-growing-next-generation-leaders

Frankenberg, E. & G. Orfield (2007). Integration lessons: realizing the promise of racial Diversity in American schools / edited by Erica Frankenberg and Gary Orfield. Charlottesville, VA, Charlottesville, VA: University of Virginia Press.

Freire, P. (2000). Pedagogy of the oppressed / Paulo Freire; translated by Myra Bergman Ramos; with an introduction by Donald Macedo. New York, New York: Continuum.

Fresh from the Field, March 1, 2018. https://content.govdelivery.com/accounts/USDANIFA/bulletins/1 de1fa2

Frumkin, P. (2004). "Institutional Isomorphism and Public Sector Organizations." Journal of Public Administration Research and Theory 14(3): 283–307.

Gardner, L., Jr. (2008). African American student affairs administrators at predominantly white institutions: Factors that contribute to their success, ProQuest Dissertations Publishing.

Garver, R. (2017). "Orienting Schools Toward Equity: Subgroup Accountability Pressure and School-Level Responses." The Educational forum (West Lafayette, Ind.) 81(2): 160–174.

GFRAS. (2012). Retrieved from http://www.g-fras.org/en/world-wide-extension-study/central-america-and-the-caribbean/central-america-list/guatemala.html

Giddens, A. (1984). The constitution of society : outline of the theory of structuration / Anthony Giddens. Cambridge [Cambridgeshire]: Cambridge Cambridgeshire : Polity Press.

Gorski, P. (2019). "Avoiding Racial Equity Detours." Educational Leadership 76(7): 56.

Gravley-Stack, K., et al. (2016). "Understanding the Subjective Experiences of the Chief Diversity Officer: A Q Method Study." Journal of Diversity in Higher Education 9(2): 95–112.

Gray, J., D. Grover, and S. Rivas. (2018). Local Systems Framework Learning Note and Presentation - Experiences from the USAID/Honduras Funded Transforming Market Systems (TMS) Activity. Tegucigalpa: Dexis Consulting Group, ACDI/VOCA, USAID/Honduras.

Greenwood, R. (2012). Institutional theory in organization studies edited by Royston Greenwood ... [et al.]. Los Angeles, [Calif.]: Los Angeles, Calif. : SAGE.

Gutierrez, G. (2012). Presumed Incompetent: The Intersections of Race and Class for Women in Academia / edited by Gabriella Gutierrez y Muhs [et al.]. Boulder, Colo.

Guzman, C. (2011). Martin Luther King Jr.: What We Can Learn From Him Today. https://core.ac.uk/download/48622574.pdf

Hallman, K., Peracca, S., Catino, J., & Ruiz, M. J. (2007). Assessing the multiple disadvantages of Mayan girls: The effects of gender, ethnicity, poverty, and residence on education in Guatemala. Promoting Healthy, Safe, and Productive Transitions To Adulthood, (16). Retrieved from https://s3.amazonaws.com/academia.edu.documents/32886541/211 .pdf?AWSAccessKeyId=AKIAIWOWYYGZ2Y53UL3A&Expires= 1509742901&Signature=g7BJ%2BTzJOSvlphuL%2F5BPq%2FERW iE%3D&response-content-disposition=inline%3B filename%3DMultiple_Disadvantages_of_Mayan_Female

Harper, S. R. (2012). Race without Racism: How Higher Education Researchers Minimize Racist Institutional Norms.(Report)(Author abstract). Review of Higher Education, 36(1), 9. doi:10.1353/rhe.2012.0047

Harvey, W. B. (2014). Chief Diversity Officers and the Wonderful World of Academe. 7(2), 92-100. doi:10.1037/a0036721

Heery, E. & M. Noon (2008). A dictionary of human resource management, Oxford University Press.

Hekman, D. R. (2017). "Does Diversity-valuing behavior result in diminished performance ratings for non-white and female leaders?" Academy of Management journal: AMJ 60(2): 771–797.

Hibbler, D. F., Jr. (2020). Managing at the Intersection: The Negotiations of Racialized Role Strain of Black Mid-Level Student Affairs Administrators at Predominantly White Institutions, ProQuest Dissertations Publishing.

Holt, M. (2018). The Kids Are at the Table: 4-H and the Making of the Modern Rural Citizen. In M. Holt (Ed.), Children and Youth in Rural America (pp. 145–168). University of Georgia Press.

Hooks, B. (1994). Teaching to Transgress. Florence, UNITED KINGDOM: Routledge.

Horne, G. (2018). The apocalypse of settler colonialism : the roots of slavery, white supremacy, and capitalism in seventeenth century North America and the Caribbean / by Gerald Horne. New York: New York : Monthly Review Press.

Husband, T. and SpringerLink (2016). However, I Do not See Color: The Perils, Practices, and Possibilities of Antiracist Education / edited by Terry Husband. Rotterdam: SensePublishers : Imprint: SensePublishers.

IDE (2020). Equity Coordinator Responsibilities Checklist. I. D. o. Education. https://educateiowa.gov/sites/files/ed/documents/Equity%20Coordinator%20Responsibilities%20Checklist%2010%2012%2020.pdf, Equity Office.

Johnson, S. & D. Hekman (2016). "Women and Minorities Are Penalized for Promoting Diversity." The Harvard Business Review.

Jones, S. M. (2014). Diversity leadership under race-neutral policies in higher education. Equality, Diversity and Inclusion: An International Journal, 33(8), 708-720. doi:10.1108/EDI-01-2013-0002

Jones, V. (2007). Roots of civic identity: 4-H and the African American experience. Journal of Extension, 45(5), Article 5COM1. https://archives.joe.org/joe/2007october/comm1.php

Kelly, E., & Dobbin, F. (1998). How Affirmative Action Became Diversity Management: Employer Response to Antidiscrimination Law, 1961 to 1996. American Behavioral Scientist, 41(7), 960-984. doi:10.1177/0002764298041007008

Kendi, I. X. (2016). Stamped from the beginning : the definitive history of racist ideas in America / Ibram X. Kendi. New York: New York : Nation Books.

Kendi, I. X. (2019). How to be an antiracist / Ibram X. Kendi (First Edition.. ed.). New York: New York : One World.

Kennedy, R. (2013). For discrimination : race, affirmative action, and the law / Randall Kennedy (First edition.. ed.). New York: New York : Pantheon Books.

Kerr, N. A. (1987). The legacy: A centennial history of the state agricultural experiment stations, 1887–1987. Missouri Agricultural Experiment Station.

Khalifa, M., et al. (2013). "Derrick Bell, CRT, and educational leadership, 1995-present." RACE ETHNIC EDUC-UK 16(4): 489–513.

Kirton, G., & Greene, A.-M. (2009). The costs and opportunities of doing diversity work in mainstream organisations. Human Resource Management Journal, 19(2), 159-175. doi:10.1111/j.1748-8583.2009.00091.x

Kofman, L., & Mather, L. (2017). The Bias of Crowds Model: Promise and Potential Challenges for Practitioners. Psychological Inquiry, 28(4), 278-280. doi:10.1080/1047840x.2017.1373560

Kohli, R., et al. (2017). "The 'New Racism' of K–12 Schools: Centering Critical Research on Racism." Review of research in education 41(1): 182-202.

Kulich, C., et al. (2014). "The Political Glass Cliff: Understanding How Seat Selection Contributes to the Underperformance of Ethnic Minority Candidates." Political research quarterly 67(1): 84–95.

Ladson-Billings, G., & Tate, W. (1995). Toward a Critical Race Theory of Education. Teachers College Record, 97(1), 47.

Ladson-Billings, G., Ed. (2003). Critical Race Theory Perspectives on the Social Studies: The Profession, Policies, and Curriculum Research in Social Education. NY, NY, Information Age Publishing

Landa Ugarte, A., Salazar, E., Quintana, M., & Herrera-Molina, R. (2018). USAID/Guatemala Gender Analysis Final Report September 2018. (September), 1–147.

Lanham, MD: Lanham : Rowman & Littlefield Publishers.

Lara, L. J. (2019). "Faculty of Color Unmask Colorblind Ideology in the Community College Faculty Search Process." Community college journal of research and practice 43(10-11): 702–717.

Leonard, J. S. (1990). The Impact of Affirmative Action Regulation and Equal Employment Law on Black Employment. Journal of Economic Perspectives, 4(4), 47-63. doi:10.1257/jep.4.4.47

Leonardo, Z., & Zembylas, M. (2013). Whiteness as Technology of Affect: Implications for Educational Praxis. Equity & Excellence in Education, 46(1), 150-165. doi:10.1080/10665684.2013.750539

Lipson, D. N. (2011). The Resilience of Affirmative Action in the 1980s: Innovation, Isomorphism, and Institutionalization in University Admissions. Political research quarterly, 64(1), 132-144. doi:10.1177/1065912909346737

Livermore, M. A., & Revesz, R. L. (2020). Retreating from Reason. Oxford University Press EBooks. https://doi.org/10.1093/oso/9780197539446.003.0005

Lozenski, B. D. (2017). "Beyond Mediocrity: The Dialectics of Crisis in the Continuing Miseducation of Black Youth." Harvard Educational Review 87(2): 161–185.

Manfred Melgar-Padilla, Simona Torretta, Ileana Grandelis, Claudia Alfaro, R. C.-A. (2016). 2016-2020 Estrategia Para La Juventud Rural del Ministerio De Agricultura, Ganaderia y Alimentacion. Retrieved from http://www.fao.org/fileadmin/user_upload/FAO-countries/Guatemala/Publicaciones/Estrategia_para_la_Juventud_R ural_Web.pdf

Marana, J. A. J. (2016). The Lived Experiences of Women of Color Chief Diversity Officers, ProQuest Dissertations Publishing.

Martin, J. L. (2015). Racial battle fatigue: insights from the front lines of social justice advocacy / Jennifer L. Martin, editor; foreword by H. Richard Milner IV. Santa Barbara, California: Praeger.

Matthew, J. M., Heidi, E. G., & Eric, L. D. (2006). Breaking the Silence: Achieving a Positive Campus Climate for Diversity from the

Staff Perspective. Res High Educ, 47(1), 63-88. doi:10.1007/s11162-004-8152-z

McDonald, M. L., et al. (2018). "One Step Forward, One Step Back: White Male Top Manager Organizational Identification and Helping Behavior toward Other Executives Following the Appointment of a Female or Racial Minority CEO." Academy of Management journal 61(2): 405-439.

Miller, E. M. (2018). Balancing Compassion Satisfaction and Compassion Fatigue: The Professional Quality of Life of Title IX Coordinators, ProQuest Dissertations Publishing.

Mills, J. H., et al. (2004). Resistance to Diversity Initiatives, Routledge.

Modica, M. (2015). "Unpacking the 'colorblind approach': accusations of racism at a friendly, mixed-race school." Race, ethnicity, and education 18(3): 396-418.

Morrill Act of 1862, ch. 130, 12 Stat. 503 (1862).archives+1

Moss, P. I. (2001). Stories employers tell: race, skill, and hiring in America / Philip Moss and Chris Tilly. New York, New York: Russell Sage Foundation.

National 4-H Council. (2020). 4-H history timeline. https://4-hhistorypreservation.com/History_Timeline/

Nayar, P. K. (2010). Postcolonialism: Postcolonialism. London: London: Bloomsbury Publishing Plc.

Norris-Hill, R. L. (2020). Chief Abolitionist Officers: An Exploration of the Lived Experiences of Black Chief Diversity Officers at Dominantly White Christian Institutions, ProQuest Dissertations Publishing.

Orfield, G. (1996). Dismantling desegregation : the quiet reversal of Brown v. Board of Education / Gary Orfield, Susan E. Eaton, and the Harvard Project on School Desegregation. New York: New York : New Press.

Orfield, G. (1996). Dismantling desegregation: the quiet reversal of Brown v. Board of Education / Gary Orfield, Susan E. Eaton, and the Harvard Project on School Desegregation. New York, New York: New Press.

Organizational Fields. American Sociological Review, 48(2), 147-160. Retrieved from http://links.jstor.org/sici?sici=0003-1224%28198304%2948%3A2%3C147%3ATICRII%3E2.0.CO%3B2-S

Ortiz, S. Y. & V. J. Roscigno (2016). "Discrimination, Women, and Work: Processes and Variations by Race and Class." Sociological Quarterly 50(2): 336–359.

OSAC. (2018). Guatemala 2018 Crime & Safety Report. Retrieved from https://www.osac.gov/pages/ContentReportDetails.aspx?cid=24030

Osei-Kofi, N., Torres, L. E., & Lui, J. (2013). Practices of whiteness: racialization in college admissions viewbooks. Race ethnicity and education, 16(3), 386-405. doi:10.1080/13613324.2011.645572

Paikeda, T. (2021). Positioning Your Chief Diversity Officer For Top Performance. https://www.russellreynolds.com/en/insights/articles/positioning-chief-Diversity-officer-top-performance, Russell Reynolds and Associates.

Plaut, V. C., et al. (2018). "Do Color Blindness and Multiculturalism Remedy or Foster Discrimination and Racism?" Current Directions in Psychological Science 27(3): 200–206.

Plaut, V., et al. (2020). Diversity Resistance Redux: The Nature and Implications of Dominant Group Threat for Diversity And Inclusion. Diversity Resistance in Organizations. K. Thomas. New York: Routledge.

Powell, W., & DiMaggio, P. (1991). The New institutionalism in organizational analysis / edited by Walter W. Powell and Paul J. DiMaggio. Chicago: Chicago : University of Chicago Press.

Ramiro Ortiz, Ottoniel Rivera, Israel Cifuentes, E. M. (2011). Estudio de sistematizacion de buenas practicas de extension en Guatemala. Guatemala City, Guatemala.

Rasmussen, W. D. (1989). Taking the university to the people: Seventy-five years of Cooperative Extension. Iowa State University Press.

Richardson, C. (2012). Diversity Performance as a Factor in Marketing Programs: A Comparative Analysis across Ethnic Group Target Audiences. Journal of Marketing Development and Competitiveness, 6(5), 62-70.

Richardson, T. (2002). The Extension Worker's Creed: A legacy of service. Journal of Extension, 40(6), Article 6COM1. https://archives.joe.org/joe/2002december/comm1.php

Rogobete, S. E. (2015). The Self, Technology and the Order of Things: In Dialogue with Heidegger, Ellul, Foucault and Taylor. Procedia - Social and Behavioral Sciences, 183, 122-128. doi:10.1016/j.sbspro.2015.04.854

Ryan, M. K., et al. (2010). "Politics and the Glass Cliff: Evidence that Women are Preferentially Selected to Contest Hard-to-Win Seats." Psychology of women quarterly 34(1): 56–64.

Ryan, T. E. (2021). Diversity Rhetoric versus the Reality of Whiteness: Educational Equity Efforts in New York and Iowa, ProQuest Dissertations Publishing.

Ryde, J. (2019). White privilege unmasked: how to be part of the solution / Judy Ryde. London, UK; Philadelphia, PA, USA, London, UK; Philadelphia, PA, USA: Jessica Kingsley Publishers.

Sablan, J. R. (2019). "Can You Really Measure That? Combining Critical Race Theory and Quantitative Methods." American Educational Research Journal 56(1): 178-203.

Samuel's, C. (2019). "The Challenging, Often Isolating Work of School District Chief Equity Officers." Education week(Oct 23, 2019).

Sanders, J. (2001). The 1890 land-grant institutions: Yesterday, today, and tomorrow. Journal of Extension, 39(6), Article 6COM1. https://archives.joe.org/joe/2001december/comm1.php

Save the Children, & USAID. (2018). Engaging Adolescents to Accelerate Progress on the First 1,000 Days. Guatemala City, Guatemala.

Schenck, L., (2011). SMALL FAMILY FARMS COUNTRY FACTSHEET. Retrieved from http://www.fao.org/family-farming/themes/small-family-farmers

Schuman, S. (2016). Seeing the land-grant university with new eyes: Toward a civic mission for the public university. University Press of America.

Scott, W. R. (2008). Institutions and organizations : ideas and interests / W. Richard Scott (Third edition.. ed.). Los Angeles: Los Angeles : Sage Publications.

Scott, W. R., & Christensen, S. (1995). The institutional construction of organizations : international and longitudinal studies / W. Richard Scott, Søren Christensen, editors. Thousand Oaks, Calif.: Thousand Oaks, Calif. : Sage Publciations.

Sensoy, Ö. and R. DiAngelo (2017). "We Are All for Diversity, but . . .": How Faculty Hiring Committees Reproduce Whiteness and Practical Suggestions for How They Can Change." Harvard Educational Review 87(4): 557-580.

Settles, I. H., et al. (2019). "Scrutinized but not recognized: (In)visibility and hypervisibility experiences of faculty of color." Journal of Vocational Behavior 113: 62–74.

Shah-Paikeday, T., et al. (2019). A Leader's Guide: Finding and Keeping Your Next Chief Diversity Officer. https://www.russellreynolds.com/insights/thought-leadership/a-leaders-guide-finding-and-keeping-your-next-chief-Diversity-officer, Russel Raynolds and Associates.

Shah-Paikeday, T., Sachar, H., & Stuart, A. (2019). A Leader's Guide: Finding and Keeping Your Next Chief Diversity Officer. Retrieved from https://www.russellreynolds.com/insights/thought-leadership/a-leaders-guide-finding-and-keeping-your-next-chief-diversity-officer: https://www.russellreynolds.com/insights/thought-leadership/a-leaders-guide-finding-and-keeping-your-next-chief-diversity-officer

Smith, A. (2012). Indigeneity, Settler Colonialism, White Supremacy. In: University of California Press.

Smith, L. T. (2012). Decolonizing methodologies : research and indigenous peoples / Linda Tuhiwai Smith (Second edition.. ed.). London: London : Zed Books.

Smith, W. A., et al. (2017). "Between Hope and Racial Battle Fatigue: African American Men and Race-Related Stress." Journal of Black Masculinity 2(1): 35–58.

Smith–Lever Act of 1914, Pub. L. No. 63–95, 38 Stat. 372 (1914).eod.ces.ncsu+1

Smith-Lever Act, 7 U.S.C. § 341 (1914).

Sniderman, P., Piazza, T., Tetlock, P., & Kendrick, A. (1991). The New Racism. American Journal of Political Science, 35(2), 423. doi:10.2307/2111369

Sobers, S. T. (2014). Can I get a witness? The resilience of four Black women senior student affairs administrators at predominantly White institutions, ProQuest Dissertations Publishing.

Steward, R. (1985). Guatemala and the CGIAR Centers: A Study of their Collaboration and Agricultural Research. Washington, DC: The International Bank for Reconstruction and Development/The World Bank.

Stewart, N. R., (1930). Extension Activities: England, Australia, France, Guatemala, Esthonia, Austria, the Soviet Union, and India. Washington DC.

Stokes, M. (2011). The career paths of African American male senior administrators in student affairs at predominantly White institutions: Formal and informal leadership experiences, ProQuest Dissertations Publishing.

Sturrock, J. (2008). Structuralism: With an Introduction by Jean-Michel Rabate (2. Aufl. ed.). Hoboken: Hoboken: Wiley-Blackwell.

Sue, D. (2004). Whiteness and ethnocentric monoculturalism making the "invisible" visible. Am. Psychol., 59(8), 761-769. doi:10.1037/0003-066X.59.8.761

Taylor, E., Gillborn, D., & Ladson-Billings, G. (2009). Foundations of critical race theory in education / edited by Edward Taylor, David Gillborn, and Gloria Ladson-Billings. New York: New York : Routledge.

The Rev. Dr. Valori Mulvey Sherer: Pentecost 2022-C: Liberating, transforming love. https://vmsherer.blogspot.com/2022/06/pentecost-2022-c-liberating.html

The World Group for Indigenous Affairs, & (IWGIA). (2019). The Indigenous Report, 2019. Retrieved from https://www.iwgia.org/images/documents/indigenous-world/IndigenousWorld2019_UK.pdf

Theoharis, G. (2008). "At Every Turn": The Resistance that Principals Face in Their Pursuit of Equity and Justice." Journal of School Leadership 18(3): 303–343.

Thomas, K. M. (2008). Diversity resistance in organizations / edited by Kecia M. Thomas. New York, New York: Lawrence Erlbaum Associates.

Thomas, K. M. (2020). Diversity Resistance in Organizations (2nd ed.): Taylor and Francis.

Thomasson, A. (2016). Structural explanations and norms: comments on Haslanger. Philos Stud, 173(1), 131-139. doi:10.1007/s11098-014-0437-2

Tintiangco-Cubales, A., et al. (2015). "Toward an Ethnic Studies Pedagogy: Implications for K-12 Schools from the Research." Urban Rev 47(1): 104–125.

Torres, L., Driscoll, M., & Burrow, A. (2010). Racial Microaggressions And Psychological Functioning Among Highly Achieving African-Americans: A Mixed-Methods Approach. Journal

241

of Social and Clinical Psychology, 29(10), 1074-1099. doi:10.1521/jscp.2010.29.10.1074

Tuhiwai-Smith, L. (2012). Decolonizing methodologies: research and indigenous peoples / Linda Tuhiwai Smith. London, London: Zed Books.

Turner, C. S. V., et al. (2008). "Faculty of Color in Academe: What 20 Years of Literature Tells Us." Journal of Diversity in Higher Education 1(3): 139-168.

U.S. Department of Agriculture, National Institute of Food and Agriculture. (2023, February 12). Extension pioneer: Thomas Monroe Campbell.nifa.usda

U.S. Department of Health & Human Services. (2018). A Checklist for Putting Positive Youth Development. Retrieved from https://www.hhs.gov/ash/oah/sites/default/files/pyd-tpp-checklist.pdf

United States Department of Agriculture. (2014). Cooperative Extension: A century of innovation. USDA National Institute of Food and   Agriculture. https://nifa.usda.gov/sites/default/files/resource/Cooperative_Extension_Century_of_Innovation.pdf

Unitedminds (2019). Chief Diversity Officers Today: Paving the Way for Diversity & Inclusion Success. https://www.webershandwick.com/wp-content/uploads/2019/09/Chief-Diversity-Officers-Today-report.pdf, KRC Research

University of Arizona Cooperative Extension. (n.d.). 4 H educational philosophy: 4 H pledge.extension.arizona

University of Maine Cooperative Extension. (2022, May 3). 4 H emblem, motto, slogan, and pledge.extension.umaine

USAID Guatemala. (2018). Sector Brief: Education. In Sector Brief: Education. Guatemala City, Guatemala.

USAID. (2012a). Guatemala Country Development Strategy, 2012-2016.

USAID. (2012b). USAID POLICY: YOUTH. Realizing the Demographic Opportunity 2012, (October).

USAID. (2019). INDIGENOUS PEOPLES ' ENGAGEMENT STRATEGY - Guatemala. Retrieved from https://www.usaid.gov/documents/1862/indigenous-peoples'-engagement-strategy

USDE (2022). Assurance of Compliance - Civil Rights Certificate of the US Department of Education. https://www2.ed.gov/about/offices/list/ocr/letters/boy-scouts-assurance-form.pdf.

Vaughan, B. (2001). HANDLE WITH CARE: On the Use of Structuration Theory within Criminology. British journal of criminology, 41(1), 185-200. doi:10.1093/bjc/41.1.185

Vinkenburg, C. J. (2017). "Engaging Gatekeepers, Optimizing Decision Making, and Mitigating Bias: Design Specifications for Systemic Diversity Interventions." J Appl Behav Sci 53(2): 212-234.

Warren, K. C. (2010). The quest for citizenship: African American and Native American education in Kansas, 1880-1935 / Kim Cary Warren. Chapel Hill: Chapel Hill: University of North Carolina Press.

Wessel, T. R., & Wessel, M. (1982). 4 H: An American idea, 1900–1980: A history of 4 H. National 4 H Council.newprairiepress+1

Williams, D. (2013). The chief Diversity officer: strategy, structure, and change management / Damon A. Williams and Katrina Wade Golden; foreword by Mark A. Emmert. Sterling, Virginia, Sterling, Virginia: Stylus.

Williams, D. A. & K. C. Wade-Golden (2008). "The Complex Mandate of a Chief Diversity Officer." The Chronicle of Higher Education 55(5).

Williams, D. A. (2013). The chief diversity officer : strategy, structure, and change management / Damon A. Williams and Katrina Wade Golden ; foreword by Mark A. Emmert (First Edition.. ed.). Sterling, Virginia: Sterling, Virginia : Stylus.

Williams, D. A., & Wade-Golden, K. C. (2008). The Complex Mandate of a Chief Diversity Officer. The Chronicle of Higher Education, 55(5).

Williams, J. (2005). Understanding Poststructuralism (1 ed.). London: London: Routledge.

Wingfield Adia, H., Hordge-Freeman, E., & Smith-Lovin, L. (2018). Does the Job Matter? Diversity Officers and Racialized Stress. In Race, Identity and Work (Vol. 32, pp. 197-215): Emerald Publishing Limited.

www.ingramcontent.com/pod-product-compliance
Lightning Source LLC
Chambersburg PA
CBHW052110030426
42335CB00025B/2922